First World War
and Army of Occupation
War Diary
France, Belgium and Germany

5 CAVALRY DIVISION
Headquarters, Branches and Services
General Staff
2 January 1917 - 21 February 1918

WO95/1162/1

The Naval & Military Press Ltd
www.nmarchive.com
Published in association with The National Archives

Published by

The Naval & Military Press Ltd

Unit 10 Ridgewood Industrial Park,

Uckfield, East Sussex,

TN22 5QE England

Tel: +44 (0) 1825 749494

www.naval-military-press.com

www.nmarchive.com

This diary has been reprinted in facsimile from the original. Any imperfections are inevitably reproduced and the quality may fall short of modern type and cartographic standards.

© Crown Copyright
Images reproduced by permission of The National Archives, London, England, 2015.

Contents

Document type	Place/Title	Date From	Date To
Heading	WO95/1162/1		
Heading	1917-1918 5th Cavalry Division General Staff Jan 1917-Feb 1918 To Egypt 29.3.18 Division Ceased To Exist 29.4.18		
Heading	War Diary of General Staff Branch The Gds. 5th Cavalry Division From 1st January 1917 To 31st January 1917		
War Diary	Dargnies	02/01/1917	28/01/1917
Miscellaneous	Cavalry Corps G/88/1	28/01/1917	28/01/1917
Miscellaneous	Table Showing How Personnel Of Corps. Bridging Train And Park Will Be Provided.		
War Diary	Darg	05/03/1917	30/03/1917
Operation(al) Order(s)	5th. Cavalry Division Operation Order No.19 Appendix 93	19/03/1917	19/03/1917
Miscellaneous	5th Cavalry Division March Table ? March (Issued with O.O. No. 19, d/19-3-17).		
Operation(al) Order(s)	5th. Cavalry Division Operation Order No.20 Appx 94	20/03/1917	20/03/1917
Miscellaneous	5th Cavalry Division March Table-21-3-17 (Issued with O.O. No. 20)		
Operation(al) Order(s)	5th. Cavalry Division Operation Order No.21 Appx 95	21/03/1917	21/03/1917
Miscellaneous	5th Cavalry Division March Table-22.3.17 (Issued with Operation Order No.21)		
Miscellaneous	No G.A./589 Headquarters 5th Cavalry Division 22nd March, 1917 Issued at Normal Operation Order Distribution.	22/03/1917	22/03/1917
Miscellaneous	No G.A./589 Headquarters 5th Cavalry Division 22nd March, 1917 Issued at Normal O.O. Distribution. Fourth Army (For Information).	22/03/1917	22/03/1917
Operation(al) Order(s)	5th Cavalry Division Operation Order No.22 Appx 96	22/03/1917	22/03/1917
Miscellaneous	No. G.A./589 Headquarters 5th Cavalry Division 23rd March, 1917 Issued at Normal O.O. Distribution Fourth Army (For Information)	23/03/1917	23/03/1917
Operation(al) Order(s)	5th Cavalry Division Operation Order No.23 Appx 98	23/03/1917	23/03/1917
Operation(al) Order(s)	5th Cavalry Division Operation Order No. 24 Appx 99	24/03/1917	24/03/1917
Miscellaneous	Messages And Signals. Appx 100		
Miscellaneous	Sec'bad Cavalry Brigade. Canadian Cavalry Brigade. Ambala Cavalry Brigade.	26/03/1917	26/03/1917
Operation(al) Order(s)	5th. Cavalry Division Operation Order No.25. Appx 101	27/03/1917	27/03/1917
Miscellaneous	Headquarters, 5th, Cavalry Division Dated 27th. March, 1917	27/03/1917	27/03/1917
Miscellaneous	Narrative of The Operations Of The 5th. Cavalry Division Between March 24th. and March 27th. Appx 102	24/03/1917	28/03/1917
Operation(al) Order(s)	5th. Cavalry Division Operation Order No.26. Appx 103	28/03/1917	28/03/1917
Miscellaneous	5th Cavalry Division March Table 29-3-17 (Issued with Op. Order No. 26)		
Operation(al) Order(s)	5th. Cavalry Division Operation Order No.27. Appx 104	30/03/1917	30/03/1917

Type	Description	Date From	Date To
Miscellaneous	5th Cavalry Division March Table 30-3-17 (Issued with O.O. No. 27)		
Operation(al) Order(s)	5th Cavalry Division Operation Order No.19. Appx 93	19/03/1917	19/03/1917
Miscellaneous	5th Cavalry Division March Table 20th March (Issued with O.O. No.19, d/19-3-17)		
Operation(al) Order(s)	5th. Cavalry Division Operation Order No.20. Appx 94	20/03/1917	20/03/1917
Miscellaneous	5th Cavalry Division March Table-21-3-17 (Issued with O.O. No 20)		
Operation(al) Order(s)	5th Cavalry Division Operation Order No.21. Appx 95	21/03/1917	21/03/1917
Miscellaneous	5th Cavalry Division March Table-22.3.17 (Issued with Operation Order No.21)		
Miscellaneous	No. G.A./589 Headquarters 5th Cavalry Division 22nd March, 1917 Issued at Normal Operation Order Distribution	22/03/1917	22/03/1917
Miscellaneous	No. G.A./589/1Headquarters 5th Cavalry Division 22nd March, 1917 Issued at Normal O.O. Distribution Fourth Army (For Information)	22/03/1917	22/03/1917
Operation(al) Order(s)	5th Cavalry Division Operation Order No.22. Appx 96	22/03/1917	22/03/1917
Miscellaneous	Issued at Norm 1 O.C. Distribution. Fourth Army (For information)	23/03/1917	23/03/1917
Operation(al) Order(s)	5th Cavalry Division Operation Order No.23. Appx 98	23/03/1917	23/03/1917
Operation(al) Order(s)	5th. Cavalry Division Operation Order No.24. Appx 99	24/03/1917	24/03/1917
Miscellaneous	Messages And Signals. Appx 100		
Miscellaneous	These instructions are preliminary and are liable to alteration.	26/03/1917	26/03/1917
Operation(al) Order(s)	5th. Cavalry Division Operation Order No.25. Appx 101	27/03/1917	27/03/1917
Miscellaneous	Headquarters, 5th. Cavalry Division Dated 27th March, 1917	27/03/1917	27/03/1917
Miscellaneous	Narrative of The Operation Of The 5th. Cavalry Division Between March 24th. and March 27th. Appx 102		
Operation(al) Order(s)	5th. Cavalry Division Operation Order No.26. Appx 103	28/03/1917	28/03/1917
Miscellaneous	5th Cavalry Division March Table 29-3-17 (Issued with Op. Order No.26)	29/03/1917	29/03/1917
Operation(al) Order(s)	5th. Cavalry Division. Operation Order No.27. Appx 104	30/03/1917	30/03/1917
Miscellaneous	5th Cavalry Division March Table 30-3-17 (Issued with O.O. No.27)		
War Diary	Incheville Beauchamps Cust. Marest Pont Marais	01/03/1917	19/03/1917
War Diary	Gamaches	07/03/1917	07/03/1917
War Diary	Beauchamps	12/03/1917	14/03/1917
War Diary	Incheville	16/03/1917	19/03/1917
War Diary	Lincheux	20/03/1917	20/03/1917
War Diary	Guienemicourt	21/03/1917	21/03/1917
War Diary	Thennes & Berteaucourt	22/03/1917	22/03/1917
War Diary	Cerisy	22/03/1917	22/03/1917
War Diary	Peronne	23/03/1917	26/03/1917
War Diary	Boucly	27/03/1917	27/03/1917
War Diary	Peronne and Neighbourhood	27/03/1917	29/03/1917
War Diary	Villers Bretonneux Lamotte Bayonviller Cappy	30/03/1917	31/03/1917
War Diary		01/04/1917	30/04/1917
Miscellaneous	No. G.A. 769 Headquarters, 5th, Cavalry Division Dated 5th. April, 1917. Appx 105	06/04/1917	06/04/1917

Type	Description	Date From	Date To
Operation(al) Order(s)	5th. Cavalry Division Operation Order No. 28. Appx 106	11/04/1917	11/04/1917
Miscellaneous	5th. Cavalry Division March Table (Issued with O.O. 28) For 12 April		
Operation(al) Order(s)	5th. Cavalry Division Operation Order No.29. Appx 104	13/04/1917	13/04/1917
Miscellaneous	5th Cavalry Division March Table 14-4-17 (Issued with O.O.)	14/04/1917	14/04/1917
Miscellaneous	Distribution As for Operation Order No. 29		
Miscellaneous	No. G.A. 844 Headquarters, 5th. Cavalry Division Dated 18th. April, 1917. Appx 108	18/04/1917	18/04/1917
Miscellaneous	5th Cavalry Division Concentration Orders-April 1917		
War Diary	Guizancourt	02/05/1917	31/05/1917
Miscellaneous	Attachment Of R.H.A. To IIIrd Corps. No. G.S.569. Headquarters, 5th. Cavalry Division Dated 8th. May, 1917. Appx 109	08/05/1917	08/05/1917
Miscellaneous	These Instructions are preliminary and are liable to alteration. Appx 110	11/05/1917	11/05/1917
Miscellaneous	5th Cavalry Division. Programme of Reliefs. 14th-17th May 1917 (Issued with G.S. 573/1)		
Miscellaneous	No. G. 531. Headquarters, 5th. Cavalry Division Dated 12th May 1917. Appx 111	12/05/1917	12/05/1917
Miscellaneous	No G. 530. 5th. Cavalry Division Instructions For Defence. Appx 112	12/05/1917	12/05/1917
Miscellaneous	No G. 535. Headquarters, 5th. Cavalry Division. Dated 14th May. 1917. Appx 113	14/05/1917	14/05/1917
Miscellaneous	No. G. 530/1. Headquarters, 5th. Cavalry Division. Dated 15th. May, 1917. Appx 113A	15/05/1917	15/05/1917
Miscellaneous	No. G. 535/1. Headquarters, 5th. Cavalry Division Dated 16th. May, 1917. Appx 114	16/05/1917	16/05/1917
Miscellaneous	No. G.-552. Headquarters, 5th. Cavalry Division Dated 20th. May, 1917. Appx 115	20/05/1917	20/05/1917
Operation(al) Order(s)	5th. Cavalry Division Operation Order No.30. Appx 116	22/05/1917	22/05/1917
Miscellaneous	No. G. 552/2 Headquarters, 5th. Cavalry Division Dated 22nd. May, 1917. Appx 114	22/05/1917	22/05/1917
Operation(al) Order(s)	5th. Cavalry Division Operation Order No.31. Appx 118	25/05/1917	25/05/1917
Miscellaneous	No. G. 552/2. Headquarters, 5th. Cavalry Divn. Dated 27th. May, 1917	27/05/1917	27/05/1917
Miscellaneous	Narrative of a Minor Enterprise carried out by the Canadian Cavalry Brigade on the night of May 26th/27th. 1917. Appx 120	27/05/1917	27/05/1917
War Diary	Nobescourt Farm	01/06/1917	09/07/1917
War Diary	Bouvincourt	10/07/1917	15/07/1917
War Diary	St Pol	16/07/1917	31/07/1917
Miscellaneous	No. G. 52/12. Headquarters, 5th. Cavalry Division. Dated July 1st 1917.	01/07/1917	01/07/1917
Miscellaneous	Suggested Arrangements For Relief.		
Miscellaneous	Account Of A Raid By Two Squadrons Canadian Cavalry Bde. On July 8th/9th 1917. Appx 123		
Operation(al) Order(s)	Canadian Cavalry Brigade. Operation Order No.39 Appendix "A"	04/07/1917	04/07/1917
Operation(al) Order(s)	Further Instructions In Continuation Of Those Issued With Operation Order No 39.	05/07/1917	05/07/1917
Map	Map to illustrate Raid of Canadian Cavalry Brigade		

Type	Description	Date From	Date To
Operation(al) Order(s)	5th. Cavalry Division Operation Order No.35 Appx 124	04/07/1917	04/07/1917
Miscellaneous	5th Cavalry Division Relief Table (Issued with Operation Order No. 35)		
Miscellaneous	No. G. 552/15. Headquarter, 5th Cavalry Division. Date 5th July, 1917. In Continuation of Operation Order No. 35, para 9,	05/07/1917	05/07/1917
Miscellaneous	No. G. 552/18. Headquarters, 5th. Cavalry Division. Dated 7th July, 1917. Reference 5th. Cavalry Division Operation No. 35,	07/07/1917	07/07/1917
Operation(al) Order(s)	5th. Cavalry Division Operation Order No.36. Appx 125	10/07/1917	10/07/1917
Miscellaneous	5th. March Division March Table, July 13th-17th (Issued with O.O. No. 36)		
Miscellaneous	No G. 636 Headquarters, 5th Cavalry Division 19th July 1917. Appx 126		
Miscellaneous	Concentration Orders.-July 1917. Appx 127		
Miscellaneous	5th Cavalry Division Concentration Orders July 19117		
War Diary	Heuchin	01/08/1917	23/08/1917
Miscellaneous	Canadian Cavalry Brigade. Sec'bad Cavalry Brigade.	02/08/1917	02/08/1917
War Diary	St. Pol Billeting Area	01/09/1917	10/09/1917
War Diary	Heuchin	01/10/1917	28/10/1917
Miscellaneous	No G.S. 690. Headquarters, 5th Cavalry Division, 3rd October 1917 5th Field Squadron. R.E. Appx 129	03/08/1917	03/08/1917
Operation(al) Order(s)	5th Cavalry Division Operation Order No.37. Appx 130	05/10/1917	05/10/1917
Operation(al) Order(s)	5th Cavalry Division March Table-(Issued with Operation Order No. 37)		
Miscellaneous	Appx 131	10/10/1917	10/10/1917
Miscellaneous	5th Cavalry Division March Table-(Issued with No. G. 735 dated 10th October, 1917)		
Miscellaneous	Headquarters, 5th Cavalry Division 11th October, 1917 In Continuation of my G. 728 dated 9th instant. Appx 132	11/10/1917	11/10/1917
Miscellaneous	List of Bivouacs-5th Cavalry Division Reference Sheet 27-1/40,000. Appx 133	12/10/1917	12/10/1917
Operation(al) Order(s)	5th Cavalry Division Operation Order No.38. Appx 134	13/10/1917	13/10/1917
Miscellaneous	5th Cavalry Division. March Table-(Issued with Operation Order No.38)		
Operation(al) Order(s)	5th Cavalry Division. Operation Order No.39. Appx 135	15/10/1917	15/10/1917
Miscellaneous	5th Cavalry Division. March Table-(Issued with Operation Order No. 39)		
Miscellaneous	Canadian Cavalry Brigade. Sec'bad Cavalry Brigade. 5th Signal Squadron. Appx 136	16/10/1917	16/10/1917
Miscellaneous	War Establishment Indian Cavalry Pioneer Battalion.		
War Diary	Cavillon	01/11/1917	01/11/1917
War Diary	Dargnies	02/11/1917	30/11/1917
Miscellaneous	Headquarters, 5th. Cavalry Division Dated 25th. November, 1916. Copy of a letter No. O.B. 1385, dated 24-11-16, From G.H.Q. (Received under cavalry Corps No. G-147, Appx 90	25/11/1916	25/11/1916
Miscellaneous	Headquarters 2nd Indian Cavalry Division. 1st November 1916. Appx 88		
Miscellaneous	Headquarters 2nd Indian Cavalry Division. 14th. November 1916. Appx 89.		
Miscellaneous	War Establishment Indian Cavalry Pioneer Battalion.		
War Diary	Fressin (Lens Sheet, 1/100000)	04/11/1917	10/11/1917

War Diary	Occoches	11/11/1917	11/11/1917
War Diary	Querrieu	12/12/1917	12/12/1917
War Diary	Bouvincourt	13/12/1917	19/12/1917
War Diary	Fins	20/12/1917	21/12/1917
War Diary	Equancourt	22/12/1917	22/12/1917
War Diary	Suzanne	23/12/1917	26/12/1917
War Diary	Monchy Lagache	27/12/1917	30/12/1917
Miscellaneous	No. G.13. Headquarters, 5th Cavalry Division, 7th November 1917. Appx 138	07/11/1917	07/11/1917
Operation(al) Order(s)	5th Cavalry Division Operation Order No.40. Appx 138	07/11/1917	07/11/1917
Miscellaneous	5th Cavalry Division March Table For Nov. 9th-(Issued with Operation Order No.40)		
Miscellaneous	5th Cavalry Division March Table For Nov.10th-(Issued with Operation Order No.40)		
Miscellaneous	5th Cavalry Division March Table For Nov.11th-(Issued with Operation Order No.40)		
Miscellaneous	Operation Orders Appx 139	08/11/1917	08/11/1917
Miscellaneous	No. G. 17. Headquarters, 5th Cavalry Division 9th November 1917. Reference Division Operation Order No.40 dated 7th Nov. Appx 140	09/11/1917	09/11/1917
Miscellaneous	Headquarters, 5th Cavalry Division 9th November 1917		
Operation(al) Order(s)	5th Cavalry Division Operation Order No.41. Appx 142	10/11/1917	10/11/1917
Miscellaneous	5th Cavalry Division. March Table For night 11/12th-(Issued with Operation Order No.41)		
Miscellaneous	5th Cavalry Division. March Table For night 12/13th-(Issued with Operation Order No.41)		
Miscellaneous	5th Cavalry Division. March Table For night 13/14th-(Issued with Operation Order No.41)		
Miscellaneous	No. G.21. Headquarters, 5th Cavalry Division, 10th November, 1917. Appx 143.		
Miscellaneous	Order For Troops Appendix L		
Miscellaneous	O.O. Distribution. Appx 149	19/11/1917	19/11/1917
Miscellaneous	O.O. Distribution. Major R.H.O'D. Paterson, 34th Horse.	19/11/1917	19/11/1917
Miscellaneous	Communications. Appx 145		
Operation(al) Order(s)	Precis Of Operations. Appx 144	17/11/1917	17/11/1917
Operation(al) Order(s)	5th Cavalry Division Operation Order No.43. Appx 147	18/11/1917	18/11/1917
Miscellaneous	Medical Instructions Issued with Operation Order No.43		
Miscellaneous	O.C. Distribution. Appx 148		
Miscellaneous	5th Cavalry Division. March Table-(Issued with G.S. No.718/11, dated 18/11/17)	18/11/1917	18/11/1917
Map	To Be Destroyed on Leaving This Area		
Miscellaneous	To Be Destroyed before Leaving Area Shewn on Attached Map. Grouping for move forward.		
Miscellaneous	5th Cavalry Division Summary of Operations November 20th to 22nd. Appx 151		
Miscellaneous	Report on action of "B" Squadron, Fort Garry Horse on November 20th 1917. Appendix "A".		
Miscellaneous	Report by Captain Lone, 7th Dragoon Guards, on Capture of Noyelles by one Squadron 7th Dragoon Guards. Appendix "B".		
Operation(al) Order(s)	5th Cavalry Division March Table-(Issued With Operation Order No.44)		
Operation(al) Order(s)	5th Cavalry Division Operation Order No.45. Appx. 153	26/11/1917	26/11/1917

Type	Description	Date	Date
Miscellaneous	5th Cavalry Division March Table Issued With O.O. No.45		
Miscellaneous	O.O. Distribution. Appx 154	28/11/1917	28/11/1917
Operation(al) Order(s)	5th Cavalry Division Operation Order No.46. Appx 155	29/11/1917	29/11/1917
Miscellaneous	Relief Table For December 1st/2nd. (Issued with O.O.46.)		
Operation(al) Order(s)	5th Cavalry Division Operation Order No.47. Appx 156	30/11/1917	30/11/1917
Operation(al) Order(s)	5th Cavalry Division Operation Order No. 40. Appx A	07/11/1917	07/11/1917
Miscellaneous	5th Cavalry Division. March Table For Nov. 9th-(Issued with Operation Order No.40)		
Miscellaneous	5th Table For 10th-(Issued with Operation Order No.40)		
Miscellaneous	Headquarters, 5th Cavalry Division. March Table For 11th November, Issued with Operation order No.40, as amended by this office No. G/17 dated 9/11/17, is cancelled and the following.	09/11/1917	09/11/1917
Miscellaneous	Headquarters, 5th Cavalry Division 7th November 1917. Appx B	07/11/1917	07/11/1917
Operation(al) Order(s)	Operation Order No.25. Appendix C	06/11/1917	06/11/1917
Miscellaneous	March Table (To accompany O.O. 25)		
Miscellaneous	H.Q. 17th Brigade R.H.A. 10th November 1917. March Orders to Divisional Troops Appendix D	10/11/1917	10/11/1917
Miscellaneous	March Table		
Miscellaneous	C.R.E. Cavalry Corps. E.A. Appendix E	10/11/1917	10/11/1917
Operation(al) Order(s)	5th Cavalry Division Operation Order No.41. Appendix F	10/11/1917	10/11/1917
Miscellaneous	5th Cavalry Division. March Table For night 12/13-(Issued with Operation Order No.41)		
Miscellaneous	5th Cavalry Division. March Table For night 13/14th-(Issued with Operation Order No.41)		
Operation(al) Order(s)	Operation Order No.27. Appendix G	11/11/1917	11/11/1917
Miscellaneous	March Table For 12th Nov. (To accompany Operation Order No.27)		
Operation(al) Order(s)	Operation Order No.28. Appendix H	13/11/1917	13/11/1917
Miscellaneous	March Table For 13th. (To accompany Operation Order No.28)		
Miscellaneous	C.R.E. Cavalry Corps. E.A. 674. Appendix J	12/11/1917	12/11/1917
Miscellaneous	C.R.E. Cavalry Corps. E.A. 710. Appendix K	15/11/1917	15/11/1917
Miscellaneous	Order For A Echelon Appendix M	19/11/1917	19/11/1917
Miscellaneous	Orders For B Echelon and Dismounted Reinforcements Appendix N	19/11/1917	19/11/1917
Operation(al) Order(s)	5th Cavalry Division Operation Order No.44. Appendix O	22/11/1917	22/11/1917
Miscellaneous	5th Cavalry Division. March Table (Issued with Operation Order No.44)		
Miscellaneous	Warning Order Appendix P	23/11/1917	23/11/1917
Miscellaneous	Q.O. Distribution. Appendix Q	25/11/1917	25/11/1917
Operation(al) Order(s)	5th Cavalry Division Operation Order No.45. Appendix R	26/11/1917	26/11/1917
Miscellaneous	5th Cavalry Division March Table Issued With O.O. No.45		
Miscellaneous	H.Q. 17th Brigade R.H.A. March Orders to Divisional Troops. Appendix S		
Miscellaneous	March Table For Divisional Troops.		
Miscellaneous	C.R.E. Cavalry Corps. E.A. 786 O.C. 5th. Field Squadron. R.E. Appendix T	28/11/1917	28/11/1917
Miscellaneous	O.O. Distribution Appendix U		

Type	Description	Date From	Date To
Operation(al) Order(s)	5th Cavalry Division Operation Order No.46. Appendix V	29/11/1917	29/11/1917
Miscellaneous	Relief Table for December 1st/2nd. (Issued with O.O.46)		
Operation(al) Order(s)	5th Cavalry Division. Operation Order No.47. Appendix W	30/11/1917	30/11/1917
Operation(al) Order(s)	5th Cavalry Division. Operation Order No.42. Appx 146	17/11/1917	17/11/1917
Miscellaneous	Appendix "A". (Issued with Operation Order No.42.) Grouping For Forward Move.		
Operation(al) Order(s)	5th Cavalry Division Operation Order No.44. Appx 152	22/11/1917	22/11/1917
Heading	War Diary 5th Cavalry Division. G.S. December 1917		
War Diary	E.5.a.	01/12/1917	01/12/1917
War Diary	Heudecourt	03/12/1917	03/12/1917
War Diary	Longavesnes	04/12/1917	08/12/1917
War Diary	Monchy Lagache	09/12/1918	31/12/1918
Miscellaneous	5th Cavalry Division Summary of Operations-30th November to 2nd December, 1917. Appx 157	30/12/1917	30/12/1917
Miscellaneous	5th Cavalry Division 6th December 1917. Intelligence Summary-30th Nov. to 2nd Dec.		
Miscellaneous	Headquarters 5th Cavalry Division 4th December 1917. Appx 158	04/12/1917	04/12/1917
Miscellaneous	Headquarters 5th Cavalry Division 6th December 1917. Appx 159	06/12/1917	06/12/1917
Operation(al) Order(s)	5th Cavalry Division. Operation Order No. 48. Appx 160	07/12/1917	07/12/1917
Miscellaneous	5th Cavalry Division March Table (Issued With Operation Order No.48)		
Miscellaneous	O.O. Distribution. Appx 161	10/12/1917	10/12/1917
Miscellaneous	Headquarters, 5th Cavalry Division. 10th December, 1917. O.O. Distribution. Appx 162	10/12/1917	10/12/1917
Miscellaneous	O.C., Dismounted Reinforcements, 5th Cavalry Division.	11/12/1917	11/12/1917
Operation(al) Order(s)	5th Cavalry Division. Operation Order No.49. Appx 164	16/12/1917	16/12/1917
Miscellaneous	5th Cavalry Division. March Table (Issued with Operation Order No.49).		
Miscellaneous	Reference G.S.722/5 pf 10th December.	19/12/1917	19/12/1917
Miscellaneous	Ambala Cavalry Brigade. Sec'bad Cavalry Brigade. A.A. and Q.M.G.	22/12/1917	22/12/1917
Miscellaneous	O.O. Distribution. Appx 167	26/12/1917	26/12/1917
Miscellaneous	O.O. Distribution. Reference this office no. G.S. 722/11 dated 26.12.17, "Instructions regarding the use of the Reserves in the Cavalry Corps Sector". Appx 168	29/12/1917	29/12/1917
Miscellaneous	Table of Duties Of Brigade (Issued with G.S. 722/14 dated 29.12.17)		
Miscellaneous	O.O. Distribution. Reference Table of Duties of Brigades Issued with this office No.G.S.722/14 dated 22nd inst., for "4p.m." read 12 noon" throughout the Table. Appx 169	30/12/1917	30/12/1917
War Diary	Monchy Lagache	01/01/1918	27/01/1918
War Diary	Bouvincourt	31/01/1918	31/01/1918
Miscellaneous	O.O. Distribution. Copy of Cavalry Crops letter No. G.X. 283/237 dated 5th January, 1918 to 5th Cavalry Divn. Forecast of probable reliefs. Appx 170	06/01/1918	06/01/1918
Miscellaneous	O.O. Distribution. Appx 171	11/01/1918	11/01/1918

Miscellaneous	O.O. Distribution. The Following instructions regarding the use of Reserves will come into force at midnight 13th/14th January and will be substituted for those issued under G.S.722/11dated 26th December 1917. Appx 172	13/01/1918	13/01/1918
Miscellaneous	O.O. Distribution.The Following Table of duties of Brigade is issued in substitution of that forwarded with this Office No.G.S. 72214 dated 29th December 1917. Appx 173	13/01/1918	13/01/1918
Miscellaneous	O.O. Distribution. Warning Order. Appx 174	23/01/1918	23/01/1918
Operation(al) Order(s)	5th Cavalry Division. Operation Order No.50 Appx 175	24/01/1918	24/01/1918
Miscellaneous	Table of Reliefs (Issued with Operation Order No. dated 24th January 1918)	24/01/1918	24/01/1918
Operation(al) Order(s)	5th Cavalry Division Operation Order No. 51. Appx 176	26/01/1918	26/01/1918
Miscellaneous	March Table. (Issued with 5th Cavalry Division Operation Order No. 51)		
War Diary	Bouvincourt	01/02/1918	16/02/1918
War Diary	Pont De Metz	17/02/1918	21/02/1918
Miscellaneous	Dismounted Divisions Locations Report. Forecasting Positions for 6 a.m. on 3rd February. Appx 177		
Miscellaneous	List of Billets 5th Cavalry Division Ref. Map. Lens 11 Abbeville 14 and Amiens 17 Appx 178		
Miscellaneous	###		
Operation(al) Order(s)	Dismounted Divisions Order No 7 Appendix 180	12/02/1918	12/02/1918
War Diary	Bouvincourt	01/02/1918	16/02/1918
War Diary	Pont De Metz	17/02/1918	21/02/1918
Miscellaneous	List of Billets-5th Cavalry Division. Ref. Map. Lens 11, Abbeville 14, and Amiens 17 Appendix 178	04/02/1918	04/02/1918
Miscellaneous	###	20/01/1918	20/01/1918
Operation(al) Order(s)	Dismounted Divisions Order No 7. Appendix 180	12/02/1918	12/02/1918
Miscellaneous	All recipients of Dis. Divns Order No. 7. Reference Dismounted Divisions, 13th February, 1918.	13/02/1918	13/02/1918

WO 95/1162/1

1917-1918
5TH CAVALRY DIVISION

GENERAL STAFF

JAN 1917 - FEB 1918

To EGYPT 29.3.18
DIVISION CEASED TO EXIST 29.4.18

SERIAL NO. 211

Confidential

War Diary

of

General Staff Branch, Hd. Qrs. 5th Cavalry Division

FROM 1st January 1917 TO 31st January 1917

Army Form C. 2118.

WAR DIARY
or
INTELLIGENCE SUMMARY.
(Erase heading not required.)

Instructions regarding War Diaries and Intelligence Summaries are contained in F.S. Regs., Part II and the Staff Manual respectively. Title pages will be prepared in manuscript.

Hour, Date, Place	Summary of Events and Information	Remarks and references to Appendices
DARGNIES.		
2nd. 10-31 am	AMBALA Pioneer Battalion left LONGROY GAMACHES by rail for XIV Corps to relieve SEC'BAD Pioneer Battalion. 2nd Series of Courses at Divisional School ended.	
3rd. 6-30 pm.	SEC'BAD Pioneer Battalion returned by rail to Divisional Area on relief by AMBALA Pioneer Battalion.	
7th.	AMBALA Pioneer Battalion transferred from XIV to VI Corps (9th Division) and located at AGNEZ les DUISANS.	
12th.	CANADIAN Pioneer Battalion transferred from XV to XIII Corps and located at AUTHIEULE (near DOULLENS).	
14th.	Third Series of Courses at Divisional School commenced.	
21st.	Approval given by G.H.Q. for the re-arming of Indian Cavalry with British Cavalry Swords. Units to be re-armed in the following order :- 20th Deccan Horse. 9th Hodson's Horse. 34th Poona Horse. 18th Lancers.	
28th.	Intimation received from Cavalry Corps that G.H.Q. have approved in principle, the formation of a Cavalry Corps Bridging Train & Park from the bridging detachments of Field Squadrons.	Appx.

Major, G.S.,
for G.O.C. 5th Cavalry Division.

<u>Cavalry Corps</u>
G/88/1.

1st. Cavalry Division.
2nd.   "   "
3rd.   "   "
4th.   "   "
5th.   "   "

The proposals forwarded to you in this office No. G.88 of 4th. November 1916, for the formation of a Cavalry Corps Bridging Train and Park, from the Bridging Detachments now attached to Field Squadrons, have been approved by G.H.Q. in principle, subject to the receipt of approval in detail to the proposed establishment from the Home Authorities.

Meanwhile sanction has been given to withdraw the Bridging Detachments from Field Squadrons, and to collect the additional personnel required. For the present, however, the detachments will not be reconstituted, no promotions will be made, and no temporary or acting rank will be granted.

The attached Table "A" shows how the personnel of the Corps Bridging Train and Park will be provided. The Lt. Col. R.E. Cavalry Corps will arrange to obtain the extra personnel required from the Base.

The Bridging Train and Park will be billeted in the villages of BOISMONT and BRETEL under arrangements which are being made by the 4th. Cavalry Division. Orders for the moves of the Bridging Detachments to those places will be issued later, when the extra accomodation now being provided, is ready.

The Bridging Train and Park, on arrival at BOISMONT and BRETEL, will be administered temporarily, by the 4th. Cavalry Division.

(Sd) A.F. Home
B.G.G.S.

Cavalry Corps,
28th. January, 1917.

Copies to,
  Cavalry Corps "Q"
  D.D.M.S.
  French Mission.
  Lt.Col.R.E.Cav.Corps.

TABLE SHOWING HOW PERSONNEL OF CORPS BRIDGING TRAIN AND PARK WILL BE PROVIDED.

	Reqd.	To be supplied by					To come from Base	Remarks
		1st. Fd. Sqn.	2nd. Fd. Sqn.	3rd. Fd. Sqn.	4th. Fd. Sqn.	5th. Fd. Sqn.		
Captain	1				1			Capt. Biggs.
Lts. or 2nd. Lts.	2			✠1			1	✠ S.S.M. WILLIS who is surplus
Sqn. Sergt. Major	1					1		
Sqn. Q.M.S.	1	1						Sergt. Thomas
Eng. Clerk	1						1	
Farrier	1		1					S.&C. Smith Corpl.
Shoeing-Smiths	5	1	1	1	1	1		
Sergts. (Sappers)	1	1						A junior Actg. Sergt.
(Drivers)	2				1	1		Sergts. Tomkins & Broad
Corporals (Sappers)	3	1	1	1				) 3 Cpls. from the base
(Drivers)	2				1	1		) base will be sent) up in lieu of 3 of) these.
2/Cpls. (Sappers)	2							
(Drivers)	2		1					
L/Cpls. (Sappers)	3	1			1	1		) To be N.C.O's) recommended for
(Drivers)	4		1	1				) promotion to 2/Cpl.
Sappers	15	3	3	3	3	3	2	
Drivers	100	21	21	21	20	20		
Rid. Horses	22	3	3	3	3	3	2	
Draught	170	35	35	35	35	35		3 horses per sqn. to be absorbed
Boat Wagons	30	6	6	6	6	6		3rd. Fd. Sqn. to
Bicycles	4	1	1	-	1	1		return 1 to Ordnance.
R.A.M.C. Ptes	2							) To be arranged by) D.D.M.S.
Interpreters	1							To be arranged by French Mission.

Sappers by trades (Including Corporals)

	Reqd.	1st. Fd. Sqn.	2nd. Fd. Sqn.	3rd. Fd. Sqn.	4th. Fd. Sqn.	5th. Fd. Sqn.	To come from Base	Remarks
Blacksmiths	2	1	1					
Carpenters	10	2	2	2	2	2		
Fitters	2					1	1	
Painters	2				1		1	
Plumbers	1				1			
Saddlers	4	1	1	1		1		
Wheelers	2	1	1					

✠ Cav. Corps G 88/2, dt. 31-1-17.

Army Form C. 2118.

WAR DIARY
INTELLIGENCE SUMMARY
(Erase heading not required.)

Instructions regarding War Diaries and Intelligence Summaries are contained in F.S. Regs, Part II and the Staff Manual respectively. Title Pages will be prepared in manuscript.

Place	Date	Hour	Summary of Events and Information	Remarks and references to Appendices
DHQ	March 5th		The 4th series of Courses at the Divisional School ended on March 5th.	
	12th		The students for the 5th General Course assembled at the Divisional School on March 12th.	
	13th		Orders received for the Division to be prepared to move in 48 hours.	
	14th		Sec'bed Pioneer Battalion arrived back from 13th Corps.	
	17th		Ambala Pioneer Battalion arrived back from 6th Corps.	
	18th		Received instructions from Cavalry Corps that Division, accompanied by "B" Echelon, would move Eastwards on 19th.	
	19th		Orders issued for closing of Divisional School.	
			Canadian Cavalry Brigade, with R.C.H.A. Brigade and Ammunition Column and Canadian Cavalry Field Ambulance moved Eastwards to area between NESLETTE and SENARPONT. 17th Bde. R.H.A. and Ammunition Column moved to area FRAMICOURT-RAMBURES-VILLEROY.	
			Orders issued at 9-30 p.m. for Division to move to the HORNOY area on 20th instant. In accordance with 5th Cavalry Division Order No.19, dated 19-3-17 attached	Appx.93.
	20th		Orders issued for the Division to move to the PONT-de-METZ - CONTY Area and concentrate along R. LA CELLE, S.W.AMIENS. 5th Cavalry Division Operation Order No.20 of 20-3-17 (attached)	Appx.94.
			5th Cavalry Division is administered by the Fourth Army from midnight 20th/21st March.	
	21st			

Army Form C. 2118.

WAR DIARY or INTELLIGENCE SUMMARY

(Erase heading not required.)

Instructions regarding War Diaries and Intelligence Summaries are contained in F. S. Regs, Part II. and the Staff Manual respectively. Title Pages will be prepared in manuscript.

Place	Date	Hour	Summary of Events and Information	Remarks and references to Appendices
	March 21st		5th Cavalry Division H.Q. moved from DARMNIES to PONT-de-METZ. Orders issued for the Division to move East on 22nd and billet as below (O.O.21 - attached)	Appx. 95.
			Canadian Cav. Brigade..........CERISY (area)	
			Secunderabad Cav. Brigade......HAMEL (area)	
			Ambala Cav. Brigade............CAIX - HANGARD (area)	
			Divisional H.Q. remains at PONT-DE-METZ.	
	22nd		Orders issued for the Division to move as follows, vide O.O. 22 - attached	Appx. 96
			Canadian Cav. Brigade........To bivouac just West of PERONNE on North banks of R. SOMME.	
			Secunderabad Cav. Brigade....Remains in old billets.	
			Ambala Cav. Brigade..........To Bois de MEREAUCOURT.	
			Divisional H.Q................To PERONNE.	
			The following troops are attached to 5th Cavalry Division :-	
			1 Coy. IV Corps Cyclists)	
			2 platoons III Corps Cyclists) Attached to Ambala Cavalry Brigade.	
			XIV Corps Cav. Regt. & Cyclist Bn. - Attached to Canadian Cavalry Brigade.	
			Cable detachment (1 Officer &)	
			37 O.R.) Joined Signal Squadron.	
			Heavy snow showers throughout the day.	
	23rd		The Division marched as ordered on March 22nd.	
			The crossings over the R. SOMME about PERONNE were not fit for Motor Transport. Division is disposed as below on the night of the 23rd/24th :-	
			Divisional H.Q................Chateau, PERONNE.	
			Canadian Cav. Bde.............	

Army Form C. 2118.

WAR DIARY
or
INTELLIGENCE SUMMARY
(Erase heading not required.)

Instructions regarding War Diaries and Intelligence Summaries are contained in F. S. Regs., Part II. and the Staff Manual respectively. Title Pages will be prepared in manuscript.

Place	Date	Hour	Summary of Events and Information	Remarks and references to Appendices
	23rd Continued	:-	Canadian Cav.Brigade............2 miles West of PERONNE near small village of HALLE.	Appx.97.
			Ambala Cav.Brigade............Bois de MEREAUCOURT.	App. 98.
			Remainder of Division as in G.A/597 of 23rd March attached	
			Weather fine, but cold.	
	24th		The Divn on moved in accordance with 5th Cav.Division Operation Order No.23 of 23-3-17 attached, and Ambala & Canadian Cavalry Brigades took over from Corps Cavalry along Fourth Army Front.	App. 99.
			Weather bright and cold; frost during the night 23rd/24th.	
			Operation Order No.24 issued (attached)	
	25th		Situation as in G.I.2, d/24-3-17, Report to Army, etc., attached Canadian Brigade occupied the small wood South of YTRES and the Bois de VALLULART one mile South of YTRES in the afternoon with only a few casualties. Weather fine and cold. XIV Corps Cav.Regt. passes under orders of 8th Division, XIV Cyclist Battalion less one platoon remains under orders of 5th Cavalry Division. Outpost reconnaissance and patrol fighting along the whole front of Fourth Army which is covered by 5th Cavalry Division.	App.100.
	26th		Two Squadrons of the 18th Lancers (Ambala Cav.Bde.) and 9th Light Armoured Car Battery co-operated with Warutt's flying Column in an attack on ROISEL.- This village was occupied, the enemy about 50 strong, being driven out. In the evening Lord Strathcona's Horse (Canadian Cav.Bde.) occupied the village of EQUANCOURT and the wood just S.E. About the same time, Royal Canadian Dragoons occupied LONGAVESNES.- In both cases the defence of the villages was handed over to the Infantry, the Cavalry covering them whilst they moved in and consolidated. Very wet all day. G.A. 658 is attached.	
			27th......Over........	

Army Form C. 2118.

WAR DIARY
or
INTELLIGENCE SUMMARY

(Erase heading not required.)

Instructions regarding War Diaries and Intelligence Summaries are contained in F. S. Regs., Part II and the Staff Manual respectively. Title Pages will be prepared in manuscript.

Place	Date	Hour	Summary of Events and Information	Remarks and references to Appendices
	27th		Operations were carried out in the afternoon in accordance with Operation Order No.25 and G.A.687, (attached). The villages of VILLERS FAUCON, SAULCOURT and GUYENCOURT were captured and 1 officer, 19% men and 2 machine guns taken. Our casualties were slight. VILLERS FAUCON was taken by the 8th Hussars in conjunction with No.9 Light Armoured Car Battery at about 5.20 p.m. Prisoners 1 officer, 10 men and 2 machine guns. GUYENCOURT was taken by the Lord Strathcona's Horse about 5.40 p.m. Prisoners, 3 men and 1 machine gun. SAULCOURT was taken by the Fort Garry Horse about 5.50 p.m. Prisoners, nil, 1 machine gun. Weather cold and showery with a heavy hail storm in the afternoon.	App.101.
	28th		As in "Narrative of Operations" for 28th(attached) 2 Platoons IV Corps Cyclists attached to Ambala Cavalry Brigade came under the orders of IV Corps Cav.Regt. on this date. Secunderabad Brigade moved to a bivouac between HEM and CLERY.	App.102.
	29th		The Division withdrew from the front line. Canadian Cavalry Brigade to bivouac near CAPPY. Ambala Cavalry Brigade to bivouac about Bois de MEREAUCOURT. 5th Cavalry Division Operation Order No.26 of 29th is attached. Captain GWATKIN appointed G.S.O. 3, 5th Cavalry Division.	App.103.
	30th		Ambala Cavalry Brigade marched to WARFUSEE (area) Secunderabad Cavalry Brigade marched to BAYONVILLERS (area). Divisional H.Q. moved to VILLERS-BRETONNEUX. 5th Cavalry Division Operation Order No.27 is attached.	App.104.

Captain, G.S.,

for G.O.C. 5th Cavalry Division.

Appx 93

SECRET

5TH. CAVALRY DIVISION
OPERATION ORDER NO. 19.

Copy No. 19.

Reference Map FRANCE 1/100,000.   19th. March, 1 9 1 7.

1. The Division will move tomorrow, the 20th. March, in accordance with the attached march table.

2. "B" Echelon will march with Brigades and Divisional Troops.

3. Divisional Troops will march under 2nd. in command of the 5th. Field Squadron.

4. No. 9 L.A.C. Battery and motors of Mhow and Sec'bad C.F.A's, and Sanitary Section will follow the Division on 21st. March, under orders which will be issued later.

5. Units not mentioned in orders or March Table will move under instructions of "Q" Staff.

6. Divisional Report Centre will remain at DARGNIES till morning 21st. March.

7. Acknowledge.

```
Nos. 1 to 21 : Normal O.O. Distribution.
        22 : Aux. H.T. Coy.
        23 : Cavalry Corps.
        24 : Fourth Army.
```

J. O'Rorke
Captain, G.S.
5th. Cavalry Division.

Issued by D.R. at 9.30, p.m.

5TH CAVALRY DIVISION.

March Table. 5th March (issued with O.O.No.19,d/19-3-17).

U N I T.	Starting Point & Time.	To.	Route.	Remarks.
Canadian Cav.Bde.	Cross roads ½ mile S. of G in BUIGNY.	POIX - BLANGY-SOUS-POIX - CROIXRAULT - ERICAMPS - THIEULLOY L'ABBAY.	LE MAZIS - LIOMER - HORNOY.	To be clear of HORNOY by 12 noon. Bde. Hdqrs. to be at POIX.
17th Bde. R.H.A.) Ammunition Col.)	Pass starting point at 10 a.m.	ST.AUBIN - LINCHEUX - GOUY L'HOPITAL.	ANDAINVILLE - VILLERS CAMPSART.	To arrive at HORNOY at 12.15 p.m. Hdqrs. to be at LINCHEUX.
Ambala Cavalry Bde.		Area :- HORNOY - SELINCOURT - DROMESNIL - VILLERS CAMPSART - LIOMER. Note.- BEZENCOURT is exclusive.	BOUTTENCOURT - SENARPONT.	Not to reach billeting area before 12 noon. Hdqrs. to be at LIOMER.
Sec'bad Cavalry Bde		Area :- LE QUESNE - ARGUEL - CAMPSART - FRESNEVILLE - ANDAINVILLE - INVAL BOIRON - ST. AUBIN RIVIERE.	MARTAINNEVILLE Stn. - OISEMONT - AUMATRE.	Hdqrs. to be at LE QUESNE.
DIVNL: TROOPS. Order of March.- Field Squadron	At 10.5 a.m.	SENARPONT - BERNAPRE.	GAMACHES - BOUTTENCOURT - SENARPONT.	"A" Echelon Divnl: Troops will march under an Officer to be detailed by O.C. Field Sqdn.
Divnl: Hdqrs.(less motors).	At 10.5 a.m.			"B" Echelon Divnl: Troops will march under an Officer to be detailed by O.C. A.S.C.
Signal Squadron	At 10.10 a.m.			H.Q. to be at SENARPONT.

DIVNL: TROOPS(Continued -

DIVNL: TROOPS (Continued -

U N I T.	Starting Point & Time.	To.	Route.	Remarks.
Mhow I.C.F.A. (less motors)	At 10.15 a.m.	See preceding page.	See preceding page.	See preceding page.
Sec'bad I.C.F.A. (less motors)	At 10.20 a.m.			
Aux: H.T.Coy.	At 10.25 a.m.			
"A" Echelon of above.	At 10.28 a.m.			
"B" Echelon of above.	at 10.30 a.m.			

Appx 94

5TH. CAVALRY DIVISION.   Copy No. 19.

OPERATION ORDER NO. 20.

SECRET   20th. March, 1917.

Reference Map 1/100,000 FRANCE.

1. The Division will continue the march Eastwards tomorrow in accordance with the attached March table.

2. "N" and "X" R.H.A. and R.C.H.A. Brigade are, from midnight 20/21st. placed under the orders of G.O's C. Secunderabad, Ambala and Canadian Cavalry Brigades respectively.

3. Canadian Section of Ammunition Column comes under orders of O.C. Ammunition Column on arrival at GUIGNEMICOURT.

4. Canadian Field Ambulance is at the disposal of A.D.M.S., but will be billetted by G.O.C. Canadian Cavalry Brigade, who will report its location in billets to A.D.M.S.

5. "A" and "B" Echelons will accompany Brigades and Divisional Troops.

6. Mounted Troops may pass Wheeled Transport on the march as long as there is no risk of blocking the road.

7. Reports to PONT DE METZ after noon.

J. O'Rorke
Capt for
Lieut-Colonel, G.S.
5th. Cavalry Division.

Nos. 1 to 21: Normal O.O. Distribution,
22: ~~Aux H.T. Coy.~~ Divisional Troops
23: Cavalry Corps.
24: 4th. Army.

Issued by D.R. at 11.30 a.m.

5TH CAVALRY DIVISION.

March Table - 21-3-17 (Issued with O.O. No.20).

U N I T.	Starting Point.	Time.	Route.	Billets.	Remarks.
Canadian Cav.Bde.) R.C.H.A.Bde.) (less Amn: Column)) Canadian C.F.A.)	-	-	FREMONTIERS or QUEVAUVILLERS.	BACOUEL - SALOUEL - CLAIRY - SAULCHUIX - CREUSE.	To be clear of THIEULLOY by 9 a.m.
Canadian Section Amn: Column.	Behind the above.	-	-	GUIGNEMICOURT -	To join remainder of Amn: Column.
2.R.H.A.) Amn: Column)	ST.AUBIN.	10 a.m.	FRESNOY AUVAL - PISSY.	GUIGNEMICOURT	
Ambala Cav.Bde. (including "X" Battery).	-	-	THIEULLOY - POIX.	CONTY - TILLOY - LOMUILLY - FREMONTIERS - FLEURY.	To be clear of THIEULLOY by 10.30 a.m.
Sec'bd.Cav.Bde. (including "N" Battery)	THIEULLOY.	10-30 am.	HORNOY - THIEULLOY - ERICAMPS.	NAMPTY - HEBECOURT - BUYON - NA'PS-au-MONT - NA'PS-au-VAL - NEUVILL.	To be clear of the line LIOMER - VILLERS CAMP-SART by 10.30 a.m.
Divnl: Hdqrs. & Signal Sqdn.(less motors)	The line LIOMER - VILLERS CAMPSART.	11 a.m.		PONT DE METZ	) To move to) starting point) in that order) in case of) clashing.
Field squadron.		11.15 am.		PISSY - FLUY.	
Fld.Ambulances (less Can:Amb. & less motors).		11.30 am.		REVELLES.	
Aux: M.T.Coy.		11.45 am		REVELLES.	

(To be allotted by A.D.M.S.)

U N I T.	Starting Point.	Time.	Route.	Billets.	Remarks.
Ammunition Park.) Supply Column.)	As ordered by A.A. & Q.M.G.			QUEVAUVILLERS.	
Motors of Divnl:) Hdqrs. & Signal) Squadron.) Motor Ambulances.) No.9 L.A.C.Bty.)	Billets.	10.30 am.	Optional.	PONT DE METZ. RIVELLES. PONT DE METZ.	Billets to be allotted by Camp Commandant.

SECRET.   5th Cavalry Division.   Copy No. 19
                           Operation Order No.21.

Reference Map 1/100,000.   21st March, 1917.

1. The Division will move Eastwards tomorrow in accordance with the attached march table.

2. "A" and "B" Echelons will accompany Brigades and Divisional Troops. "B" Echelons will probably have to be concentrated under Divisional control early on the morning of 23rd.

3. C.R.H.A. and Headquarters 17th R.H.A. Brigade form part of Divisional Headquarters from midnight 21st/22nd.

4. Representatives of units billetting in CERISY village and in Camps 55 and 131 will meet D.A.A.& Q.M.G. at the Church there at 10.30 a.m.
The Town Major of HAMEL will give information regarding Camp 60 and the Prisoners Camp.

5. Motors of Divisional Headquarters and Signal Squadron and No.9 L.A.C. Battery stand fast.

6. Report Centre remains at PONT DE METZ, but O.C. Signal Squadron will place a forwarding post at CERISY, to be established by noon.

7. Acknowledge.

                                        J. O'Rorke Capt
                                        for
                                        Lt.Colonel, G.S.,
                                        5th Cavalry Division.

Issued at 3.30 p.m by D.R.

Copies Nos. 1 - 21 at Normal Operation Order distribution.
Copy No. 22 to Cavalry Corps.
  "   "   23 " Fourth Army.
  "   "   24 " III Corps.
  "   "   25 " IV   "   .

5th Cavalry Division.
March Table - 22.3.17. (Issued with Operation Order No.21).

Unit.	Starting Point.	Time.	Route.	Billets.	Remarks.
Div.H.Q.& Signal Sqdn.(less Motors).	N.E.of SALOUEL.	9.00 am.	LONGUEAU - VILLERS BRETONNEUX	CERISY.	
Canadian Cav. Bde. & Canadian Fd. Amb.	Do.	9.30 am.	Do.	Camps 55 and 131 S. of CERISY.	May billet H.Q. in CERISY.
Field Squadron.	Do.	10.30 am.	Do.	CERISY.	Must be clear of VILLERS BRETONNEUX by 2 p.m. Not to enter VILLERS BRETONNEUX before 2 p.m.
Sec'bad Cav. Bde.	RUMIGNY.	Optional.	BOVES - VILLERS BRETONNEUX.	Camp 60 and Prisoners Camp S.& E. of HAMEL.	Billets to be allotted by D.M.S.
Field Ambulances (less Canadian). A.H.T.Company.	BEVELLES.	10.30 am.	VERS - DURY - BOVES, thence follow Sec'bad Brigade.	CACHY - GENTELLES.	
Ammunition Column.	GUIGNEMICOURT.	11.30 am.	SALEUX - DURY - BOVES.	THENNES - BERTEAUCOURT	
Ambala Cavalry Bde.	Optional.	Optional.	AILLY SUR NOYE - ROUVREL - CASTEL.	CAIX - CAYEUX - IGNAUCOURT - DEMUIN - HANGARD.	To be in billets by 1 pm.
Ammunition Park Supply Column.	Optional.As ordered by A.A.& Q.M.G.			MARCELCAVE.	Not to enter billets before 5 p.m.

SECRET.   No.G.A./589.

                                       Headquarters 5th Cavalry Division.

                                                22nd March, 1917.

Issued at Normal Operation Order Distribution.

Fourth Army.   )
III Corps.   ) For information.
IV   "   .   )
                      ----

1. In continuation of Operation Order No.22 of today's date, the following moves will take place tomorrow :-

   (a) Ambala Cavalry Brigade and attached troops as in para.2 (a).
       Starting Point - HARBONNIERES, 10 a.m.
       Route - PROYART - S. of FROISSY - CAPPY - ECLUSIER - S. of
               FRISE.
       Destination - B. DE LERBAUCOURT.

   (b) Canadian Cavalry Brigade and attached troops as in para.2 (b).
       Starting Point - CERISY, 10 a.m.
       Route - ETINEHEM - BRAY - MARICOURT - HEM - CLERY.

       Destination - HALLE.

   (c) Divisional Headquarters and Signal Squadron (less motors).
       Starting Point - CERISY, 9 a.m.
       Route - MARICOURT - S. of FROISSY - CAPPY - HERBECOURT -
               BIACHES - HALLE.
       Destination - PERONNE.

   (d) Motors of Divisional Headquarters and Signal Squadron.
       Starting Point - PONT DE METZ, 10 a.m.
       Route - VILLERS BRETONNEUX - WARFUSEE - PROYART - CAPPY,
               thence as for remainder of Divisional Headquarters.

   (e) No.9 L.A.C. Battery will move so as to reach CERISY not later
       than 1 p.m.

   (f) Supply Column and Ammunition Park as ordered by A.A.& Q.M.G.

2. The remainder of the Division will probably not move, but will be prepared to do so at half an hour's notice after 10 a.m.

3. G.Os.C. Ambala and Canadian Cavalry Brigades will reconnoitre routes forward for the following days operations in accordance with the information already given them.

Cancelled 4. ~~Echelons will accompany Brigades but will come under Divisional control on arrival in the new area.~~

5. G.Os.C. Ambala and Canadian Cavalry Brigades will issue the necessary orders to the detachments   not at present with them. In the case of R.C.H.A. Light Section, it is not necessary that it should march closed up to the rest of the Brigade.

6. Reports to PERONNE after 1 p.m.

7. Acknowledge.
                                         R.G.Howard-Vyse
                                         Lt.Colonel, G.S.,
                                         5th Cavalry Division.

SECRET.　　　　　　　　　　　　　　　　　No.G.A.589/1.

Headquarters 5th Cavalry Division.

22nd March, 1917.

Issued at Normal O.O. Distribution.

　　Fourth Army (for information).

1. Following is substituted for para.4 of G.A.589.

　　Rug wagons only of "B" Echelon will accompany Brigades and units of Divisional Troops.

2. Remainder of "B" Echelon will concentrate W. of HERBECOURT and will there come under the orders of the senior officer present.
　　This officer will receive instructions at HERBECOURT from D.A.A.& Q.M.G.

　　(a) That of Divisional Headquarters and Signal Squadron will follow those units as far as HERBECOURT.

　　(b) That of Ambala Cavalry Brigade will follow its Brigade as far as CAPPY and will thence march independently to HERBECOURT.

　　(c) That of Canadian Cavalry Brigade will march independently via MORCOURT - MERICOURT - S. of FROISSY and will thence follow the "B" Echelon of Ambala Cavalry Brigade which should reach that place about noon.

3. "B" Echelons of Ambala and Canadian Cavalry Brigades will be accompanied by 1 Sergeant per Brigade and 1 man per unit, as it is necessary to dump the contents of "B" Echelon near HERBECOURT.

　　　　　　　　　　　　　　　　　　　　　Lt.Colonel, G.S.,

　　　　　　　　　　　　　　　　　　　　　5th Cavalry Division.

App. 96

SECRET.   5th Cavalry Division.   Copy No. 19

Operation Order No.22.

Reference 1/100,000 map.   22nd March, 1917.

1. The Division will march tomorrow to an area West of PERONNE in order to pass through our infantry on the following day.

2. The following groupings take effect from receipt of this order :-

   (a) Under G.O.C. Ambala Cavalry Brigade.

      "X" R.H.A. and Light Section Ammunition Column.
      1 Field Troop.
      Mhow Field Ambulance.

   (b) Under G.O.C. Canadian Cavalry Brigade.

      R.C.H.A. Brigade and Light Section Ammunition Column.
      1 Field Troop.
      Canadian Field Ambulance.

   (c) Under G.O.C. Secunderabad Cavalry Brigade.

      "N" R.H.A. and Light Section Ammunition Column.

3. Details of the march and of bivouacs will be issued later. Canadian Cavalry Brigade and attached troops will march North of the SOMME: the remainder of the Division will march South of the SOMME.

4. The Division will march about 9 a.m. except

   (a) Motors of Divisional H.Q. and Signal Squadron and No.9 L.A.C. Battery, which will march at 10 a.m.

   (b) Supply Column and Ammunition Park, which will probably not move.

5. "B" Echelon of Canadian Cavalry Brigade will accompany its Brigade.

"B" Echelons of Ambala and Secunderabad Brigades will march under Divisional control and will be concentrated in Brigade areas by 10 a.m.

                                  Lt. Colonel, G.S.,

                                  5th Cavalry Division.

Issued at 9-15am by D.R.

Copies No.1 to 21 (incl) at Normal O.O. Distribution.
Copy No.22 to Cavalry Corps.
  " " 23 " Fourth Army.
  " " 24 " III Corps.
  " " 25 " IV ".

Appx 97

SECRET.   No. G.A./597.

Headquarters 5th Cavalry Division.

23rd March, 1917.

Issued at Norm 1 O.O. Distribution.

Fourth Army (For information)

----

1. The remainder of the Division will not move today.

2. The following troops are placed temporarily under the orders of G.O.C. Secunderabad Cavalry Brigade.

	Present Location.
Ammn. Column (less "X" and Canadian Light Sections).	THENNES – BERTEAUCOURT.
Field Squadron (less 2 Troops)	CERISY.
No. 9 L.A.C. Battery.	Moving to CERISY.
Sec'bad Field Ambulance.	CACHY – GENTELLES.
A.H.T. Company.	---Ditto----

3. The billets at CERISY and Camps 55 and 131 South of that place are placed at the disposal of G.O.C. Secunderabad Cavalry Brigade.

Lt. Colonel, G.S.,
5th Cavalry Division.

S E C R E T.   5th CAVALRY DIVISION.   COPY NO. 19

OPERATION ORDER NO. 23.

Reference Map   23:3:17.
     1
  ‾‾‾‾‾‾‾
  100,000

1.   Information as already circulated.

2.   The tasks of the Division are :-

(a) To ascertain the dispositions of the advanced
    hostile detachments.

(b) To ascertain the enemy's defences and strength.

(c) To picket the enemy so as to prevent his ad-
    vancing and so as to give instant information
    of any withdrawal.

(d) To be ready to follow up the enemy if he with-
    draws.

Brig-Gen. Rankin.

Ambala Cav. Bde.
& attached troops
1 Co.IV Corps
       Cyclists.
2 platoons III
   Corps Cyclists.

3(a) Ambala Cavalry Brigade (strength as in margin)
     will be responsible for carrying out the above
     task between the lines VIEFVILLE (inclusive) -
     VILLERS ST. CHRISTOPHE - DOUCHY - ROUPY - ST.
     QUENTIN (all exclusive) and AIZECOURT LE HAUT -
     TEMPLEUX - LONGAVESNES - EPEHY - HONNECOURT (all
     exclusive).

     Advanced detachments will be on the line
     GERMAINE - BERNES - MARQUAIX by 11.30 a.m. The
     Brigade will advance via BIACHES - HALLE -
     PERONNE.

     Touch to be established with the advanced de-
     tachments of the French.

Brig-Gen. Seely.

Canadian Cav.
Bde. & attached
troops.
XIV Corps Cav.
Regt. & Cyclist
Bn. (temporarily
only).

(b) Canadian Cavalry Brigade (strength as in
    margin) will be responsible for carrying out
    the above tasks between the lines AIZECOURT LE
    HAUT - TEMPLEUX - LONGAVESNES - EPEHY - HONNE-
    COURT (all inclusive) and LE TRANSLOY - BARASTRE
    - BERTINCOURT - HAVRINCOURT (all inclusive).

    Advanced detachments will be on the line
    TEMPLEUX - AIZECOURT - LE BAS - NURLU - BUS -
    BERTINCOURT by 11.30 a.m..

    Touch to be established with the advanced de-
    tachments of Fifth Army (Anzac Corps).

(c) Divisional Headquarters and Signal Squadron do not move.

(d) No. 9 L.A.C. Battery will move at 9.0 a.m. to FOUCAUCOURT and will there wait further orders.

Brig.Gen.GREGORY (e)

Sec'bad Cav.Bde.
& attached troops
Main Ammunition
Column.
Field Squadron
(less 2 troops)
Sec'bad Field
Amba.
A.R.T.Coy.

Remainder of Division as in margin will march under orders of G.O.C. Secunderabad Cavalry Brigade.
Starting point - X roads S.of CHUIGNOLLES,10.0 a.m.
Route - CAPPY- S.of FRISE.
Destination.- BOIS DE MERAUCOURT.

"B" Echelons will however move to FLAUCOURT and come under the orders of the senior officer there.

Attachment of Corps Mounted Troops.

4.(a) 1 Company IVth.Corps Cyclists and 2 Platoons III Corps Cyclists come under orders of G.O.C. Ambala Cavalry Brigade at 11.0 a.m. at ATHIES and ESTREES EN CHAUSSEE. They will be used *respectively* principally for establishing relay posts between the Brigade and Divisional Headquarters and within the Brigade. The Wireless Detachment of III Corps Cavalry will report at the same time and place.

(b) XIVth. Corps Cavalry Regiment and Cyclist Batn. come under orders of G.O.C. Canadian Cavalry Brigade at 10.0 a.m. at MOISLAINS. He will report assuming command. A portion of the cyclists may be used for relay posts as in (a) above. The rest will not be moved without reference to Divisional Headquarters.

Intercommunication.

5.(a) Brigades will communicate direct with Corps on whose front they are operating. For this purpose Liaison officers of Corps Cavalry will report as follows:-

To Ambala Cavalry Brigade from III Corps
ESTREES EN CHAUSSEE - 11.0 a.m.

To Ambala Cavalry Brigade from IVth.Corps
ATHIES - 11.0 a.m.

To Canadian Cavalry Brigade from XIVth. &
XVth. Corps.
MOISLAINS -10.0 a.m.

(b) Liaison Officers and Gallopers will report at Divisional Headquarters at 9.0 a.m. (Ambala and Canadian) and noon (Secunderabad)

Aeroplanes 6. R.F.C.Liaison Officer will arrange for 2 machines

to be continuously on contact patrol from 11.30 a.m. to 2.0 p.m. and from 4.30 p.m. to 6 p.m., and for as much of the rest of the day as is possible. The machines should between them work over the whole front of the Division.

Line of Resistance.	7. The Line of Resistance in case of attack will be GERMAINE-BEAUVOIS-POEUILLY-BERNES-HERVUAIX-LONGAVESNES-LIERAMONT-NURLU- thence BUSNCOURT-YERES-BRETINCOURT, if in our possession, otherwise the line at present held by the infantry.

Instructions as regards holding and strengthening the above line will be issued later. Brigades will reconnoitre it and submit proposals as early as possible. |
Situation Reports.	8. Situation Reports are required to reach Divisional Headquarters daily by 5 a.m. and 5 p.m.
Reports	9. Reports to P.MOINE.
	10. Acknowledge.

R.G. Howard Vyse

Lieut-Colonel, G.S.

5th. Cavalry Division.

Copies Nos. 1-21	Normal Distribution.
22	Cavalry Corps.
23	Fourth Army.
24	IIIrd. Corps.
25	IVth. Corps.
26	XIVth. Corps.
27	XVth. Corps.
28	Anzac Corps.
29	R.F.C. Liaison Officer.
30	O.C. "B" Echelon.

Issued by D.R. at 5.0 p.m.

Appx 99

SECRET   5TH. CAVALRY DIVISION.   COPY NO. 19

OPERATION ORDER NO. 24.

Reference Map   24th. March, 1917.
1/100,000 FRANCE.

1.   (a)   The enemy appears to be holding his advanced line on our front with weak detachments only, except about SAVY and BOIS D'HOLNON and between LONGAUESNES and SOREL, where he seems to be rather stronger.

    (b)   The Advanced Troops of the Division are on the line ETREILLERS-BEAUVOIS-CAULAINCOURT-BERNES-ROISEL-BOIS DE TINCOURT-TEMPLEUX LA FOSSE-AIZECOURT LE BAS-NURLU-BUS-BERTINCOURT. Patrols have entered YTRES.

2.   The Division will continue the tasks laid down in Operation Order No. 23. Reconnaissances will be pushed forward in all directions, and all localities not held in strength by the enemy will be occupied.

3.   (a)   <u>Ambala Cavalry Brigade and attached troops</u> will pay particular attention to

        (i)   VILLEVEQUE, the wood East of that place, and the strip of wood running East from CAULAINCOURT.

        (ii)   HESBECOURT and VILLERS FAUCON.

     (b)   <u>Canadian Cavalry Brigade and attached troops</u> will pay particular attention to the line EQUANCOURT-YTRES.

     (c)   <u>Remainder of the Division and 14th. Corps Mounted Troops</u> will be ready to move at 3 hours notice after 10.0 a.m.

4.   <u>R.F.C. Liaison Officer</u> will arrange for

     (a)   Special reconnaissances of the line VERMAND-SOYECOURT-VENDELLES (to be photographed) and of the area EQUANCOURT-GOUZEAUCOURT-METZ EN COUTURE-BERTINCOURT.

     (b)   <u>Contact Patrols</u> from   8.30 a.m. - 10.30 a.m.
                                            1.30 p.m. - 3.30 p.m.
                                            3.30 p.m. - 5.30 p.m.

5.   <u>Acknowledge.</u>

                                                            Lieut-Colonel,
                                                      5th. Cavalry Division.

Copies Nos. 1-21 Normal O.O.
             22 Fourth Army.
             23 Third Corps.
             24 Fourth Corps.
             25 Fifteenth Corps.
             26 R.F.C. Liaison Officer.
             27 O.C. "B" Echelon.
             28 OC XIV Corps Mounted Troops.

Issued by D.R. at 9.15 p.m.

MESSAGES AND SIGNALS.

Prefix.......... Code.......... m. Office of Origin and Service Instructions.	Words / Charge / Sent At...........m. To.......... By..........	This message is on a/c of: *app* Service. (Signature of "Franking Officer.")	Recd. at..........m. Date.......... From.......... By..........

TO	3rd. Corps.	Cav. Corps		
	4th. "	Fourth Army		
	15th. "			

Sender's Number	Day of Month	In reply to Number	
G.I.2	24.3.17		AAA

Ambala Bde. right Regt. H.Q. MONCHY LAGACHES. One troop at each of following places - VAUX-BEAUVOIS-TREFCON and CAULAINCOURT and POEUILLY. Left Regt. H.Q. HANCOURT and occupy LERNES-FLECHIN-ROBESCOURT FARM- POINT 114-MARQUAIX and HAMELET aaa 4th. Corps Cavalry patrols report heavily fired on from W. bank of R. OMIGON between CAULAINCOURT and MARTEVILLE aaa Patrols fired on from VENDELLES-SOYECOURT direction. They report belt of wire 20 ft. deep from rail station S.W. of JEANCOURT to SOYECOURT. Bde. H.Q. ESTREES EN CHAUSSEE aaa Canadian Bde. H.Q. MOISLAINS. Right Regt. H.Q. ST.PIERRE FARM. Occupied BOIS DE TINCOURT-AIZECOURT to HURLU exclusive-reconnaissance pushed forward to LONGAVESNES - in touch with Ambala Bde. aaa Enemy in small wood and station E. of YPRES.

From	5th. Cav. Div.		
Place			
Time			

The above may be forwarded as now corrected.

(Z) (sd) J. GWATKIN, Capt. for GS

No. G.A. 658.

Headquarters, 5th. Cavalry Division.
Dated 26th, March.1917.

To/
    Sec'bad Cavalry Brigade.
    Canadian   "   "
    Ambala   "   "
    5th. Field Squadron.
    14th. Corps Cyclists.

1. The G.O.C. Ambala Cavalry Brigade will cause the following reconnaissances to be carried out today or tonight.

    (a) With a view to occupying VERMAND and SOYECOURT. Artillery reconnaissance for two or three battery positions will be included.

    (b) Enemy's defences BOIS D'HOLNON-ATTILLY-MARTEVILLE, in order to discover whether these are wired.

2. The following attachments will take place today :-

    (a) <u>Remainder of Field Squadron</u> (H.Q. and 1 troop) to Ambala Brigade. To be employed on road repair in the area MONCHY LAGACHE - VILLEVEQUE-FLECHIN-BOUVINCOURT. The MONS EN CHAUSSEE-VERMAND road will be attended to first.

    (b) <u>1 Coy XIV Corps Cyclist Battalion</u> to Ambala Bde.

    (c) <u>XIV Corps Cyclist Btn.</u> (less 1 Coy) to Can. Bde.

3. (a) Detachments (a) and (b) above will march via HALLE-PERONNE-DOINGT, so as to reach MONS EN CHAUSSEE by 4 p.m.
        O's C. will report at H.Q. Ambala Brigade ESTREES EN CHAUSSEE as early as possible before that hour.

    (b) Detachment (c) above will march via MONT ST QUENTIN so as to reach MOISLAINS by 4 p.m. O.C. to report at H.Q. Canadian Bde. as early as possible before that hour.

4. <u>The Relay Posts</u> at present found by XIV Corps Cyclist Btn. will remain in their present position.

5. The order given verbally to <u>"N" Battery</u> to be prepared to move at short notice after 8 a.m. is cancelled.

                                  (Sd) R.G. Howard-Vyse,Lt.Col.
                                        5th. Cavalry Division.

Copy to:-
    4th. Army.
    XIV Corps
    C.R.H.A.
    Sigl. Sqdn.
    "Q"
    O.C. A.S.C.

Issued by D.R. at 6 a.m.

SECRET

Reference Map
1
100,000
FRANCE

5TH. CAVALRY DIVISION.

OPERATION ORDER NO.25.   Copy No. 19

Dated 27th. March, 1917.

1. Canadian Cavalry Brigade took LONGAVESNES and EQUANCOURT yesterday. 48th. Division, assisted by Ambala Cavalry Brigade and No. 9 L.A.C. Battery, took NOISEL.

2. The principal objects of today's operations are :-

   (a) To capture LIERAMONT.
   (b) To establish ourselves on the high ground overlooking VILLERS FAUCON, SAULCOURT and GUYENCOURT.
   (c) To occupy those places.

3. The line of demarcation will be LONGAVESNES- VILLERS FAUCON both inclusive to Canadian Brigade.

4. With the above objects in view.

   (a) Ambala Cavalry Brigade will, by 4 p.m. establish themselves on the line of the road from NOISEL to LONGAVESNES. Arrangements have been made for co-operation by the artillery of Brig.Genl! Ward's Column. C.R.H.A. is placed at the disposal of G.O.C. Ambala Cavalry Brigade, and will report to him at 10 a.m. at S. entrance to BOUCLY. A Battery should be pushed forward as soon as the first objective is taken, in order to support the advance of the Canadian Cavalry Brigade.

   (b) Canadian Cavalry Brigade with "N" Battery attached will advance at 5 p.m. to seize the high ground between LONGAVESNES and LIERAMONT.

   (c) N. Battery R.H.A. will march at 7 a.m. via BLACHES-HAUTE-ST.DENIS to AIZECOURT LE HAUT, where it will come under orders of G.O.C. Canadian Cavalry Brigade. O.C. will report to G.O.C. Canadian Cavalry Brigade at MOISLAINS at 10 a.m.

5. Arrangements must be made by Ambala and Canadian Cavalry Brigades for the closest possible liaison during the whole operation. They will report to Divisional H.Q. early their own report centres and those of the regiments taking part.

6. R.F.C. Liaison Officer will arrange for

   (a) The trench line VERMAND-BOYECOURT-VENDELLES to be photographed.

   (b) A reconnaissance at 10 a.m. of the area LONGAVESNES-VILLERS FAUCON-HEUDICOURT-EQUANCOURT with the special object of discovering hostile entrenchments.

   (c) Two machines to be continuously on contact patrol, in connection with the above operation, from 4 p.m. to 6.30 p.m.

7. (a) Secunderabad Cavalry Brigade (less "N" Battery) and Ammunition Column will march in that order, starting at 1 p.m., via BLACHES to a new bivouac near HAMEL. Representatives will meet D.A.A. & Q.M.G. at HAMEL at noon.

(b) "N" R.H.A. will return to the above bivouac on the
    conclusion of the operation.
    G.O.C. Canadian Cavalry Brigade will inform O.C. "N"
    Battery when he is free to return.

8. <u>Reports</u> to church at TEMPLEUX LA FOSSE after 4 p.m.

9. Acknowledge.

               R.Howard-Vyse

               Lieut-Colonel, G.S.

              5th. Cavalry Division.

Copies Nos. 1-21 Normal O.O.
     22 Fourth Army.
     23 III Corps.
     24 IV "
     25 Fifteenth Corps.
     26 R.F.C. Liaison Officer.
     27 O.C. "B" Echelon.
     28 48th. Division.
     29 "N" R.H.A.

Issued by D.R. at 6.0 a.m.

No. G.A. 687.

Headquarters, 5th. Cavalry Division
Dated 27th. March, 1917.

To/
Secbad Cav. Bde.   Camp Commandant.
Canadian "   "   A.P.M.
Ambala   "   "   G.S.O.1
17th. Bde. R.H.A.   Office G.S.
R.C.H.A.   War Diary.
Ammn. Column.   No. 9 L.A.C. Bty.
Fd. Squadron.
Sigl. Sqdn.
A.
O.C. A.S.C.
A.D.M.S.
A.D.C.

---

1. LIERAMONT is in our possession aaa We also hold part at least of the ROISEL-LONGAVESNES ridge, Hill 140 N.E. of LONGAVESNES, and Hill 132 North of EQUANCOURT aaa Enemy were still in SAULCOURT and GUYENCOURT at 9.30 a.m.

2. The operations this afternoon will be conducted with the objects laid down in Operation Order No. 25, paras 2 (b) and (c), and also of establishing advanced posts beyond the villages named.

3. The advanced detachments of both brigades will pass through the line of advanced posts at 5 p.m.

4. VILLERS FAUCON is inclusive to Ambala Brigade, and not to Canadian.

R.E. Howard Vyse

Lieut Colonel, G.S.
5th. Cavalry Division.

Copies to:-

Fourth Army.
III Corps.
IV "
XV "
R.F.C. Liaison Officer.
O.C. "B" Echelon.
Divisional Liaison Officers.
48th Division

App/102

NARRATIVE OF THE OPERATIONS OF THE 5TH. CAVALRY DIVISION BETWEEN MARCH 24TH. and MARCH 27TH.

March 24th. The Ambala and Canadian Cavalry Brigades took over from Corps Cavalry along the Fourth Army front. The dividing line between the Brigades was AIZECOURT LE HAUT-TEMPLEUX-LONGAVESNES-EPEHY-HONNECOURT (exclusive to Ambala Cavalry Brigade).

The front taken over was VAUX BEAUVOIS-TREFCON CAULAINCOURT-POEUILLY-FLECHIN-BERNES-ROBESCOURT FM-HAMELET-MARQUAIX-BOIS de BUIRE-AIZECOURT LE BAS-NURLU-ETRICOURT-LECHELLE-BUS. Touch was gained between the two brigades and with French on the South and Anzac infantry on the north in BERTINCOURT.

Canadian Cavalry Brigade pushed patrols into YTRES in the evening, found it unoccupied, and established posts there. The B de TINCOURT, late on the 24th, was captured.

Some shell fire and encounters between patrols along the whole front after taking over at 11.30 a.m.

H.Q. of Division and Bdes. on 24th. as follows:-

```
Division H.Q.      -   PERONNE.
Ambala Cav. Bde. H.Q.  -   ESTREES-en-CHAUSSEE.
Can.    "    "   H.Q.  -   MOISLAINS.
Sec.    "    "   H.Q.  -   BOIS de MEREAUCOURT just
                            south of FEUILLIERES.
```

March 25th. During the night 24/25th. 9th. Hodson's Horse (Ambala Cav. Bde) occupied ETREILLERS. One of their posts in this village was raided and two men were reported missing. VILLEVEQUE was also captured by the 9th. Hodson's Horse.

Canadian Cavalry Brigade aptured YTRES, small wood to the south, and the BOIS de VALLULART (P.33.a).

Front of the Ambala Cavalry Brigade extended to the N.E. to include B de TINCOURT. VILLERS-FAUCON - B. de TINCOURT were taken over by Ambala from Canadian Bde. during the day.

Outpost reconnaissance and patrol fighting along the whole front.

March 26th. A post of Royal Canadian Dragoons N. of AIZECOURT was raided on the night 25/26th, but the enemy were driven off with loss.

Canadian Cavalry Brigade captured the villages of LONGAVESNES and EQUANCOURT and wood just S.E. of the latter villages, driving out small enemy detachments. The defence of these places was then handed over to the infantry.

Two squadrons 18th. Lancers with two armoured cars (Ambala Cav.Bde) co-operated with a btn. of Ward's force

in the attack .....

in the attack on ROISEL. The Armoured Cars drove the enemy from the western exit of ROISEL, firing on them retreating N.E.

Two squadrons encircling the village north and south were held up on the flanks of the village.

The village of ROISEL was taken by our troops in the afternoon.

March 27th.
During the night 26/27th.

(a) <u>Canadian Cav. Bde.</u> took LIERAMONT, pushing out a small enemy detachment. Infantry then took over the defence of the village.

(b) <u>9th. Hodson's Horse</u> carried out a reconnaissance of BOIS D'HOLNON towards MARTEVILLE and VERMAND. Report was forwarded to Fourth Army.

About 2 p.m. a troop of <u>Royal Canadian Dragoons</u> charged a small hostile party entrenched about 1000 yards East of LONGAVESNES. Several of the enemy were killed and wounded and 9 other ranks captured.

An operation with the objective the villages of VILLERS-FANCON-SAULCOURT-GOYENCOURT, was carried out late in the afternoon.

The following troops took part :-

(a) <u>Under G.O.C. Ambala Cavalry Brigade</u>
8th. Hussars.
M.G. Squadron.
"X" R.H.A.
No. 9 L.A.C. Battery.
3 Batteries 48th. Division.

(b) <u>Under G.O.C. Canadian Cavalry Brigade</u>
The Brigade.
R.C.H.A. Brigade.
15th. Corps Cav. Regt.

<u>Lord Strathcona's Horse</u> drove the enemy from GOYENCOURT, taking 1 machine gun and 3 prisoners and occupying the village.

<u>FORT GARRY HORSE</u> captured SAULCOURT, taking 1 machine gun.

<u>8th. Hussars and 2 cars No. 9 L.A.C. Battery</u> captured VILLERS-FANCON: 2 machine guns taken and 1 officer and 10 O.R. captured.

March 28th.
<u>9th. Hodson's Horse (Ambala Cavalry Brigade)</u> carried out a reconnaissance of the enemy on their front, a report of which has been forwarded to Fourth Army. Brigade (less 1 squadron) was relieved in the afternoon.

One squadron of <u>18th. Lancers (Amb. Cav. Bde)</u> remained out as reconnaissance squadron during the day at VILLERS-FANCON, and was withdrawn after dark. The whole brigade was concentrated in the vicinity of MONCHY-LAGACHE early on 29th.

<u>Canadian Cavalry Brigade.</u> After the action

on the 27th.....

on the 27th. the Royal Canadian Dragoons returned to
MOISLAINS at 9 p.m. and "N" Battery rejoined the
Secunderabad Cavalry Brigade on the night 27/28th.
The remainder of the brigade remained in position
SAULCOURT-GUYENCOURT during the night 27th/28th. when
they withdrew to MOISLAINS, leaving out one squadron
holding advanced posts until relieved later on the
28th.

SUMMARY.

During the period covered by this narrative, 5th.
Cavalry Division occupied the villages of ETREVILLERS,
VILLEVEQUE, LONGAVESNES, VILLERS-FANCON, LIERAMONT,
SAULCOURT, GUYENCOURT, EQUANCOURT and YTRES, also co-
operating with the infantry in the capture of ROISEL
and the B de TINCOURT.

One officer and 22 O.R. were captured and 4 machine
guns taken.

The losses in the 5th. Cavalry Division during
this period were

	Killed	Wounded	Missing
Officers	--	6	--
Other ranks	4	65	15

Horse casualties   Riding - 101
                   L.D.   3

appx 103

SECRET   5TH. CAVALRY DIVISION.   Copy No. 19

OPERATION ORDER NO. 26.

Dated 28th. March, 1917.

Reference Map

$\frac{1}{100,000}$ FRANCE.

1.   (a)   Ambala and Canadian Brigades took VILLERS FAUCON, SAULCOURT, GUYENCOURT yesterday. Advanced posts were established at STE. EMILIE (North of the Railway) and one mile East of SAULCOURT.
           HEUDICOURT and SOREL were found by Corps Cavalry to be still held by the enemy.

     (b)   Infantry Advanced Guards have now taken over the line held by the Division.

2.   The Division is being withdrawn to a position of assembly West of PERONNE.

3.   In consequence

     (a)   Secunderabad Cavalry Brigade, (including Light Section Ammunition Column and Sec'bad Fd. Ambs) marches at 3 p.m. today to a bivouac between CLERY and HEM.

     (b)   Divisional Headquarters and Signal Squadron remain in their present position.

     (c)   No. 9 L.A.C. Battery will move to FAUBOURG DE BRETAGNE at 5 p.m., where it will remain until the cars at present at VILLERS FAUCON have rejoined. Further orders will then be issued.

     (d)   Supply Column and Ammunition Park will not move.

     (e)   Remainder of Division will move tomorrow in accordance with attached March Table.

     (f)   14th. Corps Cyclist Battalion will assemble at 10 a.m. at MT. ST. QUENTIN and march thence independently to report for orders to O.C. 14th. Corps Mounted Troops at LE MESNIL-EN ARROUAISE.

4.   Intervals of 100 yds. will be maintained between squadrons or equivalent units.

..............5.

5. Representatives of Formations and Units bivouacking at Cp. 57 N. of CAPPY will report to D.A.A. & Q.M.G. at CAPPY CH. at 10 a.m.

6. <u>Field Troops</u> attached to Brigades are to be used for improving shelters and bivouacs and communications in the vicinity of bivouacs. One Field Troop is placed under orders of G.O.C. Sec'bad Cav. Bde. from arrival in their bivouac at CLERY-HEM.

7. Liaison officers and gallopers will rejoin their units in bivouacs tomorrow evening.

8. Acknowledge.

                                                Lieut-Colonel, G.S.
                                                5th. Cavalry Division.

Nos. 1 to 21. Normal O.O.
        22 XIV Corps Cyclist Btn.
        23 III Corps.
        24 IV "
        25 XV "
        26 R.F.C. Liaison Officer.
        27 O.C. "B" Echelon.
        28 Fourth Army.
        29 Cavalry Corps.

Issued by D.R. at 5-30 p.m.

5th Cavalry Division
March Tables 29-3-17 (Issued with Op: Order No 26)

Formation & Unit	Starting Point	Time	Route	Destination	Remarks
"B" Echelon (less Div H.Q and Sig'l Sqn) and A.H.T. Coys.	Bivouacs	8 am	HALLE–BIACHES– HERBÉCOURT– CAPPY.	Camp 5b, N. of CAPPY.	—
Main Amm'n Col.	Bridge S. of HALLE.	8 am	"	"	—
Reserve Park	"	8-15 am	"	"	Move to starting point behind Amm'n Column.
Under G.O.C. Can. Cav. Bde.					
Can. Cav. Bde. R.C.H.A. Bde. Right Section Amm" Col. 1 Field Troop Cav. Field Amb.	"	11 am	ALLAINES– MT. ST QUENTIN, thence as above.	"	
Under G.O.C. Ambala Cav. Bde.					
Ambala Cav. Bde. X Bty R.H.A. Right Section Amm" Column Field Sqdn (less 1 Troop) 1 how. Cav. Field Amb.	DOINGT.	1 am	PERONNE– HALLE– BIACHES– HERBÉCOURT.	BOIS de MEREAUCOURT	1 Field Troop to join Sec'ond Bde in CLERY-HEM bivouac.

Appx 104

SECRET

5TH. CAVALRY DIVISION.
OPERATION ORDER NO.27

Copy No. 19

Reference Map

$$\frac{1}{100,000}$$

FRANCE

Dated 30th. March, 1917.

1. The Division, less troops now at CAPPY, will move Westwards today, in accordance with the attached march table.

2. Secunderabad Brigade and Canadian Brigade will be prepared to exchange billets in the course of two or three days, under orders which will be issued later.

3. B. Echelon will remain for the present at CAPPY.
A.A. & Q.M.G. will arrange to move the "B" Echelon kits by lorry.

4. The Conference ordered for 4 p.m. today is postponed.

5. Reports to VILLERS BRETONNEUX after 2 p.m.

Lieut-Colonel, G.S.

5th. Cavalry Division.

Copies Nos. 1 - 21 Normal O.O.
22 Fourth Army.
23 Cavalry Corps.
24 III Corps.
25 48th. Division.
26 O.C. "B" Echelon.
27 R.F.C. Liaison Officer.

Issued by D.R. at 12.30 a.m.

5th Cavalry Division

March Table 30-3-18. (Issued with O.O. H29 Y).

Formations & units	Starting Point	Time	Route	Destination	Remarks
Under K.O.C. Ambala Bde. Ambala Cav. Bde. X Bty R.H.A. Light Sec. Am. Col. F.A. Sqdn (less 2 troops) Man Cav Fd. Amb.	Bois de MÉRICOURT	10:30 am	FRISÉ - CAPPY - PROYART.	MARFUSÉE ABANCOURT.	Not to enter PROYART before noon.
Div. H.Qrs and Sig: Squadron (less motors)	PÉRONNE	10:30 am	Fbg de PARIS - BIACHES - HERBÉCOURT - CAPPY - PROYART.	VILLERS - BRETONNEUX.	Follow Ambala Bde from CAPPY.
Under G.O.C. Sec. Bde. Sec. Cav. Bde. N. Bty R.H.A. Light Sec. Amm Col. Field Troop Section Cav. Fd. Amb.	HEM	11:30 am	FRISÉ - CAPPY - PROYART.	BAYON - VILLERS.	Div. H.Q. have precedence
Motors of Div. H.Qrs & Signal Squadron. No 9 2nd Battery	PÉRONNE	2 pm 2:15 pm	Fbg de PARIS - VILLERS CARBONNEL - FOUCAUCOURT.	VILLERS BRETONNEUX. — do —	Billets to be allotted by Camp Comdt. — do —

App 93

SECRET

5TH. CAVALRY DIVISION
OPERATION ORDER NO. 19.

Copy No. 20.

Reference Map FRANCE 1/100,000.   19th. March, 1917.

1. The Division will move tomorrow, the 20th. March, in accordance with the attached march table.

2. "B" Echelon will march with Brigades and Divisional Troops.

3. Divisional Troops will march under 2nd. in command of the 5th. Field Squadron.

4. No. 9 L.A.C. Battery and motors of Mhow and Sec'bad C.F.A's, and Sanitary Section will follow the Division on 21st. March, under orders which will be issued later.

5. Units not mentioned in orders or March Table will move under instructions of "Q" Staff.

6. Divisional Report Centre will remain at DARGNIES till morning 21st. March.

7. Acknowledge.

Nos. 1 to 21 : Normal O.O. Distribution.
     22 : Aux. H.T. Coy.
     23 : Cavalry Corps.
     24 : Fourth Army.

J. O'Rorke
Captain, G.S.
5th. Cavalry Division.

Issued by D.R. at 9.30, p.m.

5TH CAVALRY DIVISION.

March Table. 20th March (issued with O.O.No.19,d/19-3-17).

UNIT.	Starting Point & Time.	To.	Route.	Remarks.
Canadian Cav.Bde.	—	POIX - BLANGY-SOUS-POIX - CROIXRAULT - FRICAMPS - THIEULLOY L'ABBAY.	LE MAZIS - LIOMER - HORNOY.	To be clear of HORNOY by 12 noon. Bde. Hdqrs. to be at POIX.
17th Bde. R.H.A.) Ammunition Col.)	—	ST.AUBIN - LINCHEUX - GOUY L'HOPITAL.	ANDAINVILLE - VILLERS CAMPSART.	To arrive at HORNOY at 12.15 p.m. Hdqrs. to be at LINCHEUX.
Ambala Cavalry Bde.	—	Area :- HORNOY - SELINCOURT - DROMESNIL - VILLERS CAMPSART - LIOMER. Note.- BEZENCOURT is exclusive.	BOUTTENCOURT - SENARPONT.	Not to reach billeting area before 12 noon. Hdqrs. to be at LIOMER.
Sec'bad Cavalry Bde.	—	Area :- LE QUESNE - ARGIEL CAMPSART - FRESNEVILLE - ANDAINVILLE - INVAL BOIRON - ST. AUBIN RIVIERE.	MARTAINNEVILLE Stn. - OISEMONT - AUMATRE.	Hdqrs. to be at LE QUESNE.
DIVNL: TROOPS. Order of March.- Field Squadron	Cross roads ½ mile S. of G in BUIGNY.	SENARPONT - BERNAPRE.	GAMACHES - BOUTTENCOURT - SENARPONT.	"A" Echelon Divnl: Troops will march under an officer to be detailed by O.C. Field Sqdn.
Di\'vnl: Hdqrs.(less motors).	Pass starting point at 10 a.m.			
	At 10.5 a.m.			"B" Echelon Divnl: Troops will march under an officer to be detailed by O.C. A.S.C.
Signal Squadron	At 10.10 a.m.			H.Q. to be at SENARPONT.

DIVNL: TROOPS(Continued -

DIVNL TROOPS (Continued -

UNIT.	Starting Point & Time.	To.	Route.	Remarks.
Mhow I.C.F.A. (less motors)	At 10.15 a.m.	See preceding page.	See preceding page.	See preceding page.
Sec'bad I.C.F.A. (less motors)	At 10.20 a.m.			
Aux: H.T.Coy.	At 10.25 a.m.			
"A" Echelon of above.	At 10.28 a.m.			
"B" Echelon of above.	at 10.30 a.m.			

Appx 94

5TH. CAVALRY DIVISION.   Copy No. 20.

OPERATION ORDER NO. 20.

S E C R E T   20th. March, 1917.

Reference Map 1/100,000 FRANCE.

1. The Division will continue the march Eastwards tomorrow in accordance with the attached March table.

2. "N" and "X" R.H.A. and R.C.H.A. Brigade are, from midnight 20/21st. placed under the orders of G.O's C. Secunderabad, Ambala and Canadian Cavalry Brigades respectively.

3. Canadian Section of Ammunition Column comes under orders of O.C. Ammunition Column on arrival at GUIGNEMICOURT.

4. Canadian Field Ambulance is at the disposal of A.D.M.S., but will be billetted by G.O.C. Canadian Cavalry Brigade, who will report its location in billets to A.D.M.S.

5. "A" and "B" Echelons will accompany Brigades and Divisional Troops.

6. Mounted Troops may pass Wheeled Transport on the march as long as there is no risk of blocking the road.

7. Reports to PONT DE METZ after noon.

J. O'Rorke
Capt for
Lieut-Colonel, G.S.

Nos. 1 to 21: Normal O.O. Distribution,   5th. Cavalry Division.
       22:   Aux H.T. Coy. Colonel Troop
       23:   Cavalry Corps.
       24:   4th. Army.

Issued by D.R. at 11.30 a.m.

5TH CAVALRY DIVISION.

March Table - 21-3-17 (Issued with O.O.No.20).

UNIT.	Starting Point.	Time.	Route.	Billets.	Remarks.
Canadian Cav.Bde. R.C.H.A.Bde.(less Amn: Column) Canadian C.F.A.	-	-	FREMONTIERS or QUEVAUVILLERS.	BACOUEL - SALOUEL - CLAIRY - SAULCHUIX CREUSE.	To be clear of THIEULLOY by 9 a.m.
Canadian Section Amn: Column.	Behind the above.	-	-	GUIGNEMICOURT -	To join remainder of Amn: Column.
C.R.H.A. Amn: Column	ST.AUBIN.	10 a.m.	PRESNOY AUVAL - PISSY.	GUIGNEMICOURT	
Ambala Cav.Bde. (including "X" Battery).	-	-	THIEULLOY - POIX.	CONTY - TILLOY - LOEUILLY - FREMONTIERS FLEURY.	To be clear of THIEULLOY by 10.30 a.m.
Sec'bed Cav.Bde. (including "N" Battery.)	THIEULLOY.	10-30 am.	HORNOY - THIEULLOY - BRICAMPS.	NAMPTY - HEBECOURT - BUYON - NAMPS-au-MONT NAMPS-au-VAL - NEUVILLE	To be clear of the line LIOMER - VILLERS CAMPSART by 10.30 a.m.
Divnl: Hdqrs. & Signal Sqdn.(less motors)	The line LIOMER - VILLERS CAMPSART.	11 a.m.		PONT DE METZ	To move to starting point in that order in case of clashing.
Field Squadron.		11.15 am.		PISSY - FLUY.	
Fld.Ambulances (less Can:Amb. & less motors).		11.30 am.		REVELLES.	
Aux: M.T.Coy.		11.45 am.		REVELLES (To be allotted by A.D.M.S.)	

U N I T.	Starting point.	Time.	Route.	Billets.	Remarks.
Ammunition Park.) Supply Column.)	As ordered by A.A. & Q.M.G.			QUEVAUVILLERS.	
Motors of Divnl:) Hdqrs. & Signal) Squadron.) Motor Ambulances.) H.Q. I.A.C.Bty.)	Billets.	10.30 am.	Optional.	PONT DE METZ. RIVELLES. PONT DE METZ.	Billets to be allotted by Camp Commandant.

Appx 95

SECRET.   5th Cavalry Division.   Copy No. 20

Operation Order No.21.

Reference Map 1/100,000.   21st March, 1917.

1. The Division will move Eastwards tomorrow in accordance with the attached march table.

2. "A" and "B" Echelons will accompany Brigades and Divisional Troops. "B" Echelons will probably have to be concentrated under Divisional control early on the morning of 23rd.

3. C.R.H.A. and Headquarters 17th R.H.A.Brigade form part of Divisional Headquarters from midnight 21st/22nd.

4. Representatives of units billetting in CERISY village and in Camps 55 and 131 will meet D.A.A.& Q.M.G. at the Church there at 10.30 a.m.
The Town Major of HAMEL will give information regarding Camp 60 and the Prisoners Camp.

5. Motors of Divisional Headquarters and Signal Squadron and No.9 L.A.C.Battery stand fast.

6. Report Centre remains at PONT DE METZ, but O.C.Signal Squadron will place a forwarding post at CERISY, to be established by noon.

7. Acknowledge.

J. O'Rorke Capt
for
Lt.Colonel, G.S.,
5th Cavalry Division.

Issued at 3.30 p.m by D.R.

Copies Nos.1 - 21 at Normal Operation Order distribution.
Copy No.22 to Cavalry Corps.
  "   "   23 " Fourth Army.
  "   "   24 " III Corps.
  "   "   25 " IV   " .

5th Cavalry Division.
March Table - 22.3.17. (Issued with Operation Order No.21.)

Unit.	Starting Point.	Time.	Route.	Billets.	Remarks.
Div.H.Q.& Signal Sqdn.(less Motors).	N.E.of SALOUEL.	9.00 am.	LONGUEAU - VILLERS BRETONNEUX	CERISY.	
Canadian Cav.Bde. & Canadian Fd.Amb.	Do.	9.30 am.	Do.	Camps 55 and 131 S. of CERISY.	May billet H.Q. in CERISY.
Field Squadron.	Do.	10.30 am.	Do.	CERISY.	Must be clear of VILLERS BRETONNEUX by 2 p.m.
Sec'bad Cav.Bde.	RUMIGNY.	Optional.	BOVES - VILLERS BRETONNEUX.	Camp 60 and Prisoners Camp S.& E. of HAMEL.	Not to enter VILLERS BRETONNEUX before 2 p.m. Billets to be allotted by D.M.S.
Field Ambulances (less Canadian). A.H.T.Company.	REVELLES.	10.30 am.	VERS - DURY - BOVES, thence follow Sec'bad Brigade.	CACHY - GENTELLES.	
Ammunition Column.	GUIGNEMICOURT.	11.30 am.	SALEUX - DURY - BOVES.	THENNES - BERTEAUCOURT	
Ambala Cavalry Bde.	Optional.	Optional.	AILLY SUR NOYE - ROUVREL - CASTEL.	CAIX - CAYEUX - IGNAUCOURT - DEMUIN - HANGARD.	To be in billets by 1 p.m.
Ammunition Park Supply Column.	Optional.As ordered by A.A.& Q.M.G.			MARCELCAVE.	Not to enter billets before 5 p.m.

SECRET.   No.G.A./589.

Headquarters 5th Cavalry Division.

22nd March, 1917.

Issued at Normal Operation Order Distribution.

Fourth Army.   )
III Corps.   ) For information.
IV   " .   )
                    ----

1. In continuation of Operation Order No.22 of today's date, the following moves will take place tomorrow :-

   (a) Ambala Cavalry Brigade and attached troops as in para.2 (a).
       Starting Point - HARBONNIERES, 10 a.m.
       Route - PROYART - S. of FROISSY - CAPPY - ECLUSIER - S. of FEISE.
       Destination - B.DE HEREAUCOURT.

   (b) Canadian Cavalry Brigade and attached troops as in para.2 (b).
       Starting Point - CERISY, 10 a.m.
       Route - ETINEHEM - BRAY - MARICOURT - HEM - CLERY
       Destination - HALLE.

   (c) Divisional Headquarters and Signal Squadron (less motors).
       Starting Point - CERISY, 9 a.m.
       Route - MARICOURT - S. of FROISSY - CAPPY - HERBECOURT - BIACHES - HALLE.
       Destination - PERONNE.

   (d) Motors of Divisional Headquarters and Signal Squadron.
       Starting Point - PONT DE METZ, 10 a.m.
       Route - VILLERS BRETONNEUX - WARFUSEE - PROYART - CAPPY,
               thence as for remainder of Divisional Headquarters.

   (e) No.9 L.A.C.Battery will move so as to reach CERISY not later than 1 p.m.

   (f) Supply Column and Ammunition Park as ordered by A.A.& Q.M.G.

2. The Remainder of the Division will probably not move, but will be prepared to do so at half an hour's notice after 10 a.m.

3. G.Os.C.Ambala and Canadian Cavalry Brigades will reconnoitre routes forward for the following days operations in accordance with the information already given them.

4. ~~Batteries will accompany Brigades but will come under Divisional control on arrival in the new area.~~ *(Cancelled)*

5. G.Os.C.Ambala and Canadian Cavalry Brigades will issue the necessary orders to the detachments not at present with them. In the case of R.C.H.A.Light Section, it is not necessary that it should march closed up to the rest of the Brigade.

6. Reports to PERONNE after 1 p.m.

7. Acknowledge.

                                           R.G.Howard Vyse
                                           Lt.Colonel, G.S.,
                                           5th Cavalry Division.

SECRET.

No.G.A.589/1.

Headquarters 5th Cavalry Division.

22nd March, 1917.

Issued at Normal O.O.Distribution.

Fourth Army (for information).

----

1. Following is substituted for para.4 of G.A.589.

Rug wagons only of "B" Echelon will accompany Brigades and units of Divisional Troops.

2. Remainder of "B" Echelon will concentrate W. of HERBECOURT and will there come under the orders of the senior officer present.
This officer will receive instructions at HERBECOURT from D.A.A.& Q.M.G.

(a) That of Divisional Headquarters and Signal Squadron will follow those units as far as HERBECOURT.

(b) That of Ambala Cavalry Brigade will follow its Brigade as far as CAPPY and will thence march independently to HERBECOURT.

(c) That of Canadian Cavalry Brigade will march independently via HORCOURT - MERICOURT - S. of FROISSY and will thence follow the "B" Echelon of Ambala Cavalry Brigade which should reach that place about noon.

3. "B" Echelons of Ambala and Canadian Cavalry Brigades will be accompanied by 1 Sergeant per Brigade and 1 man per unit, as it is necessary to dump the contents of "B" Echelon near HERBECOURT.

Lt.Colonel, G.S.,

5th Cavalry Division.

Appx 96

SECRET. 5th Cavalry Division. Copy No. 20

Operation Order No.22.

Reference 1/100,000 map. 22nd March, 1917.

1. The Division will march tomorrow to an area West of PERONNE in order to pass through our infantry on the following day.

2. The following groupings take effect from receipt of this order :-

   (a) <u>Under G.O.C. Ambala Cavalry Brigade.</u>

   "X" R.H.A. and Light Section Ammunition Column.
   1 Field Troop.
   Mhow Field Ambulance.

   (b) <u>Under G.O.C. Canadian Cavalry Brigade.</u>

   R.C.H.A. Brigade and Light Section Ammunition Column.
   1 Field Troop.
   Canadian Field Ambulance.

   (c) <u>Under G.O.C. Secunderabad Cavalry Brigade.</u>

   "N" R.H.A. and Light Section Ammunition Column.

3. Details of the march and of bivouacs will be issued later. Canadian Cavalry Brigade and attached troops will march North of the SOMME: the remainder of the Division will march South of the SOMME.

4. The Division will march about 9 a.m. except

   (a) Motors of Divisional H.Q. and Signal Squadron and No.9 L.A.C. Battery, which will march at 10 a.m.

   (b) Supply Column and Ammunition Park, which will probably not move.

5. "B" Echelon of Canadian Cavalry Brigade will accompany its Brigade.

"B" Echelons of Ambala and Secunderabad Brigades will march under Divisional control and will be concentrated in Brigade areas by 10 a.m.

Lt. Colonel, G.S.,
5th Cavalry Division.

Issued at 9-15am by D.R.

Copies No.1 to 21 (incl) at Normal O.O. Distribution.
Copy No.22 to Cavalry Corps.
"   " 23 " Fourth Army.
"   " 24 " III Corps.
"   " 25 " IV ".

App. 94

SECRET.   No.G.A./597.

Headquarters 5th Cavalry Division.

23rd March, 1917.

Issued at Norm 1 O.O.Distribution.

Fourth Army (For information)

----

1. The remainder of the Division will not move today.

2. The following troops are placed temporarily under the orders of G.O.C.Secunderabad Cavalry Brigade.

	Present Location.
Ammn.Column (less "X" and Canadian Light Sections).	THENNES - BERTEAUCOURT.
Field Squadron (less 2 Troops)	CERISY.
No.9 L.A.C.Battery.	Moving to CERISY.
Sec'bad Field Ambulance.	CACHY - GENTELLES.
A.H.T.Company.	---Ditto----

3. The billets at CERISY and Camps 55 and 131 South of that place are placed at the disposal of G.O.C.Secunderabad Cavalry Brigade.

Lt.Colonel, G.S.,
5th Cavalry Division.

appx 98

SECRET.   COPY NO. 20

5th CAVALRY DIVISION.

OPERATION ORDER NO. 23.

Reference Map   23:3:17.
$\frac{1}{100,000}$

1. Information as already circulated.

2. The tasks of the Division are :-

   (a) To ascertain the dispositions of the advanced hostile detachments.

   (b) To ascertain the enemy's defences and strength.

   (c) To picket the enemy so as to prevent his advancing and so as to give instant information of any withdrawal.

   (d) To be ready to follow up the enemy if he withdraws.

Brig-Gen. Rankin.

Ambala Cav. Bde. & attached troops
1 Co. IV Corps Cyclists.
2 platoons III Corps Cyclists.

3(a) Ambala Cavalry Brigade (strength as in margin) will be responsible for carrying out the above task between the lines VIEFVILLE (inclusive) - VILLERS ST. CHRISTOPHE - DOUCHY - ROUPY - ST. QUENTIN (all exclusive) and AIZECOURT LE HAUT - TEMPLEUX - LONGAVESNES - EPEHY - HONNECOURT (all exclusive).

Advanced detachments will be on the line GERMAINE - BERNES - MARQUAIX by 11.30 a.m. The Brigade will advance via BIACHES - HALLE - PERONNE.

Touch to be established with the advanced detachments of the French.

Brig-Gen. Seely.

Canadian Cav. Bde. & attached troops.
XIV Corps Cav. Regt. & Cyclist Bn. (temporarily only).

(b) Canadian Cavalry Brigade (strength as in margin) will be responsible for carrying out the above tasks between the lines AIZECOURT LE HAUT - TEMPLEUX - LONGAVESNES - EPEHY - HONNECOURT (all inclusive) and LE TRANSLOY - BARASTRE - BERTINCOURT - HAVRINCOURT (all inclusive).

Advanced detachments will be on the line TEMPLEUX - AIZECOURT - LE BAS - NURLU - BUS - BERTINCOURT by 11.30 a.m..

Touch to be established with the advanced detachments of Fifth Army (Anzac Corps).

(c) Divisional Headquarters and Signal Squadron do not move.

(d) No. 9 L.A.C. Battery will move at 9.0 a.m. to FOUCAUCOURT and will there await further orders.

Brig.Gen.GREGORY

Sec'bad Cav.Bde.
& attached troops
Main Ammunition
Column.
Field Squadron
(less 2 troops)
Sec'bad Field
Amba.
A.R.T.Coy.

(e) Remainder of Division as in margin will march under orders of G.O.C. Secunderabad Cavalry Brigade.
Starting point - X roads N.of CHUIGNOLLES, 10.0 a.m.
Route - CAPPY- W.of FRISE.
Destination.- BOIS DEMETAUCOURT.

"B" Echelons will however move to HERBECOURT and come under the orders of the senior officer there.

Attachment of Corps Mounted Troops.

4.(a) 1 Company IVth.Corps Cyclists and 2 Platoons III Corps Cyclists come under orders of G.O.C. Ambala Cavalry Brigade at 11.0 a.m. at ATHIES and ESTREES EN CHAUSSEE. They will be used respectively principally for establishing relay posts between the Brigade and Divisional Headquarters and within the Brigade. The Wireless detachment of III Corps Cavalry will report at the same time and place.

(b) XIVth. Corps Cavalry Regiment and Cyclist Batn. come under orders of G.O.C. Canadian Cavalry Brigade at 10.0 a.m. at MOISLAINS. He will report assuming command. A portion of the cyclists may be used for relay posts as in (a) above. The rest will not be moved without reference to Divisional Headquarters.

Intercommunication.

5.(a) Brigades will communicate direct with Corps on whose front they are operating. For this purpose Liaison officers of Corps Cavalry will report as follows:-

To Ambala Cavalry Brigade from III Corps
  ESTREES EN CHAUSSEE - 11.0 a.m.

To Ambala Cavalry Brigade from IVth.Corps
  ATHIES - 11.0 a.m.

To Canadian Cavalry Brigade from XIVth. &
  XVth. Corps.
  MOISLAINS -10.0 a.m.

(b) Liaison Officers and Gallopers will report at Divisional Headquarters at 9.0 a.m. (Ambala and Canadian) and noon (Secunderabad)

Aeroplanes

6. R.F.C.Liaison Officer will arrange for 2 machines to be continuously on contact patrol from 11.30 a.m. to 2.0 p.m. and from 4.30 p.m. to 6 p.m., and for as much of the rest of the day as is possible. The machines should between them work over the whole front of the Division.

Line of resistance.

7. The Line of Resistance in case of attack will be GERMAINE-BEAUVOIS-POEUILLY-BERNES-MARQUAIX-LONGAVESNES-LIERAMONT-NURLU- thence D'UANCOURT-YERES-BETINCOURT, if in our possession, otherwise the line at present held by the infantry.

Instructions as regards holding and strengthening the above line will be issued later. Brigades will reconnoitre it and submit proposals as early as possible.

Situation reports.

8. Situation Reports are required to reach Divisional Headquarters daily by 5 a.m. and 5 p.m.

Reports

9. Reports to P.ROMME.

10. Acknowledge.

R.E.Howard Vyse

Lieut-Colonel, G.S.

5th. Cavalry Division.

```
Copies Nos. 1-21    Normal Distribution.
            22      Cavalry Corps.
            23      Fourth Army.
            24      IIIrd. Corps.
            25      IVth. Corps.
            26      XIVth. Corps.
            27      XVth. Corps.
            28      Anzac Corps.
            29      R.F.C. Liaison Officer.
            30      O.C. "B" Echelon.
```

Issued by D.R. at 5.0 p.m.

SECRET   5TH. CAVALRY DIVISION.   COPY NO. 20.

Appx 99

OPERATION ORDER NO. 24.

Reference Map
1/100,000 FRANCE.   24th. March, 1917.

1. (a) The enemy appears to be holding his advanced line on our front with weak detachments only, except about SAVY and BOIS D'HOLNON and between LONGAUESNES and SOREL, where he seems to be rather stronger.

(b) The Advanced Troops of the Division are on the line ETREILLERS-BEAUVOIS-CAULAINCOURT-BERNES-ROISEL-BOIS DE TINCOURT-TEMPLEUX LA FOSSE-AIZECOURT LE BAS-NURLU-BUS-BERTINCOURT. Patrols have entered YTRES.

2. The Division will continue the tasks laid down in Operation Order No. 23. Reconnaissances will be pushed forward in all directions, and all localities not held in strength by the enemy will be occupied.

3. (a) Ambala Cavalry Brigade and attached troops will pay particular attention to

   (i) VILLEVEQUE, the wood East of that place, and the strip of wood running East from CAULAINCOURT.

   (ii) HESBECOURT and VILLERS FAUCON.

(b) Canadian Cavalry Brigade and attached troops will pay particular attention to the line EQUANCOURT-YTRES.

(c) Remainder of the Division and 14th. Corps Mounted Troops will be ready to move at 3 hours notice after 10.0 a.m.

4. R.F.C. Liaison Officer will arrange for

(a) Special reconnaissances of the line VERMAND-SOYECOURT-VENDELLES (to be photographed) and of the area EQUANCOURT-GOUZEAUCOURT-METZ EN COUTURE-BERTINCOURT.

(b) Contact Patrols from   8.30 a.m. - 10.30 a.m.
                                  1.30 p.m. - 3.30 p.m.
                                  3.30 p.m. - 5.30 p.m.

5. Acknowledge.

                                      Lieut-Colonel,
                                      5th. Cavalry Division.

Copies Nos. 1-21 Normal O.O.
           22 Fourth Army.
           23 Third Corps.
           24 Fourth Corps.
           25 Fifteenth Corps.
           26 R.F.C. Liaison Officer.
           27 O.C. "B" Echelon.
           28 OC XIV Corps Mounted Troops.

Issued by D.R. at 9.15 p.m.

MESSAGES AND SIGNALS.

Prefix...... Code......m.	Words	Charge	This message is on a/c of:	Recd. at......m.
Office of Origin and Service Instructions.	Sent			Date
	At......m.		Service.	From
	To......		*OYYX*	
	By......		(Signature of "Franking Officer.")	By

TO	3rd. Corps.	Cav. Corps		
	4th. "	Fourth Army		
	15th. "			

Sender's Number	Day of Month	In reply to Number	
C.I.2	24.3.17		AAA

Ambala Bde. right Regt. H.Q. MONCHY LAGACHES.
One troop at each of following places - VAUX-
BEAUVOIS-TREFCON and CAULAINCOURT and POEUILLY.
Left Regt. H.Q. HANCOURT. and occupy BRIE-MACHIN-
ROBESCOURT FARM- POINT 114-MARQUAIX and HAMLET and
4th. Corps Cavalry patrols report heavily fired on
from E. bank of R. OMIGON between CAULAINCOURT
and BANTEVILLE and patrols fired on from VENDELLES
BOYLECOURT direction. They report belt of wire
20 ft. deep from rail station S. of LIANCOURT
to BOYNCOURT. Bde. H.Q. ETTERBE EN CHAUSSEE and
Canadian Bde. H.Q. BOISLAIRS. Right Regt. H.Q.
ST. PIERRE FARM. Occupied BOIS DE TINCOURT-
AIZECOURT to MURIN exclusive-reconnaissance pushed
forward to LONGAVESNES - in touch with Ambala Bde. and
Enemy in small wood and station E. of YTRES.

From	5th. Cav. Div.			
Place				
Time				

The above may be forwarded as now corrected.   (Z)(sd) J. GWATKIN, Capt for GS

Censor.   Signature of Addressor or person authorised to telegraph in his name.

No. G.A. 658.

Headquarters, 5th. Cavalry Division.
Dated 26th, March.1917.

To/
    Sec'bad Cavalry Brigade.
    Canadian   "   "
    Ambala   "   "
    5th. Field Squadron.
    14th. Corps Cyclists.

1. The G.O.C. Ambala Cavalry Brigade will cause the following reconnaissances to be carried out today or tonight.

    (a) With a view to occupying VERMAND and SOYECOURT. Artillery reconnaissance for two or three battery positions will be included.

    (b) Enemy's defences BOIS D'HOLNON-ATTILLY-MARTEVILLE, in order to discover whether these are wired.

2. The following attachments will take place today :-

    (a) Remainder of Field Squadron (H.Q. and 1 troop) to Ambala Brigade. To be employed on road repair in the area MONCHY LAGACHE - VILLEVEQUE-FLECHIN-BOUVINCOURT. The MONS EN CHAUSSEE-VERMAND road will be attended to first.

    (b) 1 Coy XIV Corps Cyclist Battalion to Ambala Bde.

    (c) XIV Corps Cyclist Btn. (less 1 Coy) to Can. Bde.

3. (a) Detachments (a) and (b) above will march via HALLE-PERONNE-DOINGT, so as to reach MONS EN CHAUSSEE by 4 p.m.
    O's C. will report at H.Q. Ambala Brigade ESTREES EN CHAUSSEE as early as possible before that hour.

    (b) Detachment (c) above will march via MONT ST QUENTIN so as to reach MOISLAINS by 4 p.m. O.C. to report at H.Q. Canadian Bde. as early as possible before that hour.

4. The Relay Posts at present found by XIV Corps Cyclist Btn. will remain in their present position.

5. The order given verbally to "N" Battery to be prepared to move at short notice after 8 a.m. is cancelled.

                                (Sd) R.G. Howard-Vyse, Lt. Col.
                                    5th. Cavalry Division.

Copy to:-
    4th. Army.
    XIV Corps
    C.R.H.A.
    Sigl. Sqdn.
    "Q"
    O.C. A.S.C.

Issued by D.R. at 6 a.m.

SECRET

Reference Map
1 / 100,000
FRANCE

5TH. CAVALRY DIVISION.

OPERATION ORDER NO.25.   Copy No. 20

Dated 27th. March, 1917.

1. Canadian Cavalry Brigade took LONGAVESNES and EQUANCOURT yesterday. 48th. Division, assisted by Ambala Cavalry Brigade and No. 9 L.A.C. Battery, took ROISEL.

2. The principal objects of today's operations are :-

   (a) To capture LIERAMONT.
   (b) To establish ourselves on the high ground overlooking VILLERS FAUCON, SAULCOURT and GUYENCOURT.
   (c) To occupy those places.

3. The line of demarcation will be LONGAVESNES- VILLERS FAUCON both inclusive to Canadian Brigade.

4. With the above objects in view

   (a) Ambala Cavalry Brigade will, by 4 p.m. establish themselves on the line of the road from ROISEL to LONGAVESNES. Arrangements have been made for co-operation by the artillery of Brig.Genl! Ward's Column. C.R.H.A. is placed at the disposal of G.O.C. Ambala Cavalry Brigade, and will report to him at 10 a.m. at S. entrance to BOUCLY. A Battery should be pushed forward as soon as the first objective is taken, in order to support the advance of the Canadian Cavalry Brigade.

   (b) Canadian Cavalry Brigade with "N" Battery attached will advance at 5 p.m. to seize the high ground between LONGAVESNES and LIERAMONT.

   (c) N. Battery R.H.A. will march at 7 a.m. via BIACHES-HAME-ST.DENIS to AIZECOURT LE HAUT, where it will come under orders of G.O.C. Canadian Cavalry Brigade. O.C. will report to G.O.C. Canadian Cavalry Brigade at MOISLAINS at 10 a.m.

5. Arrangements must be made by Ambala and Canadian Cavalry Brigades for the closest possible liaison during the whole operation. They will report to Divisional H.Q. early their own report centres and those of the regiments taking part.

6. R.F.C. Liaison Officer will arrange for

   (a) The trench line VERMAND-BOYSCOURT-VENDELLES to be photographed.

   (b) A reconnaissance at 10 a.m. of the area LONGAVESNES-VILLERS FAUCON-HEUDICOURT-EQUANCOURT with the special object of discovering hostile entrenchments.

   (c) Two machines to be continuously on contact patrol, in connection with the above operation, from 4 p.m. to 6.30 p.m.

7. (a) Secunderabad Cavalry Brigade (less "N" Battery) and Ammunition Column will march in that order, starting at 1 p.m., via BIACHES to a new bivouac near HAME. Representatives will meet D.A.A. & Q.M.G. at HAME at noon.

(b) "N" R.H.A. will return to the above bivouac on the
 conclusion of the operation.
 G.O.C. Canadian Cavalry Brigade will inform O.C. "N"
 Battery when he is free to return.

8. Reports to church at TEMPLEUX LA FOSSE after 4 p.m.

9. Acknowledge.

R.G.Howard-Vyse

Lieut-Colonel, G.S.

5th. Cavalry Division.

Copies Nos. 1-21 Normal O.O.
         22 Fourth Army.
         23 III Corps.
         24 IV   "
         25 Fifteenth Corps.
         26 R.F.C. Liaison Officer.
         27 O.C. "B" Echelon.
         28 48th. Division.
         29 "N" R.H.A.

Issued by D.R. at 5.0 a.m.

No. G.A. 687.

Headquarters, 5th. Cavalry Division
Dated 27th. March, 1917.

To/
Secbad Cav. Bde.
Canadian   "   "
Ambala   "   "
17th. Bde. R.H.A.
R.C.H.A.
Amm. Column.
Fd. Squadron.
Sigl. Sqdn.
A.
O.C. A.S.C.
A.D.M.S.
A.D.C.

Camp Commandant.
A.P.M.
G.S.O.1
Office G.S.
War Diary.
No. 9 L.A.C. Bty.

----

1. LIERAMONT is in our possession aaa We also hold part at least of the ROISEL-LONGAVESNES ridge, Hill 140 N.E. of LONGAVESNES, and Hill 132 North of EQUANCOURT aaa Enemy were still in SAULCOURT and GUYENCOURT at 9.30 a.m.

2. The operations this afternoon will be conducted with the objects laid down in Operation Order No. 25, paras 2 (b) and (c), and also of establishing advanced posts beyond the villages named.

3. The advanced detachments of both brigades will pass through the line of advanced posts at 5 p.m.

4. VILLERS FAUCON is inclusive to Ambala Brigade, and not to Canadian.

R.G. Howard Vyse

Lieut Colonel, G.S.
5th. Cavalry Division.

Copies to:-

Fourth Army.
III Corps.
IV   "
XV   "
R.F.C. Liaison Officer.
O.C. "B" Echelon.
Divisional Liaison Officers.
48th Division

NARRATIVE OF THE OPERATIONS OF THE 5TH. CAVALRY DIVISION BETWEEN MARCH 24TH. and MARCH 27TH.

March 24th. The Ambala and Canadian Cavalry Brigades took over from Corps Cavalry along the Fourth Army front. The dividing line between the Brigades was AIZECOURT LE HAUT-TEMPLEUX-LONGAVESNES-EPEHY-HONNECOURT (exclusive to Ambala Cavalry Brigade).

The front taken over was VAUX BEAUVOIS-TREFCON CAULAINCOURT-POEUILLY-FLAMICHE-BERNES-ROBESCOURT EN HAMELET-MARQUAIX-BOIS de BUIRE-AIZECOURT-LE BAS-NURLU-ETRICOURT-LECHELLE-BUS. Touch was gained between the two brigades and with French on the South and Anzac infantry on the north in BERTINCOURT.

Canadian Cavalry Brigade pushed patrols into YTRES in the evening, found it unoccupied, and established posts there. The B de TINCOURT, late on the 24th, was captured.

Some shell fire and encounters between patrols along the whole front after taking over at 11.30 a.m.

H.Q. of Division and Bdes. on 24th. as follows:-

    Division H.Q.   - PERONNE.
    Ambala Cav. Bde. H.Q.   - ESTREES-en-CHAUSSEE.
    Can. " " H.Q.   - MOISLAINS.
    Sec. " " H.Q.   - BOIS de MEREAUCOURT just south of FEUILLIERES.

March 25th. During the night 24/25th. 9th. Hodson's Horse (Ambala Cav. Bde) occupied ETREILLERS. One of their posts in this village was raided and two men were reported missing. VILLEVEQUE was also captured by the 9th. Hodson's Horse.

Canadian Cavalry Brigade captured YTRES, small wood to the south, and the BOIS de VALLULART (P.33.a).

Front of the Ambala Cavalry Brigade extended to the N.E. to include B de TINCOURT. VILLERS-FAUCON - B. de TINCOURT were taken over by Ambala from Canadian Bde. during the day.

Outpost reconnaissance and patrol fighting along the whole front.

March 26th. A post of Royal Canadian Dragoons N. of AIZECOURT was raided on the night 25/26th, but the enemy were driven off with loss.

Canadian Cavalry Brigade captured the villages of LONGAVESNES and EQUANCOURT and wood just S.E. of the latter villages, driving out small enemy detachments. The defence of these places was then handed over to the infantry.

Two squadrons 18th. Lancers with two armoured cars (Ambala Cav.Bde) co-operated with a btn. of Ward's force

in the attack.....

in the attack on ROISEL. The Armoured Cars drove the enemy from the western exit of ROISEL, firing on them retreating N.E.

Two squadrons encircling the village north and south were held up on the flanks of the village.

The village of ROISEL was taken by our troops in the afternoon.

March 27th.   During the night 26/27th.

(a) <u>Canadian Cav. Bde.</u> took LIERAMONT, pushing out a small enemy detachment. Infantry then took over the defence of the village.

(b) <u>9th. Hodson's Horse</u> carried out a reconnaissance of BOIS D'HOLNON towards HANTEVILLE and VERMAND. Report was forwarded to Fourth Army.

About 2 p.m. a troop of <u>Royal Canadian Dragoons</u> charged a small hostile party entrenched about 1000 yards East of LONGAVESNES. Several of the enemy were killed and wounded and 9 other ranks captured.

An operation with the objective the villages of VILLERS-FAUCON-SAULCOURT-GOYENCOURT, was carried out late in the afternoon.

The following troops took part :-

(a) <u>Under G.O.C. Ambala Cavalry Brigade</u>
8th. Hussars.
M.G. Squadron.
"X" R.H.A.
No. 9 L.A.C. Battery.
3 Batteries 48th. Division.

(b) <u>Under G.O.C. Canadian Cavalry Brigade</u>
The Brigade.
R.C.H.A. Brigade.
15th. Corps Cav.Regt.

<u>Lord Strathcona's Horse</u> drove the enemy from GOYENCOURT, taking 1 machine gun and 3 prisoners and occupying the village.

<u>FORT GARRY HORSE</u> captured SAULCOURT, taking 1 machine gun.

<u>8th. Hussars</u> and 2 cars No. 9 L.A.C. Battery captured VILLERS-FAUCON; 2 machine guns taken and 1 officer and 10 O.R. captured.

March 28th.   <u>9th. Hodson's Horse (Ambala Cavalry Brigade)</u> carried out a reconnaissance of the enemy on their front, a report of which has been forwarded to Fourth Army. Brigade (less 1 squadron) was relieved in the afternoon.

One squadron of <u>15th. Lancers (Amb. Cav. Bde)</u> remained out as reconnaissance squadron during the day at VILLERS-FAUCON, and was withdrawn after dark. The whole brigade was concentrated in the vicinity of ROUCHY-LAGACHE early on 29th.

<u>Canadian Cavalry Brigade.</u>   After the action
on the 27th.....

on the 27th. the Royal Canadian Dragoons returned to
MOISLAINS at 9 p.m. and "N" Battery rejoined the
Secunderabad Cavalry Brigade on the night 27/28th.
The remainder of the brigade remained in position
SAULCOURT-GUYENCOURT during the night 27th/28th. when
they withdrew to MOISLAINS, leaving out one squadron
holding advanced posts until relieved later on the
28th.

SUMMARY.

During the period covered by this narrative, 5th.
Cavalry Division occupied the villages of GUREVILLERS,
VILLEVEQUE, LONGAVESNES, VILLERS-FAUCON, LIERAMONT,
SAULCOURT, GUYENCOURT, EQUANCOURT and YPRES, also co-
operating with the infantry in the capture of ROISEL
and the B de TINCOURT.

One officer and 25 O.R. were captured and 4 machine
guns taken.

The losses in the 5th. Cavalry Division during
this period were

	Killed	Wounded	Missing
Officers	-	6	-
Other ranks	4	65	15

Horse casualties   Riding - 101
                   L.D.   3

appx 103

SECRET   5TH. CAVALRY DIVISION.   Copy No. 20

OPERATION ORDER NO. 26.

Dated 28th. March, 1917.

Reference Map

$\frac{1}{100,000}$ FRANCE.

1. (a) Ambala and Canadian Brigades took VILLERS FAUCON, SAULCOURT, GUYENCOURT yesterday. Advanced posts were established at STE. EMILIE (North of the Railway) and one mile East of SAULCOURT.
          HEUDICOURT and SOREL were found by Corps Cavalry to be still held by the enemy.

   (b) Infantry Advanced Guards have now taken over the line held by the Division.

2. The Division is being withdrawn to a position of assembly West of PERONNE.

3. In consequence

   (a) Secunderabad Cavalry Brigade, (including Light Section Ammunition Column and Sec'bad Fd. Ambs) marches at 3 p.m. today to a bivouac between CLERY and HEM.

   (b) Divisional Headquarters and Signal Squadron remain in their present position.

   (c) No. 9 L.A.C. Battery will move to FAUBOURG DE BRETAGNE at 5 p.m., where it will remain until the cars at present at VILLERS FAUCON have rejoined. Further orders will then be issued.

   (d) Supply Column and Ammunition Park will not move.

   (e) Remainder of Division will move tomorrow in accordance with attached March Table.

   (f) 14th. Corps Cyclist Battalion will assemble at 10 a.m. at MT. ST. QUENTIN and march thence independently to report for orders to O.C. 14th. Corps Mounted Troops at LE MESNIL EN ARROUSSE.

4. Intervals of 100 yds. will be maintained between squadrons or equivalent units.

                                                        ....5.

5. Representatives of Formations and Units bivouacking at Cp. 57 N. of CAPPY will report to D.A.A. & Q.M.G. at CAPPY CH. at 10 a.m.

6. <u>Field Troops</u> attached to Brigades are to be used for improving shelters and bivouacs and communications in the vicinity of bivouacs. One Field Troop is placed under orders of G.O.C. Sec'bad Cav.Bde. from arrival in their bivouac at CLERY-HEM.

7. Liaison officers and gallopers will rejoin their units in bivouacs tomorrow evening.

8. Acknowledge.

                                    Lieut-Colonel, G.S.
                                    5th. Cavalry Division.

Nos. 1 to 21. Normal O.O.
     22 XIV Corps Cyclist Btn.
     23 III Corps.
     24 IV   "
     25 XV   "
     26 R.F.C. Liaison Officer.
     27 O.C. "B" Echelon.
     28 Fourth Army.
     29 Cavalry Corps.

Issued by D.R. at 5-30 p.m.

5th Cavalry Division

March Tables 29-3-17 (Issued with Op: Order No 36)

Formation or Unit	Starting Point	Time	Route	Destination	Remarks
"B" Echelon (less two H.Q. and Sig: Sqdn) and A.H. Coy.	Bivouacs	8 a.m.	HALLE - BIACHES - HERBECOURT - CAPPY.	Camp 56, N of CAPPY.	—
Main Ammⁿ Colⁿ	Bridge S. of HALLE.	8 a.m.	"	"	—
Reserve Park	"	8-15 a.m.	"	"	Move to starting point behind Ammⁿ Column.
Under G.O.C. Cav. Cav. Bde. Can. Cav. Bde. R.C.H.A. Bde. Right Section Ammⁿ Col. 1 Field Troop. Can. Cav. Field Amb.		11 a.m.	ALLAINES - MT. ST QUENTIN, thence as above.	"	
Under G.O.C. Ambala Cav Bde. Ambala Cav Bde. X Bty R.H.A. Right Section Ammⁿ Column. Field Sqdn (less 1 troop.) Lucknow Cav Field Amb.	DOINGT.	1 p.m.	PERONNE - HALLE - BIACHES - HERBECOURT.	BOIS de MEREAUCOURT	1 Field Troop to join Sec'ond Bde in CLERY-HEM bivouac.

appx 104

SECRET

5TH. CAVALRY DIVISION.
OPERATION ORDER NO.27   Copy No. 20.

Reference Map

$$\frac{1}{100,000}$$
FRANCE

Dated 30th. March, 1917.

1. The Division, less troops now at CAPPY, will move Westwards today, in accordance with the attached march table.

2. Secunderabad Brigade and Canadian Brigade will be prepared to exchange billets in the course of two or three days, under orders which will be issued later.

3. B. Echelon will remain for the present at CAPPY.
A.A. & Q.M.G. will arrange to move the "B" Echelon kits by lorry.

4. The Conference ordered for 4 p.m. today is postponed.

5. Reports to VILLERS BRETONNEUX after 2 p.m.

Lieut-Colonel, G.S.

5th. Cavalry Division.

Copies Nos. 1 - 21 Normal C.O.
             22 Fourth Army.
             23 Cavalry Corps.
             24 III Corps.
             25 48th. Division.
             26 O.C. "B" Echelon.
             27 R.F.C. Liaison Officer.

Issued by D.R. at 12.30 a.m.

8th Cavalry Division

March Table 30-3-17 (Issued with O.O. No 24.)

Formation & unit	Starting point	Time	Route	Destination	Remarks
Under G.O.C. Ambala Bde: Ambala Cav. Bde, X.(By) R.H.A., Right Sec. Amn Col, F.A.: 3 gdns (less 2 troops), Mton Cav Fd. Amb.	Bois de MERICOURT	10·30 am	FRISE – CAPPY – PROYART	WARFUSÉE ABANCOURT	Not to enter PROYART before noon.
Div H Qrs and Sig: Squadron (less motors)	PÉRONNE	10·30 am	Flg de PARIS – BIRCHES – HERBÉCOURT – CAPPY – PROYART	VILLERS-BRETONNEUX	Yellow Ambala to be from CAPPY.
Under G.O.C. Sec. Bde. Sec. Cav. Bde. N. (By) R.H.A., Left Sec. Amn Col, Field Troop, Secnd Cav Fd Amb.	HEM	11·30 am	FRISE – CAPPY – PROYART	BAYON – VILLERS	Div H.Q. have precedence
Motors of Div. H.qrs & Signal Squadron. No 9 Cav. Battery.	PÉRONNE	2 pm / 2·15 pm	Flg de PARIS – VILLERS CARBONNEL – FOUCAUCOURT	VILLERS BRETONNEUX – do –	Billets to be allotted by Camp Condt. – do – Camp Condt

Army Form C. 2118.

WAR DIARY
or
INTELLIGENCE SUMMARY
(Erase heading not required.)

17th R.H.A. Brigade. — March 1917.   Vol XI

Place	Date	Hour	Summary of Events and Information	Remarks and references to Appendices
INCHEVILLE BEAUCHAMPS OUST-MAREST PONTH MARAIS	1st 15th 19th	—	Rest billets.	
GAMACHES	7th	—	Distribution of medals to Ambala Cav. Bde. by Brig. Gen. Rankin. The following men of the 17th R.H.A. Bde. received were decorated:— B.S.M. Evans N. Battery R.H.A. and Sergt. Barrett Bde. Ammn. Col. D.C.M. Sergt. Gardiner X " " Cpl. Haynes X "Battery R.H.A and Cpl. Barnes N. Battery R.H.A. — Military Medal.	
BEAUCHAMPS	12th	—	Major I.N. FRENCH R.H.A. relinquished command of N Battery R.H.A. on posting to the 41st Divl. Artillery and left the brigade to join that formation. The Divn. placed under 48 hours notice to move.	
BEAUCHAMPS	14th	—	Major G.M. Spencer-Smith R.F.A. arrived from 41st Divnl. Artillery to join the brigade, and took over command of N Battery R.H.A.	
INCHEVILLE	16th	—	2nd Lt. Musgrave rejoined Hd. Qrs. from a signalling course at Cavalry Corps. Hd. Qrs.	
"	19th	—	Orders received to move east. The brigade marched at 12.0 noon, five hours after receipt of orders, via GAMACHES and LE TRANSLAY, to the area FRAMICOURT-RAMBURES-VILLEROY, and billetted there for the night.	
LINCHEUX	20th	—	Continued the march eastwards at 9.0 a.m. to the area LINCHEUX-ST AUBIN and billetted for the night.	
GUIGNEMICOURT	21st	—	Continued the march eastwards. Batteries placed under the orders of their own Cavalry Brigadiers from mid-night 20-21st, in consequently to their respective brigade billeting areas. Hd. Qrs and Ammn. Column billetted for the night in GUIGNEMICOURT.	

2449. Wt. W14957/M90 750,000 1/16 J.B.C. & A. Form A C 2118/12
Mid-night 20-21st.

Army Form C. 2118.

Instructions regarding War Diaries and Intelligence Summaries are contained in F. S. Regs., Part II. and the Staff Manual respectively. Title Pages will be prepared in manuscript.

WAR DIARY
or
INTELLIGENCE SUMMARY
(Erase heading not required.)

17th Bde R.H.A.   March 1917

Place	Date	Hour	Summary of Events and Information	Remarks and references to Appendices
THENNES & BERTEAUCOURT.	21st	—	Captain H.W. Barnes R.F.A. joined the brigade from 28th Army Field Artillery, and took over command of the Bde. Ammunition Column.	
PERONNE ~~or~~ CERISY.	22nd	—	Continued the march eastwards to CERISY. with Div.HQ., troops being now attached to A Divisional Head. Qrs. Batteries with their own Cavalry Brigades. Light section of the ammunition column attached to Batteries. Main column remained at BERTEAUCOURT.	
PERONNE.	23rd	—	Marched with Divl. Hd. Qrs. to PÉRONNE and billeted there. Batteries continued their march east with their own Cavalry brigades to billets & bivouacs west of PERONNE. N. Dickson X Battery evacuated sick. Little Lyons joined X Battery from the Reinforcements for the R.H.A.Bde.	
"	24th	—	Head Quarters remained in PERONNE. AMBALA and CANADIAN CAVALRY Bdes. moved forward to cover the IV Army Front, and took over the forward outpost line from Corps Cavalry. In consequence of this X Battery moved to DEVISE in reserve with Ambala Cav. Bde. N. Battery in Divisional reserve with Secunderabad Cav. Bde. Reconnaissance of the northern (Canadian) sector by C.R.H.A.	
"	25th	—	Reconnaissance of the southern (Ambala) sector by C.R.H.A. 27. EASTWOOD X Battery R.H.A. rejoins his Brigade from leave and sick.	
"	26th	—	Bad weather prevented further reconnaissance. Remained in PÉRONNE.	
BOUVE LY.	27th	—	Conference with Gen. Ambala Cav. Bde. 10.0 a.m. Reconnoitred forward roads and east of BOIS TINCOURT for artillery positions to support an attack in the afternoon.	

Army Form C. 2118.

WAR DIARY
or
INTELLIGENCE SUMMARY
(Erase heading not required.)

17th Bde R.H.A. March 1917

Place	Date	Hour	Summary of Events and Information	Remarks and references to Appendices
PERONNE and neighbourhood	27th	—	N. Battery detached under command of the OC. RCHA Bde. 1st Cavalry in support of an attack on SAILCOURT and GUYENCOURT by Canadian Cav. Bde. The battery was in action during the afternoon and evening till about 9.0 p.m. when they ceased firing about 500 rounds fired. Both villages were taken, and battery was withdrawn and returned to Bivouac which was reached at 2.30 a.m. on 28th. X. Battery R.H.A. under CRHA supported an attack by VIII Hussars on VILLERS FAUCON. One 18 pdr battery, and one 4.5" Howitzer battery R.F.A. from 48th Divn. and one section of 21st Heavy Battery R.G.A. were included in the group. The attack was successful and the battery withdrew about 7 p.m. after firing 250 rounds, to TINCOURT village where it remained for the night under the orders of OC. VIII Hussars.	
"	28th	—	X. Battery withdrew from TINCOURT to DEVISE when VILLERS FAUCON was taken over by the infantry & the Cavalry relieved. N. Battery marched west to Bivouac near CHERY in the Leinster Cav. Bde. Hd. Qrs. remained in PERONNE.	
"	29th	—	X Battery marched west with Ambala Cav. Bde. to Bivouac near BOIS de MEREAUCOURT.	

Army Form C. 2118.

WAR DIARY
or
INTELLIGENCE SUMMARY
(Erase heading not required.)

19th Brigade R.H.A.   March 1917

Place	Date	Hour	Summary of Events and Information	Remarks and references to Appendices
VILLERS-BRETONNEUX LAMOTTE. BAYONVILLERS CAPPY	30th		Division withdrawn to rest in area west of PERONNE. Batteries still with their Cavalry brigades. Bde. Hd. Qrs. marched from PERONNE at 10.30 a.m. via. BIACHES - HEBECOURT - CAPPY - PROYART to VILLERS BRETONNEUX. 2/Lt. Robinson X. Battery R.H.A. evacuated to Field Ambulance sick.	
— do —	31st		Resting & refitting.	

Wistuting
Lt. Col. R.H.A.
Comg. 19th Bde R.H.A.

Army Form C. 2118.

Vol 10

WAR DIARY
or
INTELLIGENCE SUMMARY.
(Erase heading not required.)

Instructions regarding War Diaries and Intelligence Summaries are contained in F.S. Regs., Part II. and the Staff Manual respectively. Title pages will be prepared in manuscript.

Hour, Date, Place	Summary of Events and Information	Remarks and references to Appendices
APRIL 1st. to 4th.	Division resting in VILLERS BRETONNEUX Area.	
4th.	Dismounted Reinforcements rejoined Division.	
4th.	Information received from G.H.Q. that GERMAN Summer Time will be introduced at 2 a.m. on 16th April.	Appx 105
5th.	Warning Order "Move of Division Eastwards", probably on 8th April issued at 1-30 p.m.	
7th.	Four Armoured Cars sent for modification of armour to No.3 A.S.C. Workshops.	
8th.	Units informed that Division would not move on 8th, but would be prepared to move at 6 hours notice from midnight 8th/9th - G.A. 769 of 6th cancelled.	
9th.	Dismounted Reinforcements concentrated at FOUCAUCOURT.	
10th.	The Field Squadron moved to new billets at RAINECOURT.	
11th.	The Division received orders from Fourth Army to move East. Orders for the move (O.O.28) were issued at 4-30 p.m., but the move was cancelled by Fourth Army at 10 p.m., and the Division was put on eight hours notice to move. Operation Order No. 28 was cancelled.	Appx 106
12th.	Field Squadron moved to forward area and bivouaced at TREFCON - Squadron to be employed in improvising horse shelters in the CAULAINCOURT DEVISE Area pending the arrival of the Division.	

13th......Over

Army Form C. 2118.

WAR DIARY
or
INTELLIGENCE SUMMARY.

(Erase heading not required.)

Instructions regarding War Diaries and Intelligence Summaries are contained in F.S. Regs., Part II. and the Staff Manual respectively. Title pages will be prepared in manuscript.

Hour, Date, Place	Summary of Events and Information	Remarks and references to Appendices
APRIL 13th.	Division (less Field Squadron) resting in VILLER BRETONNEUX, and Field Squadron in bivouac about TERTRY Area. Orders received from Fourth Army in the afternoon for the Division to move to the TERTRY Area on the 14th. Captain R.G.P.Wood, 7th D.Guards took over duties of G.S.O.3 from Captain Gwatkin, on forenoon 13th., the latter officer returning to regimental duty.	Appx 104
14th.	The Division less Field Squadron (already in forward area) and 1 Battery R.C.H.A. (remained at CAPPY owing to horse shortage) moved to the area ATHIES CAULAINCOURT in accordance with 5th Cavalry Division Operation Order No. 29, attached in appendix. 104	
15th.	The Division remains in ATHIES CAULAINCOURT Area - Men are largely employed in repair of roads, filling in of craters and cross roads, the making of horse standings and shelters, all buildings in the area having been wrecked by the enemy. Weather very windy and wet.	
16th.	"A" Battery R.C.H.A. marches from CAPPY and joined R.C.H.A.Bde. Weather very bad. Dismounted Reinforcements of the Division arrived at Camp at BRIE from FOUCAUCOURT Area. They are employed on road repair in Fourth Army Area.	
17th. 18th. 19th.	Weather very bad. Weather continues bad, nothing to report. Orders for concentration in event of a move E. S.E.,etc. issued under G.A.844 of 19-4-17.	Appx 108

Army Form C. 2118.

WAR DIARY
or
INTELLIGENCE SUMMARY.
(Erase heading not required.)

Instructions regarding War Diaries and Intelligence Summaries are contained in F.S. Regs., Part II. and the Staff Manual respectively. Title pages will be prepared in manuscript.

Hour, Date, Place	Summary of Events and Information	Remarks and references to Appendices
APRIL.		
26th.	Armoured Cars reported all returned after modification of Armour plating.	
28th.	Work commenced on CAULAINCOURT - POEUILLY Sector of "RED LINE" defences by 200 men per each Brigade under O.C. Field Squadron.	
20th. to 30th.	Division engaged in training in GUIZANCOURT Area.	

J.D'Arke Capt
Major, G.S.,
5th. Cavalry Division.

Appx 105

No. G.A. 789.

SECRET

Headquarters, 5th. Cavalry Division.
Dated 5th. April, 1917.

To/
    Sec'bad Cavalry Brigade.
    Canadian   "   "
    Ambala   "   "
    C.R.H.A.
    O.C. A.S.C.
    5th. Signal Sqdn.
    Camp Commandant.
    "Q"

1. The Division will move, probably on April 8th., to the following billets and bivouacs.

    (a) Divisional H.Q.) PERONNE.
        Signal Squadron)

    (b) Can. Cav. Bde.) DOINGT - FAUBOURG BRETAGNE and slopes
        & attd. troops)   to North.

    (c) Amb. Cav. Bde.) Between the line DOINGT (exclusive) -
        & attd. troops) FLAMICOURT (inclusive) and BOIS d'AULNAIES
                              (exclusive)

    (d) Sec. Cav. Bde.) Between the line BOIS d'AULNAIES (incl)
        & attd. troops) and a line drawn along the top of the
                             ridge from PRUSLE to ETERPIGNY.

    (e) Divl. Troops) Between the above line and the BRIE-PRUSLE
        (less Div.H.Q. &) road (exclusive)
        Sigl. Sqdn, and)
        less troops at)
        present attd. to)
        Bdes.)

2. (a) The above areas will be reconnoitred early tomorrow, the 7th. inst. by Camp Commandant, representatives of Bdes. and D.A.A. & Q.M.G. respectively.

3. (a) No troops of detachments (c) (d) and (e) are to be East of the DOINGT-ATHIES road.

   (b) Units are to be spread out as much as possible, in view of aeroplane attack.

4. A limited number of tents will be available. A.A. & Q.M.G. will inform Brigades early of the number of tents which will be at their disposal. Brigades will inform A.A. & Q.M.G. where they wish the tents sent to.

                                              Capt. for
                                              Lieut-Colonel, G.S.
                                              5th. Cavalry Division.

Copy to:-
Fourth Army
III Corps.

App 106

SECRET   5TH. CAVALRY DIVISION   11th. April, 1917.   COPY No. 19

Reference Map   OPERATION ORDER NO. 28

$\frac{1}{100,000}$

FRANCE

1. The Division will move East tomorrow in accordance with the attached March Table. The condition of the roads being in some cases uncertain, advanced reconnaissances should be made. Routes may be altered where necessary so long as no clashing is risked.

2. The Crossing of BRIE is allotted to the Division for one hour at a time and is then closed for 20 minutes to allow of return traffic. Consequently it is of particular importance that Units should arrive at BRIE punctually. In the event of delay at the crossing, units will clear the road.

3. O.C. Signal Squadron will arrange to synchronise watches not later than 7.0 a.m.

4. Advanced Parties may be sent forward to pitch tents, but must cross during the times allotted to the Division (except in case of Secunderabad Brigade, whose parties may cross at ST. CHRIST at any time).

5. A.P.M. will co-operate with A.P.M. 3rd. Corps in regulating traffic at BRIE, under instructions already issued.

6. Field Squadron, on arrival in the bivouac area, will be disposed as follows:-

     (a) 1 Field Troop under orders of G.O.C. Ambala Cav. Bde.
     (b) Remainder   "   "   "   "   Secunderabad Cav. Bde.

7. Motors of Divisional Headquarters and Signal Squadron

     No. 9 L.A.C. Battery

will move independently, so as to arrive at TERTRY not later than 3 p.m. No. 9 L.A.C. Battery will come under direct orders of Divisional Headquarters from arrival in bivouac.

8. Liaison Officers and Gallopers will report at Divisional Headquarters by 4 p.m.

9. Reports to TERTRY after 3 p.m.

10. Acknowledge.

R.G. Howard Vyse

Lieut-Colonel, G.S.
5th. Cavalry Division.

Nos. 1 - 21   Normal O.O. distribution.
        22   Fourth Army.
        23   Third Corps.
        24   Fourth Corps.
        25   Cavalry Corps.
        26   R.F.C. Liaison Officer (for No 9 Squadron R.F.C.)
        27   Div. Limbered Train.
        28   Reserve Park.

Issued by D.R. at 4.30 p.m.

March Table (issued with O.O.B.ks 13th April)

Formation of Unit	Starting Point	Time	Route	Destination	Remarks
5th Field Sqdn	RAINCOURT	8-15am	FOUCAUCOURT – BRIE – MONS en CHAUSSEE	1 Troop to COULAINCOURT – Remainder to TREFCON	(a) Cross at BRIE between 11-0 and 11-45am (b) 1 Troop to be allotted by 2nd A.M.Cy.
Ambered Train	"	8-20am	— ditto —	DENISE	
Main Am Col	Camp nr CAPPY	7-45am	HERBECOURT – BARLEUX	— " —	
Reserve Park	— " —	7-50am	2nd (lasso) road to N of HERBECOURT	— " —	
A.H.T. Coy	— " —	8-0am	ESTERPIGNY – VILLERS CARBONNEL – BRIE – MONS en CHAUSSEE.	— " —	
B Echelon Comi Van B32	— " —	8-15am	— ditto —	See below	Cross at BRIE between 11-45am and 9 noon
Com: Van: P.do and attached troops (less B echelon)	CAPPY	9-30am	— ditto —	MONCHY LAGACHE – MERAUCOURT – MONTECOURT.	Cross at BRIE between 12-20 and 1-10pm
Divnl HDQrs & Signal Squadron (less motors)	VILLERS BRETONNEUX	7-45am	FOUCAUCOURT – BRIE – ESTREES EN CHAUSSEE, TERTRY	(a) To be clear of MARFUSEE by 8-45am (b) Cross at BRIE between 1-10 and 1-20pm
B Echelon Sec: BRIE	BAYONVILLERS	9am	— ditto —	TREFCON	Cross at BRIE between 1-40 and 1-50pm
B Echelon Amb: BRIE	MARFUSEE	9am	— ditto —	COULAINCOURT	Cross at BRIE between 1-50 and 2pm
Ambulance rearguard troops (less B echelon)	— " —	10.30am	— ditto —	— ditto —	Cross at BRIE between 2 and 2-40pm Cont/-

Formation or Unit	Starting Point	Time	ROUTE	Destination	Remarks
Sechos Corr B&C & attd Troops (Rear Echelon)	RAYONVILLERS	8-30 am	LIHONS – CHAULNES – ST CHRIST – ENNEMAIN – S. side of MONCHY LAGACHE	TREFCON	(a) 20th Div and M.G. Sqdn going en route (b) Not to cross at ST CHRIST before 1pm.

Appx 104

SECRET   5TH. CAVALRY DIVISION.   COPY NO. 18

Reference Map   OPERATION ORDER NO.29
     1   Dated 13th. April, 1917.
100,000
FRANCE.

1. The Division will move East tomorrow in accordance with the attached March Table. The condition of the roads being in some cases uncertain, advanced reconnaissances should be made. Routes may be altered where necessary so long as no clashing is risked.

2. Bivouac Areas are allotted in every case exclusive of accommodation and ground at present occupied by other troops.

3. The Crossing of BRIE is allotted to the Division for one hour at a time and is then closed for 20 minutes to allow of return traffic. Consequently it is of particular importance that units should arrive at BRIE punctually. In the event of delay at the crossing, units will clear the road.

4. O.C. Signal Squadron will arrange to synchronise watches not later than 7 a.m.

5. Advanced Parties may be sent forward. At BRIE they will not be allowed to cross between noon and 12.20 p.m., or between 1.20 and 1.40 p.m.

6. A.P.M. will co-operate with A.P.M. 3rd. Corps in regulating traffic at BRIE, under instructions already issued.

7. O.C. Field Squadron (already at TERTRY) will, early tomorrow morning, send one troop to improvise as many shelters as possible in each Brigade area. The troops will rejoin their squadrons in the evening.

8. Motors of Divisional Headquarters and Signal Squadron

       No. 9 L.A.C. Battery

will move independently via BRIE-ESTREES EN CHAUSSEE-MONCHY LAGACHE, so as to arrive at GUIZANCOURT not later than 3 p.m. No. 9 L.A.C. Battery will come under direct orders of Divisional Headquarters from arrival in bivouac.

9. Liaison Officers and Gallopers will report at Divisional Headquarters by 4 p.m.

10. Reports to GUIZANCOURT after 3 p.m.

11. Acknowledge.

                                                             Lieut-Colonel, G.S.
Nos. 1 to 25 Normal O.O. dist'n.   5th. Cavalry Division.
      26 Fourth Army.
      27 Third Corps
      28 Fourth Corps
      29 Cavalry Corps
      30 R.F.C. Liaison Officer.

Issued by D.R. at 5-15 p.m.

5th Cavalry Division
March Table 14-4-17 (Issued with O.O.   )

Formation/Unit	Starting point	Time	Route	Destination	Remarks
Canadian Horse Artillery Brigade.	TRAINECOURT.	4-15 A.m.	FOUCAUCOURT - ESTREES trans PARGNY. (following two columns)	PARGNY.	(a) To be clear of PONT LES BRIE by 11 A.m. and of ST CHRIST by 12-30 P.m.
Fusign. Amm. Column.	CAPPY.	4-0 A.m.	FAY - ESTREES - VILLERS CARBONNEL - PONT LES BRIE - FALVY GUIZANCOURT.	FALVY	
Reserve Park and H.Q. A.V.T. Coy.	— do —	7-15 A.m.	— ditto —	EPENANCOURT	
"B" Echelon, Canadian Cav: Brigade.	CAPPY.	4-45 A.m.	FAY - ESTREES - VILLERS CARBONNEL - BRIE.	See below.	Cross at BRIE between 11-0 & 11-15 A.m.
Canadian Cav: Ads.	— do —	9-15 A.m.	— ditto —	West E. of DENISE(incl) MONS EN CHAUSSEE (excl) ATHIES - FOUQUES (both inclusive)	Cross at BRIE between 11-15 A.m. and noon
Divnl. H.Q. & Sig. Sqdn.; VILLERS (less 1 troop)	VILLERS BRETONNEUX.	9-45 A.m.	FOUCAUCOURT - VILLERS CARBONNEL - BRIE - ATHIES.	GUIZANCOURT.	(a) May pass "B" echelon Seabrad and Ambula en route (b) Cross at BRIE at 12-20 P.m.
"B" Echelon Seabrad Bde & Sec to 3rd Cav. Ambr.	BAYONVILLERS.	8-0 A.m.	FOUCAUCOURT - A RIE - ESTREES EN CHAUSSEE.	See below.	Cross at BRIE at 12 - 30 P.m.
"A" Echelon Ambula bec Brigade.	MARFUSEE.	7-0 A.m.	— ditto —	CAULAUCOURT-POEUILLY. West West of TERNY all inclusive	Cross at BRIE between 12-40 and 1-20 P.m. and (if necessary) after 1-40 P.m.

cont'd.

Formation of unit	Starting point	Time	Route	Destination	Remarks
Stabs Escadre & 6 troops (less 2n dand 3rd Echelon	BAYONVILLERS	Notional	HARBONNIÈRES - CHAULNES - MARCHÉ-LE-POT - ST CHRIST - FOURQUES - S. of MONCHY LAGACHE	TREFCON - MONCHY LAGACHE	To cross at ST CHRIST not earlier than 12-30 pm

C.R.R.O.   Distribution - As for Operation Order No 29.

The following should be added to the March Table issued with Operation Order No 29.

1st Indian Cavalry Brigade & attached troops (less B. Echelon)	WARFUSÉE	9.30 a.m.	FOUCAUCOURT - ESTRÉES EN CHAUSSÉE	CAULAINCOURT - PEUILLY-Wood N. of TERTRY all inclusive	Cross at BRIE (inclusive) 12.40-1.20 p.m. and (if necessary) after 1.40 pm

5th Cavalry Division
13:4:17.
5.30 p.m.

R.G.Howard Vyse Lt Col G.S.

Appx 108

SECRET   NO. G.A. 244.

                                          Headquarters, 5th. Cavalry Division.
                                          Dated 19th. April, 1917.

1.   Concentration orders for moves in various directions are forwarded herewith.

2.   These orders will be acted on on the receipt of the order "Concentrate for move East, South East, etc."

3.   Unless otherwise stated

       (a)   All troops at present attached to Brigades will remain under their orders, except that Motor Ambulances will come under the orders of A.D.M.S.

       (b)   A Echelons will accompany Brigades.

       (c)   B. Echelons will be assembled off the road at the end of Brigade Areas from which the move forward is taking place. They will be assembled within 3 hours of the Brigade concentrating.

       (d)   Horse Rugs will be collected under orders which are being issued by A.A. & Q.M.G.

4.   On receipt of Concentration Orders Captain J.E. BLAKISTON HOUSTON 8th. Hussars will assume command of B. Echelons and will establish his Headquarters at CAULAINCOURT CHATEAU (in the case of a move S.E., East or N.E.) or at ATHIES CHURCH (in the case of a move West). If Captain HOUSTON is not available, Ambala Brigade will detail another officer of similar seniority.

5.   O.C. Signal Squadron will detail a motor cyclist for duty with O.C. "B" Echelon, to report at the Headquarters laid down above.

6.   Reports of Arrival at the place of concentration will be sent without delay to Divisional Headquarters. Whenever possible troops will close up off the road.

7.   Report Centres of Brigades should not move till further orders are issued.

                                                   R.E. Howard Vyse

                                                      Lieut-Colonel, G.S.

                                                      5th. Cavalry Division.

Issued at O.O. Distribution

       and :-

       Fourth Army.
       III Corps.
       IV Corps.
       Cavalry Corps.

SECRET.

5th Cavalry Division.
Concentration Orders — April, 1917.

Unit or Formation	Secunderabad Cav. Bde.	Ambala Cav. Bde.	Canadian Cav. Bde.	Main Amm. Column.	Field Squadron.	Limbered Train Reserve Park. Aux. H.T. Coy. (in that order)
Move South East	BEAUVOIS	CAULAINCOURT.	South entrance to MONCHY LAGACHE	Stand to in bivouacs	Stand to in bivouacs.	Stand to in bivouacs
Move East	VILLEVEQUE	"	"	MONTECOURT (via ENNEMAIN)	"	DEVISE.
Move North East.	Xroads ½ m. W. of TREFCON.	Xroads CAULAINCOURT– SOYECOURT and POEUILLY– VERMAND	ESTREES EN CHAUSSEE	"	"	DEVISE
Move West	½ road ½ m. W. of TREFCON	Xroads East of ESTREES EN CHAUSSEE	East of BRIE	Stand to in bivouacs	"	Stand to in bivouacs

Army Form C. 2118.

General Staff
H.Q. 5th Cav. Divn.
Vol. XI

WAR DIARY
or
INTELLIGENCE SUMMARY
(Erase heading not required.)

Instructions regarding War Diaries and Intelligence Summaries are contained in F. S. Regs., Part II. and the Staff Manual respectively. Title Pages will be prepared in manuscript.

Place	Date	Hour	Summary of Events and Information	Remarks and references to Appendices
GEZAINCOURT	2nd.		Dismounted Re-inforcements of Canadian Cavalry Brigade moved to new bivouacs in vicinity BOIS de HOLNON where they commenced work on the "Brown Line" of defences on 4th May.	
	7th.		Fourth Army ordered that R.H.A. Batteries be placed at disposal of IIIrd Corps. Instructions issued for movement of R.H.A. units (G.S.569 dated 8/5/17 - copy attached) on 8th May.	Appx 109
	8th.		Cavalry Corps, May 8th, G.X.148/1 received stating Cavalry Corps probably taking over IIIrd Corps front; in which case front of 59th Infantry Division will be allotted to 5th Cavalry Division. R.H.A. units moved to IIIrd Corps. Warning order is issued to all concerned.	
	9th.		Instructions re taking over from 59th Division are issued. An order is received from Fourth Army in which Cavalry Corps take over IIIrd Corps front and also that part of IVth Corps front North of the R. OMIGNON.	
	10th.		R.H.A. units returned from IIIrd Corps to forward billeting area.	
	11th.		In accordance with orders received from Fourth Army and Cavalry Corps Instructions for taking over revised front are issued under G.S.573/1 attached and later on Amendment G.A.924 is issued. R.F.C. Liaison Officer, R.F.C. personnel with all connected material attached to Division returned to R.F.C.	Appx 110
	12th.		Further amendments to G.S.573/1 necessitated by orders received from Cavalry Corps are issued under G.551 attached. Policy of defending front to be taken over are issued under G.530 attached. Canadian Cavalry Brigade dismounted re-inforcements withdrawn from work on "Brown Line" after work today.	Appx 111 Appx 112
	13th.		Indian Regiment dismounted re-inforcements withdrawn from work on "Brown Line" after work today.	

Army Form C. 2118.

WAR DIARY
or
INTELLIGENCE SUMMARY

(Erase heading not required.)

Instructions regarding War Diaries and Intelligence Summaries are contained in F.S. Regs., Part II. and the Staff Manual respectively. Title Pages will be prepared in manuscript.

Place	Date	Hour	Summary of Events and Information	Remarks and references to Appendices
	14th.		No. G.535 is issued and is attached as appendix showing disposition of 178th Infantry Brigade which is allotted as Reserve to 5th Cavalry Division.	Appx 113.
	15th.		The Canadian Cavalry Brigade (with 8th Hussars and 1 Field Troop No. 9 L.A.C. Battery attached) relieved the 104th Infantry Brigade 35th Division on the night of the 14th/15th without incident. The section taken over from 104th Infantry Brigade which was left Brigade of IVth Corps is N. of R. OMIGNON from the river to R.5.d.3.5. The H.Q. 5th Cavalry Division moved from GUIZANCOURT to NOBESCOURT Fm. K.32.b.9.1. where report centre opens at 5 pm. G.530/1 issued and attached as appx	Appx 113.A.
	16th.		The Secunderabad Cavalry Brigade (with 9th Hodsons Horse, 18th Lancers, No. 14 M.G. Sqdn. and 1 Field Troop attached) relieved the 177th Infantry Brigade in the line without incident on the night of the 15th/16th. The sector taken over is R.5.d.3.5. to L.22.a. The 5th Cavalry Division take over command of the 59th Division front at 9 a.m. No. G.535/1 issued and attached as appendix containing instructions reference R.E. Situation quiet, slight shelling along the Divisional front. Weather very wet and foggy.	Appx 114
	17th.		Situation normal. Signallers from 4th Cavalry Division joined 5th Cavalry Division on attachment to that Division while holding the line. Three dismounted Field Troops from 4th Cavalry Division are attached for work with 5th Cavalry Division.	
	18th.		Situation normal.	
	19th.		Cavalry Corps take over command of III Corps Front. 5th Cavalry Division take over command of Canadian Cavalry Brigade and Sub-sector A.1. from the 35th Division. Situation normal.	
	20th.		L.S.H. Canadian Cavalry Brigade captured two prisoners during the night 19th/20th in Sub-sector A.1. In accordance with orders received from Cavalry Corps-No. G. 552 (in appx) is issued. Situation quiet.	Appx 115

Army Form C. 2118.

WAR DIARY
INTELLIGENCE SUMMARY
(Erase heading not required.)

Instructions regarding War Diaries and Intelligence Summaries are contained in F. S. Regs., Part II. and the Staff Manual respectively. Title Pages will be prepared in manuscript.

Place	Date	Hour	Summary of Events and Information	Remarks and references to Appendices
	21st		During the night a party of the enemy attempted to raid SOMERVILLE WOOD (G.32) but were driven off without reaching the position. Situation normal.	App. 116 – 117
	22nd.		Situation normal. Hostile shelling slight. Operation Order No. 30 issued and attached as appendix. G. 552/1 issued in continuation of G. 552 of the 20th instant.	
	23rd.		Situation quiet.	
	24th.		During the night 23rd/24th a patrol encounter took place in the Sub-sector held by the Secunderabad Cavalry Brigade. Two of the enemy were bayoneted and three captured by the Deccan Horse patrol. Identification of prisoners was normal. The 4th Cavalry Division took over the Sub-sector A.3. from 176th Infantry Brigade which passed from command of 5th Cavalry Division. The relief took place without incident.	App. 118
	25th.		Divisional Operation Order, attached as appendix, is issued. A quiet day hostile artillery being less active than usual.	
	26th.		Situation normal - nothing to report.	
	27th.		G. 552/2 is issued and attached as an appendix. A raid was carried out in Sub-sector A.1. by the Canadian Cavalry Brigade. 17 prisoners were taken and 10 of the enemy bayoneted. His total casualties were estimated at 50. Our losses 1 killed and 3 wounded. An account of this minor operation is attached as appendix.	App. 119 App. 120
	28th.		Situation quiet.	
	29th.		On the night of the 28th/29th the 4th Cavalry Division took over the northern part of Sub-sector A.2. from Secunderabad Cavalry Brigade and the Canadian Cavalry Brigade extended their front slightly northward taking over similar portion of Sub-sector A.2. from Secunderabad Cavalry Brigade. Reliefs were carried out without incident in accordance with Divisional Operation Order 31 dated 26/5/1917. (App "B")	
	30th.		Situation normal.	

Army Form C. 2118.

WAR DIARY
or
INTELLIGENCE SUMMARY
(Erase heading not required.)

Instructions regarding War Diaries and Intelligence Summaries are contained in F. S. Regs., Part II. and the Staff Manual respectively. Title Pages will be prepared in manuscript.

Place	Date	Hour	Summary of Events and Information	Remarks and references to Appendices
	31st.		Hostile artillery fire above normal. About 180 shells fell about L.28.c.c. close to H.Q. Poona Horse. No damage was done. The enemy were probably searching for a 6" howitzer battery in the vicinity, otherwise situation normal.	

J. M. Rokke Major GS
5th Cavalry Division

SUBJECT: ATTACHMENT OF R.H.A.   No. G.S. 569.
TO IIIrd. CORPS.

SECRET   app+109

Headquarters, 5th. Cavalry Division.
Dated 8th. May, 1917.

To/
    Sec'bad Cav. Bde.
    Canadian " "
    Ambala " "
    C.R.H.A.
    Ammunition Column (Main).

Reference this office G.A. 893.

1.   C.R.H.A. will report to B.G.R.A. IIIrd. Corps at 10.30 a.m. today 8th. for detailed instructions.

2.   R.H.A. will move to wagon lines in Squares K.19.a.and b. and K.20.a.and b. (all South of the River COLOGNE) as follows:-

Unit	Starting Point	Time	Route
"N" R.H.A.	CAULAINCOURT	1 p.m.	POEUILLY-BERNES-HAMELET
"X" R.H.A.	"	1.30 p.m.	Do
R.C.H.A. Bde.	ATHIES	1.0 p.m.	MONS EN CHAUSSEE-VRAIGNES-HANCOURT-HAMELET.
Main Ammn. Col.	FALVY	12.30 p.m.	ATHIES- thence follow R.C.H.A.

17th.H.A.Bde.
   H.Q.   - as ordered by C.R.H.A.

3.   Tents can be drawn from O.C. Battalion at HAMELET. Advanced Parties will meet the Adjutant at that place at 1 p.m.

4.   The above force will continue to be administered by this Division. A.A. & Q.M.G. will issue the necessary orders as regards *Ammunition Park*.

5.   S.A.A. wagons of Light Sections Ammunition Column will start from their bivouacs for FALVY 2 hours after their batteries have moved.

6.   2nd. Lieut. MELLINGS "N" Battery will assume command of the S.A. Ammunition Column at noon and will report at FALVY on receipt of this order.

7.   Rugs will be dumped in accordance with orders already issued in the event of a forward move.

Lieut-Colonel, G.S.
5th. Cavalry Division.

Copy to:-
    IIIrd. Corps.
    "Q"
    O.C. A.S.C.
    A.D.M.S.
    A.D.V.S.
    D.A.D.O.S.
    Am'n Park

Appx 110

SECRET   No. G.S. 573/1.

Headquarters, 5th. Cavalry Division.
Dated 11th. May, 1917.

N.B. These instructions are preliminary
and are liable to alteration.

1. The Division will take over the front now occupied by the left Brigade 35th. Division and the 59th. Division in accordance with the attached Table of Reliefs.

2. 176th. Infantry Brigade remains for the present in the line and comes under command of the Division when the latter relieves 59th. Division.

3. Brigadiers will make all arrangements direct with Infantry Brigadiers concerned, and will get into touch with them forthwith.

4. Brigades will select positions for the troops which they are ordered to place in Divisional Reserve, and will submit their proposals to this office for approval. Positions will be selected with a view to these troops being available to work on the Main Line of Resistance and to strengthen the garrison of it.

5. 17th. R.H.A. Bde. and R.C.H.A. Bde. are placed from midnight 12th/13th. at the disposal of C.R.H.A., who will issue the necessary orders for moves and reliefs.

6. Moves will be carried out mounted, the horses extra to Dismounted War Establishment returning to their present bivouacs.

    (a) Brigadier Generals SEELY and GREGORY will issue the necessary orders for the move of the troops placed under their command, giving this office 24 hours' notice.

    (b) Div. H.Q. and Signal Sqdn. will move to NOBESCOURT Farm (K.32.b.) on May 16th.

    (c) 5th. Field Squadron (less 2 troops) will move on a date and to a destination which will be notified later.

    (d) A.A. & Q.M.G. will issue instructions regarding Ammunition Park and other A.S.C. Units.

7. Instructions regarding the POLICY OF DEFENCE will be issued later.

                                                  Lieut-Colonel, G.S.
                                                  5th. Cavalry Division.

To/
    Normal O.O. Distribution.
                    Copies to:-
                    Fourth Army.
                    Cavalry Corps.
                    IIIrd. Corps.
                    IVth. Corps.
                    35th. Division.
                    59th. Division.

5TH CAVALRY DIVISION.

Programme of Reliefs. 14th - 17th May 1917. (Issued with G.S. 573/1)

Relieving Force.	Formation to be relieved.	Frontage.	Date.	Remarks.	Artillery Allotment.
Brig.-Gen. SEELY. Canadian Cav. Bde. 8th Hussars. No. 9 L.A.C. Battery. 1 Field Troop.	104th Infantry Brigade.	M.8.c. - G.32.d.1.9.	14th/15th	(a) Command passes at midnight 14th/15th (b) 1 Regt. & 4 Vickers. Divisional Reserve. (c) Under 55th Division till 8 a.m., 17th.	16th H.A. Bde. (less 1 Battery) (12-13 prs.)
Brig.-Gen. GREGORY. Secunderabad Cav. Bde. 9th Hodson's Horse. 18th Lancers. No. 14 M.G. Squadron. 1 Field Troop.	177th Infantry Brigade.	G.32.d.1.9.- L.24.a.2.9.	15th/16th (Right Bn.) 16th/17th (Left Bn.)	(a) Command passes at midnight 16th/17th. (b) 1 Indian Regt. and 4 Vickers in Divisional Reserve.	17th H.A. Bde. (12-13 prs.) R.C.H.A. Bde. (8-13 prs.)
Headquarters, 5th Cavalry Division.	H.Q. 59th Division.	M.8.c. - F.29.d. central.	8 a.m. 17th.	Takes over command of *left* Brigade of 59th Division (176th) as well as above two frontages.	

P.R. Howard Wyee M.A. 3p

"SECRET" Appx III

No. G. 531.

Headquarters, 5th. Cavalry Division.
Dated 12th. May, 1917.

The following additions and alterations are made to this office No.G.S. 573/1, and the attached Table of Reliefs :-

A. Additions

1. (a) Cavalry Corps takes over from IIIrd. Corps at 9.0 a.m. on 19th. May.

   (b) 2nd. Cavalry Division relieves left (42nd.) Division of IIIrd. Corps on nights 17th/18th. and 18th/19th. May, beginning at the right.

2. 178th. Infantry Brigade is in Divisional Reserve to the Division until 9.0 a.m. May 19th.

3. (a) 1 Bde. 59th. Divisional Artillery, covering the left (178th.) Infantry Brigade of 59th. Div., comes under orders of C.R.H.A. when that officer relieves B.G.R.A. 59th. Division.

   (b) 15th. H.A. Bde. comes under orders of G.O.C. 35th. Division from the time of going into the line until 9.0 a.m. May 19th.

4. No. 9 L.A.C. Battery (less that portion which accompanies the Vickers Guns and less the Motor Car) will move at 2.0 p.m. on May 14th., under an officer, to the bivouac of the Ammunition Column East of TERTRY.
   The motor car is placed at the disposal of C.R.H.A. from receipt of this order.

5. Field Squadron (less 2 troops) will move to MONTIGNY FARM on 15th., under squadron arrangements.

6. A.D.M.S. will issue the necessary orders for move of Field Ambulances (already ordered in G.S. 573/2).

7. " All troops allotted to Brigadier Generals SEELY
   " and GREGORY come under their orders at midnight on
   " the night preceding the move."

B. Alterations

8. Para 6 (b) Div. H.Q. and Signal Squadron will now move to NOBESCOURT FARM on May 15th. Reports to that place after 5.0 p.m.

9. Table of Reliefs.

   (a) In "Remarks" column opposite Brig.Gen. SEELY

      (i) Erase sub-para (b)
      (ii) For "8.0 a.m. 17th", substitute "9.0 a.m. 19th."

   (b) In "Date" Column opposite Brig.Gen. GREGORY, for the whole detail substitute "15/16th."

   (c) In "Remarks" column opposite Brig.Genl. GREGORY, for "Midnight 16th/17th" substitute "9 a.m. 16th" (cancels G.A. 934)

   (d) ....

(d) In "Frontage" Column, opposite "Div.Hqrs." for whole detail substitute

"(i) Up to 9.0 a.m. 19th, G.32.d.1.9 – F.29.d. Central.

"(ii) Afterwards, M.8.c.–F.29.d.central".

(e) In "Date" Column opposite Divisional Headquarters – for "8.0 a.m.17th." substitute "9.0 a.m.18th."

R.E.Howard Wyse

Lieut-Colonel, G.S.

5th. Cavalry Division.

To/
Normal O.O. Distribution.

Fourth Army.
Cavalry Corps.
IIIrd. Corps.
IVth. Corps.
35th. Division.
59th. Division.

SECRET　　　　　　　appx 112　　　　　　NO. G. 530.
　　　　　　　　　　　　　　　　　　　　　　12-5-14

5TH. CAVALRY DIVISION.
INSTRUCTIONS FOR DEFENCE.

1. **PLAN OF DEFENCE.**

    (a) An Outpost Line.

    (b) A Main Line of Resistance.

    (c) A Second Line.

    Maps showing these lines will be issued shortly.

2. **GENERAL POLICY.**

    (a) The Outpost Line will be held with a succession of small posts, mutually supporting one another, and with supporting troops close behind, ready to counter-attack if a part is rushed. If an immediate counter-attack fails no further effort will usually be made except under Divisional arrangements.

    (b) The Main Line will be held by a succession of similar, but larger and stronger, posts. The Brigade Reserves will be in or near this line. If an immediate counter-attack fails no further effort will usually be made

    except under Divisional arrangements.

    (c) Patrols will be pushed out constantly in front of the Outpost Line in order

    　　(i) To establish a moral superiority over the hostile patrols.

    　　(ii) To discover the strength of his defences, with a view to arranging enterprises against any weak points.

    (d) The Major-General expects every commander, down to Troop Leaders to be able to say without hesitation what his action will be in the event of any part of his front being lost to the enemy, and also what arrangements have been made for artillery support. This is to be very thoroughly impressed on all officers.

3. **WORK TO BE CARRIED OUT.**

    The following are the most important items of work to be carried out :-

    (a) Posts to be wired in all round.

    (b) Posts to be connected by continuous rays of wire to provide enfilade machine gun or Hotchkiss fire. The rays should run obliquely forward thus

    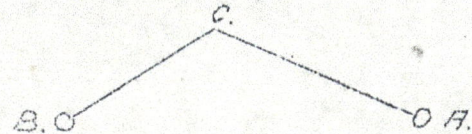

    The distance A-C or B-C should not exceed 300 yards and should usually be less.

    　　　　　　　　　　　　　　　　　............(c)

- (c) Night lines to be laid out and communication trenches dug where necessary, to allow of counter-attack troops being brought up.

- (d) Earthworks of posts to be deepened and strengthened. Alternative positions to be prepared for occupation in case of hostile bombardment.

- (e) Where there is no accommodation for counter-attack troops close behind the Outpost Line, this must be provided as early as possible, in the form of Strong Posts which will, besides affording cover to counter-attack troops, form a retrenchment, if necessary, to the Outpost Line.

- (f) Points (a) (b) and (c) apply to the Outpost Line as well as the Main Line of Resistance. The latter is the most important, and the wire on that line must be strengthened and made continuous with all speed.

4. The Divisional Reserve located in Brigade areas and not employed under Divisional arrangements, will be at the disposal of Brigadiers for work not further forward than the Main Line. The Division will use every endeavour to let Brigades know early what portion of the Divisional Reserve is required for other work.

5. The Divisional Commander wishes all ranks to be impressed with the fact that their comfort and safety depends directly upon their patrolling activity and upon the amount of work they do. In the latter respect he intends to set a high standard, and he wishes again to remind officers that they must invariably set an example to their men by themselves working.

6. MISCELLANEOUS POINTS.

- (a) Any guns in front of the Main Line are to be wired in, under Brigade arrangements.

- (b) Vickers guns should not be placed in the Outpost Line till the posts are thoroughly strong. They can however be used for long range fire from intermediate positions between the Outpost and Main Lines.

- (c) Artillery communications and barrage arrangements will be tested frequently.

To/

R.G. Howard de Vyse

Lieut-Colonel, G.S.
5th. Cavalry Division.

Canadian Cav. Bde.		5
Sec'bad " "		5
Ambala " "		5
C.R.H.A.		3
R.C.H.A.Bde.		3
No. 9 LAC Bty.		1
Field Squadron		1
Q		1
A.D.M.S.		1

No. G. 535.

Headquarters, 5th. Cavalry Division.
Dated 14th. May, 1917.

To/

Normal O.C. Distribution.

1. The Brigade of the 59th. Divisional Artillery referred to in this office G.531 of May. 12th. is 295th. F.A. Brigade.

2. Major F.I. COLLIN, 5th. Field Squadron R.E. will assume the duties of C.R.E. 5th. Cavalry Division at 9.0 a.m. on May 16th., at which hour he will relieve C.R.E. 59th. Division. The following R.E. Units will be at his disposal :-

    (a) 5th. Field Squadron.

    (b) 2 sections 469th. Field Coy, which will continue to be employed in the sub sector of the 176th. Inf. Bde.

    (c) 3 troops 4th. Field Squadron, which will arrive on a date to be notified later.

3. This office G.533 of May 13th. is cancelled.

178th. Inf. Bde. will be in Divisional Reserve from 9.0 a.m. May 16th. 1 Battalion moves to VENDELLES and JEANCOURT on May 15th., and will be at the disposal of C.R.E. for work on May 16th. The remainder of the Brigade is located at VRAIGNES (Hqrs) - HANCOURT - BERNES and KARELET.

4. R.A.M.C. details now attached to 176th. Inf. Bde. come under the control of A.D.M.S. this Division at 9.0 a.m. May 16th.

Lieut-Colonel, G.S.
5th. Cavalry Division.

Copy to:-

    176th. Inf. Bde.
    178th. " "
    Cavalry Corps.
    IIIrd. Corps.
    35th. Division.
    59th. Division.

Appx 113A

No. G. 530/1.

Headquarters, 5th. Cavalry Division.
Dated 15th. May, 1917.

To/
Canadian Cavalry Brigade.   8
Sec'bad Cavalry Brigade.   8
Ambala Cavalry Brigade.   1
C.R.H.A.   3
Field Squadron   1
"Q"   1
A.D.M.S.   1

The following instructions are in amplification of this Office No. G.530.

1. NOMENCLATURE.

   (a) The front commanded by the Major-General will be known as Sector A.

   (b) The front of Canadian Cavalry Brigade will be called (after May 18th) subsector A-1.

       That of Secunderabad Cavalry Bde. - Subsector A-2

       That of 176th. Inf. Bde. - subsector A-3.

   (c) If it is found necessary to number posts, this will be done from right to left, throughout the Brigade front.

2. PLAN OF DEFENCE.

   (a) The Outpost Line is the line of the most advanced posts.

   (b) The Main Line of Resistance is what is now known as the Brown Line.

   (c) The Second Line is not yet settled.

3. GENERAL POLICY.

   (a) Brigadiers are responsible for all defence work in, and in front of the present front trenches of the Brown Line.

   (b) A Support Trench already exists behind part of the Brown Line, and this will be improved and extended under Divisional arrangements. For the present Brigadiers will concentrate on work on the front trenches of the Brown Line, but will be prepared to submit proposals as regards the Support Trenches.

4. ARRANGEMENTS IN CASE OF ATTACK.

   (a) "Battle Headquarters" will be settled upon immediately by all commanders. In case of attack they will move to them and will remain there, remembering that if they leave for any but the shortest interval of time, they will inevitably lose control of the force which it is their duty to command.

   (b) Battle Headquarters, and the routes to them, must be well known to all subordinate commanders, by all runners, and, in the case of squadrons, by every man.

..............(c)

(c) Brigadiers and Regimental Commanders will, in addition, select and construct Observation Posts, which should be close to their Battle Headquarters. A sentry should be constantly on duty by day near these observation posts, to prevent other officers (except General Officers) using them.

(d) COUNTER-ATTACKS across the open will be practised by all units detailed as counter-attack troops, on the first night after they take up their position. They must be continued until every possible eventuality has been dealt with. Lines of Posts, painted white on one side, will be laid out to direct such counter-attacks.

5. DUTIES OF R.E. - WORKING PARTIES.

(a) The senior R.E. officer in a brigade subsector acts as the technical adviser of the Brigadier, just as the C.R.E. acts as the technical adviser of the Divisional Commander.

(b) In both cases it is for the R.E. to point out what working parties are required, and for the Brigade or Divisional Staff to decide whether they should be provided, and to issue the necessary orders.

(c) Instructions given to his subordinates by the C.R.E. should be regarded as emanating from the Staff of the Division, so far as policy is concerned. Such instructions do not convey a definite order to provide a working party, but a request for one will not be refused without reference to the Division.

6. GAS ALARM.

Small shell cases, such as 18 pdr. as Gas Gongs, do not make sufficient noise. Either large shell-cases or railway rails will be used. The latter will be provided by the R.E. on demand.

7. MEDICAL.

(a) In spite of the time of year, a number of cases of "Trench feet" are still reported every week in the Army. A.D.M.S. is issuing instructions on this subject as a reminder.

(b) The Division which is being relieved has suffered considerably from dysentery. In view of this fact, strict measures of sanitation are of paramount importance.

(sd) R.C.Howard Vyse, Lieut-Col.
G.S. 5th. Cav. Division.

Copy to:-
178th. Inf. Bde.

Appx 114

No. G. 535/1.

Secret.

Headquarters, 5th. Cavalry Division,
Dated 16th. May, 1917.

To/

O.O. Distribution.
----

1. In continuation of this office No. G. 535 of May 14th.

(a) 2 additional sections 469th. Field Coy are attached to the Division and will work in the Intermediate Line in subsector A-2 under Divisional arrangements.

(b) The three troops of 4th. Field Squadron have arrived and have been distributed by C.R.E.

(c) 180th. Tunnelling Company R.E. (less 2 sections) is attached to the Division for work. It will be administered by 59th. Division.

2. All troops of 59th. Division in the sector 5th. Cav. Div. will be administered by 59th. Division.

J. O'Rorke. Capt. for
Lieut-Colonel, G.S.
5th. Cavalry Division.

Copy to:-
    Cavalry Corps.
    IIIrd. Corps.
    59th. Division.
    176th. Inf. Bde.
    178th. Inf. Bde.

SECRET

Appx 115

No. G-552.

Headquarters, 5th. Cavalry Division.
Dated 20th. May, 1917.

To/
Sec'bad Cavalry Brigade.
Canadian   "   "
176th. Infantry Brigade.
178th.   "   "
C.R.H.A.
C.R.E.
Signal Squadron.

---

1. Consequent upon the withdrawal of 59th. Division, the Cavalry Corps front is being taken over by all four cavalry divisions, each of which will have one brigade in reserve for training.

2. 176th. Infantry Brigade will be relieved by 4th. Cavalry Divn. by dawn May 24th. Details will be notified later. Preparations to hand over will be made at once.

3. 176th. and 178th. Infantry Brigades will be at disposal of Cavalry Divisions for work on wire in the Intermediate Line from May 25th. to about 28th., as follows:-

   (a) 2 Btns 176th. Brigade, now in Brigade Reserve, to 4th. Cavalry Division.

   (b) 2 Btns 176th. Brigade, on relief, to 2nd. Cavalry Divn.

   (c) 2 Btns. 178th. Bde., now with 2nd. Cavalry Divn. to 3rd. Cavalry Division.

   (d) 2 Btns. 178th. Bde. now with 5th. Cav. Divn., remain.

4. Artillery will be re-allotted under instructions to be issued by G.O.C. R.H.A. Cavalry Corps.

5. (a) 3 Field Troops of 4th. Field Squadron will be returned to the command of 4th. Cavalry Division by 9.0 p.m. 22nd. Details will be notified later.

   (b) Instructions regarding R.E. 59th. Division and sections of Tunnelling Company will be forwarded later.

6. Signal Personnel will be transferred under arrangements to be made by A.D. Signals Cavalry Corps.

7. On a date to be notified later

   (a) 4th. Cavalry Division will take over the front of Secunderabad Cavalry Brigade as far as the line N. edge of PIEUMEL WOOD - N. edge of GRAND PRIEL FM.- G.20 central.

   (b) Canadian Cavalry Brigade will extend their front Northwards. The new line of demarcation in contemplation is R.5.central- N. side of PURPLE COPSE (including post at N. corner) - G.27 central.

   (c) Units of Ambala Cavalry Brigade will be withdrawn for training.

..............8.

8. In consequence of para 7

   G.O's C. Canadian and Sec'bad Cavalry Brigades will

   (a) Meet the Divisional Commander at Headquarters 7th. Dragoon Guards L.5.a.5.1 at 11 a.m. on May 21st. prepared to discuss the alteration of fronts.

   (b) Make the necessary preparations for handing over.

   (c) Arrange their reliefs in such a way that units of Ambala Cavalry Bde. can be withdrawn on May 25th.

9. Divisional Headquarters will not move.

10. ACKNOWLEDGE.

R. Howard Vyse

Copy to:-
   4th. Cavalry Division.
   59th. Division.
   "Q"
   A.D.M.S.
   Ambala Cavalry Brigade.

Lieut-Colonel, C.S.
5th. Cavalry Division.

appx 116

SECRET   5TH. CAVALRY DIVISION.

OPERATION ORDER NO. 30.   Copy No. 20
                                                22-5-17

Reference Map
$\frac{1}{20,000}$
F R A N C E

1. The front at present held by the Cavalry Corps is to be taken over by all four Cavalry Divisions, the 59th. Division being withdrawn.

2. 176th. Infantry Brigade will be relieved by two brigades of 4th. Cavalry Division on the night of May 23rd/24th. The command of this Subsector passes from 5th. Cavalry Division to 4th. Cavalry Division at 8 a.m. May 24th.

3. (a) Details of Infantry reliefs will be arranged between G.O.C. 176th. Infantry Brigade and Brigadier General N.W. HAIG, C.M.G. Completion of relief and hour of handing over will be reported to this office.

   (b) Details of Artillery reliefs are being arranged between C.R.H.A's concerned.

   (c) Details of R.E. Reliefs are being arranged between O.C. 4th. Field Squadron and O.C. 176th. Field Company.

4. The 176th. and 178th. Infantry Brigades are at the disposal of the Cavalry Corps for wiring the Intermediate Line up to May 28th. inclusive.

   (a) G.O.C. 176th. Infantry Brigade will leave 2 Btns. at HERVILLY, HESBECOURT and POISEL, at the disposal of G.O.C. 4th. Cavalry Division, and will place the other two at the disposal of G.O.C. 2nd. Cavalry Division, who will issue instructions for their move direct.
      Remainder of the Brigade will move, on completion of relief, to BOUVINCOURT, and will revert to command of 59th. Division on arrival there.

   (b) 2 Btns. 178th. Infantry Brigade now with 2nd. Cavalry Division will be transferred to 3rd. Cavalry Division under orders to be issued by 2nd. Cavalry Division.
      The remainder of the brigade will remain in their present position, 2 Btns. being at the disposal of this Division for work.

5. ACKNOWLEDGE.

                                         R.G. Howard Vyse
                                         Lieut-Colonel, G.S.
                                         5th. Cavalry Division.

Normal O.O. Dist'n. 1-27.   4th. Cav. Division 31.
Cavalry Corps   28.   59th. Division   32.
2nd. Cav. Division   29.   87th. French Division. 33.
3rd. Cav.   "   30.

Appx 114

No. G. 552/1.

Headquarters, 5th. Cavalry Division.
Dated 22nd. May, 1917.

To/
Canadian Cavalry Brigade.
Sec'bad Cavalry Brigade.

Reference this office G.552 of May 20th., para 7.d.

1. The new line of demarcation will be

CAUBRIERES WOOD No. 2 (Secunderabad) - trench junction R.5.c.9.8 - present H.Q. of 9th. Hodson's Horse, R.5.b.3.2 (Canadian) - RED HOUSE (Secunderabad) - trench at N.W. corner of PURPLE COPSE (see para 3 below) - bottom of valley which runs through G.26. central.

2. The date of the readjustment, and details of the relief, will be notified later.

3. Secunderabad Brigade will, before May 25th., arrange to extend the trench at the N.W. corner of PURPLE COPSE so as to provide room for one troop Canadian Cavalry Brigade in addition to the present garrison.

R.E. Howard Wyse
Lieut-Colonel, G.S.
5th. Cavalry Division.

Copy to:-
Ambala Cavalry Brigade.
C.R.H.A.
C.R.E.

Appx 118

5TH. CAVALRY DIVISION.   Copy No. 20

OPERATION ORDER -NO. 31.   25-5-17.

Reference Map
1
20,000
F R A N C E.

1. 4th. Cavalry Division is taking over part of Subsector A.2.

2. The following reliefs will take place on the night of May 28/29th.

   (a) Canadian Cavalry Brigade will take over from Secunderabad Cavalry Brigade as far North as the line Trench junction R.5.c.9.7 - RED HOUSE (Sec'bad) - PURPLE COPSE (Canadian) - Valley which runs through G.26. central.
   The trench at the N.W. corner of PURPLE COPSE will be occupied conjointly by the two Brigades.
   Code word for completion of relief - AULT.

   (b) Mhow Cavalry Brigade will take over from Secunderabad Cavalry Brigade as far south as the line L.27.b.9.5 - N. side of PIEUMEL WOOD- GRAND PRIEL FM.- G.20 central, all inclusive to Sec'bad Bde.
   Code word for completion of relief - TREFCON.

3. All arrangements will be made direct by Brigadiers concerned.

4. Command passes on completion of relief.

5. The troops of Ambala Cavalry Brigade now in the line, less Subsections 14th. Machine Gun Squadron, will return to bivouacs near CAULAINCOURT and TERTRY on May 29th. and revert to command of G.O.C. that brigade as Divisional Reserve.
   Orders for the move will be issued by G.O's C. Canadian and Secunderabad Cavalry Brigades, who will make all arrangements direct with G.O.C. Ambala Cavalry Brigade.

6. 3 Subsections of 14th. Machine Gun Squadron will remain at the disposal of G.O.C. Secunderabad Cavalry Brigade.

7. A.D.M.S. will issue instructions as regards any necessary readjustment of medical details.

8. Acknowledge.

                                       Lieut-Colonel, G.S.
                                       5th. Cavalry Division.

To/
   O.C. Bgt'n.   1- 25.
   Cavalry Corps   26.
   4th. Cavalry Div. 27.
   87th. French Div. 28.

Issued by D.R. at ....

SECRET

copy119

No. G. 552/2.

Headquarters, 5th. Cavalry Divn.
Dated 27th. May, 1917.

To/
    Canadian Cavalry Brigade.
    Sec'bad Cavalry Brigade.
    Ambala Cavalry Brigade.

In amplification of this office No. G.A. 45 of today's date.

1. The Dismounted Reinforcements (i.e. other ranks surplus to the authorised establishment for operations) of the Brigade in Divisional reserve will remain in the forward area, and will be employed under Divisional arrangements on work on the Intermediate Line.

2. Consequently, when units of Ambala Cavalry Brigade are withdrawn in accordance with Operation Order No. 31, the above details will remain with the Brigades to which they are at present attached.

3. The following will remain

    (a) <u>Officers</u>, as laid down in Organisation Table "G", except that the officer in command of the whole party must have not less than 8 years' service.

    (b) <u>Transport</u>.   1 Wagon L.G.S. per Regiment.
                               1 Water Cart from Mhow Field Ambs.

4. (a) <u>Ambala Cavalry Brigade</u> will notify Secunderabad and Canadian Cavalry Brigades the exact numbers which will remain.

    (b) Secunderabad and Canadian Cavalry Brigades will notify this office and Ambala Cavalry Brigade the exact location of the parties.

5. In the course of a day or two all three parties will be concentrated near VENDELLES under instructions which will be issued by A.A. & Q.M.G.

6. Meanwhile 8th. Hussars party is at the disposal of G.O.C. Canadian Cavalry Brigade for work not further forward than the Intermediate Line. Parties of 9th. Hodson's Horse and 18th. Lancers will be employed under C.R.E. after tomorrow night 28th/29th.

                                             R. Howard Wyse

                                          Lieut-Colonel, G.S.

Copy to:-   5th. Cavalry Division.
    C.R.E.   A.D.M.S.
    Signals. O.C. A.S.C.
    "Q"   Cavalry Corps.

Appx 120.

Narrative of a Minor Enterprise carried out by the Canadian Cavalry Brigade on the night of May 26th/27th., 1917.

OBJECT.

The object of the raid was to kill and capture Germans holding advanced posts (G.32.d., G.33.c. and M.2.d.) in front of the ST.HELENE trench line and to destroy their works.

Reference 1/20,000
Map of HINDENBURG
Line, sheet 4.
BELLENGLISE.

PRELIMINARY ARRANGEMENTS.

1. RECONNAISSANCE.

The ground, the enemy's habits and dispositions, had been carefully studied for some days previously. The two regiments concerned had already been in front line for a tour of duty of five days and had just begun their second tour. They therefore knew the ground well and were fresh.

2. STRENGTH AND POSITION OF RAIDING PARTIES AT ZERO HOUR AND THEIR OBJECTIVE.

(a) L.S.H. Raiding Party. One officer and one troop in position 200 x W. of FISHERS CRATER (M.2.d.7.4.) with the objective FISHERS CRATER, small works N. and S. and the ruins W. of it — all about 200 x from the Crater.

In addition to above one officer and 10 men accompanied the raiders to act as covering party and to take over prisoners.

(b) F.G.H. Raiding Party. Two officers and two troops in position S.E. corner of SOMERVILLE WOOD (G.32.d.6.3) with the objective MAX WOOD (G.32.d.9.0) and sunken road East of the wood (G.32.d).

50% of each troop carried two P bombs.
25% " " " " electric torches.

3. ARTILLERY.

Three batteries of French 75's to barrage ST.HELENE trench- M.3.c.9.9, G.33.b.2.6 from Zero to Zero + 30 minutes. These batteries firing from S. of R. OMIGNON with oblique enfilade fire.
X and N Batteries R.H.A. and A. and B. Batteries R.C.H.A. to put up a barrage to cover the raiding parties from Zero onwards. Fire to be directed :-

Firstly - on objectives of raiding parties.
Secondly- on tactical points, M.G. emplacements and trenches beyond the zone of the raiding parties.

Heavy Artillery

(a) Seven- 6 inch Hows: from 109 and 40 (S) Batteries, to co-operate by fire firstly on the objectives of raiding party and afterwards on enemy works in rear.

.... (b)

(b) One Battery of 60-pdrs to search and sweep the approaches from the HINDENBURG to the ST.HELENE line throughout the operation.

4. MACHINE GUN BARRAGE. Six M.G's were placed S. of river OMIGNON near BERTHAUCOURT to cover the raiders by sweeping ST.HELENE trench with enfilade fire.

5. LIGHT SIGNALS. It was previously decided that raiders should withdraw clear of their objectives by Zero + 28 minutes. The commander of the right party was given a red rocket as the signal to withdraw: the commander of the left party was given a green one. In addition, both a red and a green rocket were to be fired from our trenches, as nearly as possible over the raiding parties, in case either commander should be killed, lose his rocket, or forget the time.

6. ZERO HOUR was fixed at 2.15 a.m. as it was considered that the increasing light at 2.45 a.m. would assist the withdrawal of our troops.

-:-----:-oOo-:-----:-

NARRATIVE OF EVENTS.

7. Raiding Parties.

(a) The L.S.H. Raiding Party met with some opposition near FISHERS CRATER, where the enemy encountered were more numerous than the raiders - at least six of the enemy were bayonetted in and around the crater and nine prisoners were taken of whom one died on the way back. Our casualties in this party amounted to one man killed and two men wounded.

(b) The F.G.H. Raiding Party met with little opposition; at least five of the enemy were killed by this party and nine prisoners taken. This party had no casualties.

8. Artillery.

Reports from both raiding parties testify as to the accuracy and destructiveness of our artillery fire. Many Germans were found killed by our artillery fire and those who fled back to ST.HELENE trench came under the M.G. and artillery barrage which was on that trench throughout the operation.

9. M.G. Barrage.

M.G. Barrage was maintained throughout. One machine gunner was wounded.

10. Action of the enemy.

About 5 minutes after Zero the enemy fired a red rocket(it has since been ascertained from prisoners that this was the signal for all in advance of the main line to fall back there) which received no apparent answer. About Zero plus 20 minutes the enemy began to send up green lights on a front of about 1000 x extending from both sides of the R. OMIGNON Northwards. No apparent increase of their artillery fire was noted. The action of hostile artillery throughout was extremely feeble there being nothing in the nature of a barrage employed.

................11.

11. The garrison of the hostile advanced posts is known to have been 54. It is considered that at least 50 of the enemy have been accounted for with a loss of one killed and three wounded only.

CONCLUSIONS.

12. The success of this operation was due to

(a) Thorough familiarity with the ground.

(b) Careful arrangements and definite instructions as to the line of withdrawal.

(c) Facilities for enfilade machine gun and artillery fire from the S. bank of the OMIGNON.

(d) The short bombardment which gave the enemy no warning of the raid.

(e) Bold leading.

-:------:-oOo-:------:-

S E C R E T

Instructions regarding War Diaries and Intelligence Summaries are contained in F.S. Regs., Part II. and the Staff Manual respectively. Title Pages will be prepared in manuscript.

Army Form C. 2118.

WAR DIARY of 5TH. CAVALRY DIVISION.
or
INTELLIGENCE SUMMARY
(Erase heading not required.)

June, 1916.

Place	Date	Hour	Summary of Events and Information	Remarks and references to Appendices
NOBESCOURT FARM.	June 1st		Situation quiet.	
	2nd		Wire cutting and a bombardment of the enemy's trenches about ST. HELENE was carried out during the afternoon. One of our aeroplanes was brought down by hostile A.A. fire near VILLERET - pilot and observer killed. Rain fell in the evening - first for ten days. German trenches about ST. HELENE bombarded during the night 2nd/3rd. Canadian patrol went up to German wire but found trenches occupied.	Appx 121 O.O.32
	3rd		Situation quiet. Slight increase in hostile artillery fire.	
	4th		The enemy shelled LEVERGUIER fairly heavy during the morning.	
	5th		The enemy shelled LEVERGUIER during the morning.	
	6th		During the night 5th/6th the Ambala Cavalry Brigade relieved the Canadian Cavalry Brigade in Subsector A-1. The Germans bombarded PONTRUET about 1 a.m., and launched an attack by one Company on that village, which they occupied. They were however immediately driven out by counter-attack by the French.	
	7th		Enemy activity normal.	
	8th		Situation unchanged.	
	9th		Situation unchanged.	
	10th		During night of 9th/10th, after a bombardment with guns and trench mortars, enemy attempted a raid on SOMERVILLE WOOD and LONE TREE Post. He was repulsed. No prisoners were taken.	
	11th		During night 10th/11th, enemy bombarded GUILLEMONT Farm on front of 2nd. Cav. Div. Artillery of Division cooperated in retaliation by bombarding BUISSON GAULAINE. A very severe thunder storm with heavy rain during the night.	

Army Form C. 2118.

WAR DIARY
or
INTELLIGENCE SUMMARY

(Erase heading not required.)

Instructions regarding War Diaries and Intelligence Summaries are contained in F. S. Regs., Part II. and the Staff Manual respectively. Title Pages will be prepared in manuscript.

Place	Date	Hour	Summary of Events and Information	Remarks and references to Appendices
NOBESCOURT FARM	June 12th.		100 dismounted men were placed at the disposal of the Division for work on roads in Divisional area on June 11th.	
	13th		During the night 12th/13th., after a heavy bombardment, a small raid was carried out on ASCENSION WOOD by a squadron of the 20th. Deccan Horse under Capt.N.F.C. MULLOY, 32nd.Lancers. The party entered the wood from the North East and worked back. They destroyed some wire and shelters. On the way back they met a party of Germans, which they charged. A hand to hand and bombing fight ensued in which considerable casualties were inflicted on the enemy. The following identifications were obtained. 75th/184 Regiments - MARNE. Our losses were 4 killed and 22 wounded.	Appx 122 O.O.33
	14th		Weather very hot. Our artillery fired about 150 rounds at BIG BILL with a view to harassing the enemy.	
	15th		During the night 14th/15th. the Canadian Cavalry Brigade relieved the Sec'bad Cavalry Bde. in Subsector A.2. without incident. Last night hostile artillery was above normal in Subsector A.1.	
	16th		Very quiet day on Divisional front.	
	17th		Enemy aeroplanes very active in early morning. A very quiet day.	
	18th		A very quiet day on Divisional front. Enemy artillery activity was below normal.	
	19th		Early on morning of 19th. a raid was carried out on the enemy trenches in the vicinity of ST.HELENE by two squadrons of the 9th. Horse under Capt. M.D. VIGORS, 9th. Hodson's Horse. Of the enemy garrison of 18, 5 were bayonetted, 10 were bombed in dugouts - the dugouts being burnt - and three prisoners of the 164th. Regt. were brought back. Our casualties - 3 slightly wounded. Enemy garrison reduced the previous night from 60 to 18.	
	20th		Enemy shelled TUMULUS and SOMERVILLE wood during the morning.	
	21st		A good deal of rain during the day. The enemy shelled ASCENSION WOOD during the early part of last night.	

2449 Wt. W14957/M90 750,000 1/16 J.B.C. & A. Forms/C.2118/12.

Army Form C. 2118.

WAR DIARY
or
INTELLIGENCE SUMMARY

(Erase heading not required.)

Instructions regarding War Diaries and Intelligence Summaries are contained in F. S. Regs., Part II. and the Staff Manual respectively. Title Pages will be prepared in manuscript.

Place	Date	Hour	Summary of Events and Information	Remarks and references to Appendices
NOEESCOURT FARM.	22nd June		A very quiet day along whole front.	
	23rd		Enemy shelled VERMAND during the morning.	
	24th		Last night the Sec'bad Cavalry Brigade relieved the Ambala Cavalry Brigade in Subsector A-1. The enemy shelled ROISEL during the afternoon without incident.	Appx 123 O.O.34
	25th		One of our aeroplanes was brought down by enemy machine gun fire just in front of LEVERGUIER, the observer and pilot were not injured.	
	26th		Situation normal on Divisional front.	
	27th		GRAHAM post heavily shelled during the afternoon with H.E.	
	28th		Two guns of No. 9 L.A.C. Battery relieved two guns of No. 7 L.A.C. Battery at TINCOURT. Very heavy rain during the afternoon.	
	29th		Some rain during the day.	
	30th		Very heavy rain during the day.	

Moriarty
Major for G.O.C.
5th. Cavalry Division.

SECRET.

Instructions regarding War Diaries and Intelligence Summaries are contained in F.S. Regs., Part II. and the Staff Manual respectively. Title pages will be prepared in manuscript.

GENERAL STAFF, 5TH CAVALRY DIVISION.

WAR DIARY
or
INTELLIGENCE / SUMMARY.

(Erase heading not required.)

Army Form C. 2118.

Hour, Date, Place	Summary of Events and Information	Remarks and references to Appendices
1917.		
July 1st. NOBESCOURT FARM.	Enemy artillery activity was below normal. A good deal of rain fell during the day.	
July 2nd. do.	Enemy artillery was very active during the afternoon and evening. TUMULUS Intermediate Line and PONTRUET - VADENCOURT VALLEY were shelled intermittently.	
July 3rd. do.	Nothing to report.	
July 4th. do.	Enemy aeroplanes were more active than usual. Several came over our lines, some quite low, evidently taking photographs.	
July 5th. do.	Hostile artillery fire was above normal about ASCENSION WOOD; DRAGOON POST, SOMERVILLE WOOD, and RED WOOD were shelled during the early morning and again in the evening.	
July 6th. do.	Enemy shelled the Intermediate Line just South of LE VERGUIER in the afternoon.	
July 7th. do.	No change. A very heavy thunderstorm and rain during the night.	
July 8th. do.	A raid was carried out in Sub-Sector A.2. by the Canadian Cavalry Brigade. Two squadrons (1from Lord Strathcona's Horse and 1 from Fort Garry Horse) took part; the whole under the command of Captain CONNOLLY, Lord Strathcona's Horse. 1 Officer, 35 O.R. of the enemy were taken prisoners and one Machine Gun was captured. Many Germans were bayonetted and a great many bombed in dug-outs. Enemy's total casualties were estimated at over a hundred. Our casualties were - 1 Officer, killed; 5 Officers, wounded(2 slightly, at duty); 23 O.R.	

SECRET.

Army Form C. 2118.

GENERAL STAFF, 5TH CAVALRY DIVISION.

WAR DIARY
or
INTELLIGENCE SUMMARY.

(Erase heading not required.)

Instructions regarding War Diaries and Intelligence
Summaries are contained in F.S. Regs., Part II
and the Staff Manual respectively. Title pages
will be prepared in manuscript.

Hour, Date, Place	Summary of Events and Information	Remarks and references to Appendices
1917.		
July 8th. NOBESCOURT (cont'd) FARM.	25 O.R., wounded, only 3 seriously. See Appx 123	Appendix 123
July 9th. do.	Very quiet day on whole divisional front.	
July 10th. BOUVINCOURT.	During the night of the 9th/10th the Division (less Artillery) was relieved by the 34th Division without incident, and moved to their back area bivouacs. Divisional Headquarters to BOUVINCOURT. (See O.o.35) Orders received from Cavalry Corps for Division to move Northwards between July 15th and 18th. (see O.O.56)	Appendix 124 Appendix 125
July 11th. do.	No change. On night 10th/11th 17th Brigade, R.H.A. and R.C.H.A. Brigade relieved by 34th Divisional Artillery and moved to back area bivouacs.	
July 12th. do.	No change. Following detail of casualties, prisoners and decorations awarded, during the Division's recent employment in the line :—	

(a) CASUALTIES.

	Killed.	Wounded.	Missing.
B.Os.	1	26	1
I.Os.	—	6	—
O.R.Bs.	11	127	—
O.Rs.I.	23	88	7
Totals.	35	247	8

(b) PRISONERS ....

SECRET.

GENERAL STAFF, 5TH CAVALRY DIVISION.

WAR DIARY
INTELLIGENCE SUMMARY.

(Erase heading not required.)

Army Form C. 2118.

Instructions regarding War Diaries and Intelligence Summaries are contained in F.S. Regs., Part II. and the Staff Manual respectively. Title pages will be prepared in manuscript.

Hour, Date, Place	Summary of Events and Information	Remarks and references to Appendices
1917.		

July 12th. BOUVINCOURT. (cont'd)	(b) PRISONERS TAKEN. 1 Officer and 58 O.Rs. (c) Approximately the following DECORATIONS were awarded :-
	
	  D.S.O. M.C. D.C.M. M.M. I.D.S.M. I.O.M.
	   4 17 8 27 15 2	

July 13th. do.	Field Squadron inspected in morning by Divisional Commander. Ambala Brigade moved to area CARTIGNY, BUIRE, COURCELLES in afternoon.	
July 14th. do.	Secunderabad Brigade moved to area CARTIGNY, BUIRE, COURCELLES in afternoon. Canadian Brigade moved to CAPPY area in morning. Ambala Brigade moved to area VAUX.- SUZANNE. Wet night.	
July 15th. do.	Ambala Brigade moved to TREUX, BUIRE, RIBEMONT ###### area. Secunderabad Brigade moved to VAUX, SUZANNE area. Canadian Brigade moved to MERICOURT, HEILLY area. 17th Brigade, R.H.A. and R.C.H.A. Brigade moved to CAPPY area. Intermediate report centre opened at TREUX at 12 noon. July 16th	

S E C R E T.

GENERAL STAFF, 5TH CAVALRY DIVISION.

WAR DIARY
or
INTELLIGENCE SUMMARY.
(Erase heading not required.)

Army Form C. 2118.

Instructions regarding War Diaries and Intelligence Summaries are contained in F.S.Regs., Part II. and the Staff Manual respectively. Title pages will be prepared in manuscript.

Hour, Date, Place	Summary of Events and Information	Remarks and references to Appendices
1917.		
July 16th. ST POL.	Report centre opened at 14 Rue des PROCUREURS, ST POL, at 12 noon. Ambala Brigade moved to SARTON area. Secunderabad Brigade moved to BUIRE area. Canadian Brigade moved to ORVILLE area. 17th Brigade, R.H.A. and R.C.H.A. Brigade moved to HEILLY area.	
July 17th. do.	Ambala Brigade moved to BRYAS area. Secunderabad Brigade moved to SARTON area. Canadian Brigade moved to GAUCHIN - HERNICOURT - CROIX area with Headquarters in ST POL. 17th Brigade R.H.A. and R.C.H.A. Brigade moved to ORVILLE area. Intermediate report centre closed at TREUX at 8 a.m.	
July 18th. do.	Secunderabad Brigade moved to RAMECOURT area with Headquarters at RAMECOURT. Ambala Brigade Headquarters at ROELLECOURT. Canadian Brigade Headquarters at ST POL. The Artillery of the division arrived in divisional area, the Batteries joining their respective Cavalry Brigades and Headquarters, 17th Brigade R.H.A. and R.C.H.A. Brigade, being established in ST POL.	
July 19th. do.	Further changes in billeting area were made - (vide G.636 attached). Concentration orders for moves in various directions issued as shown in G.S.649 attached.	Appx: 126 Appx: 124
July 20th. do.	Changes indicated above were carried out.	
July 21st. do.	No change. July 22nd.	

Army Form C. 2118.

WAR DIARY
or
INTELLIGENCE SUMMARY.

(Erase heading not required.)

Instructions regarding War Diaries and Intelligence Summaries are contained in F.S. Regs., Part II. and the Staff Manual respectively. Title pages will be prepared in manuscript.

Place	Date	Hour	Summary of Events and Information	Remarks and references to Appendices
	July 22nd.		Further changes in billeting area were made. Fort Garry Horse moved from CROIX to WAVRANS and BETHONVAL, Canadian Brigade Headquarters to CROIX.	
	23rd-26th.		No change.	
	27th.		17th Bde R.H.A. and R.C.H.A. Brigade (and Ammunition Column (less S.A.A.Section) placed at disposal of First Army and moved to-day to First Army Area where they come under orders of Canadian Corps. 3rd Brigade R.H.A. and Ammunition Column from 2nd Cavalry Division moved into area vacated by 17th Bde R.H.A. and R.C.H.A. Brigade.	
	28th.		3rd Brigade R.H.A. and Ammunition Column moved from this Divisional Area to join First Army. Very heavy rain storm in afternoon	
	29th.		No change. Much rain and thunder during the day.	
	30th.		Heavy rain at night.	
	31st.		Divisional Hdqrs. moved from ST.POL to HEUCHIN. The Major-General visited the 17th Bde R.H.A. and R.C.H.A. Brigade in the Canadian Corps Area and saw their horses.	

M.M.Cherty Major,

for General Staff, 5th Cavalry Division.

SECRET

No. G.552/12.

Headquarters, 5th. Cavalry Division.
Dated July 1st., 1917.

To/
    101st. Infantry Brigade.
    5th. Signal Squadron.

101 Inf) 1.   101st. Infantry Brigade Group, strength as in margin, will
Bde.)
1 Fd.Co) detrain in the Corps area (station uncertain) on July 5th. and come
R.E.)
1 Fd.) temporarily under orders of G.O.C. 5th. Cavalry Division.
Ambs.)
1 Coy) 2.   It will billet and bivouac in the area SOYECOURT-POEUILLY-
Train.)
    VRAIGNES - FLECHIN, under instructions to be issued by A.A. & Q.M.G.

3.   Headquarters will be at VRAIGNES. O.C. Signal Squadron will
arrange telephonic communication.

                                                          Lieut-Colonel, G.S.
                                                          5th. Cavalry Division.

Copy to:-
    Cavalry Corps.
    34th. Div.
    4th. Cav. Division.
    Can. Cav. Bde.
    Sec'bad Cav. Bde.
    Ambala Cav. Bde.
    C.R.E.
    "A"
    O.C. A.S.C.
    A.D.M.S.

SUGGESTED ARRANGEMENTS FOR RELIEF.

1. 101st. Bde. Group on arrival goes to the area FLECHIN- POUILLY- VRAIGNES (Hqrs. VRAIGNES).

2. Relief - night 9th/10th.

    1 Btn. to relieve Sec'bad Cav. Bde (less Reserve Regt).
    1 " " " Canadian " " " " "
    1 " " " Reserve Regt. Can. Cav. Bde. and garrisons of LE VERGUIER keeps.
    1 " " VENDELLES.

Reserve Regt. Sec'bad Cav. Bde. withdraws without relief.

3. Machine Guns relief under arrangements to be made between Machine Gun Officers.

Field Coy relief by arrangements between O.C. 207th. Field Coy and C.R.E. 5th. Cav. Div.

Field Ambulances relief by day on 9th, under arrangements of A.D's M.S.

4. Command passes from Brigadiers to O's C. Btns. and from 5th. Cav. Div. to G.O.C. 101st. Inf. Bde. at 9.0 a.m. 10th.
101st. Inf. Bde. Headquarters MONTIGNY FARM.

5. C.R.H.A. 5th. Cav. Div. moves to MONTIGNY FARM as a Group Commander at 9.0 a.m. 10th.

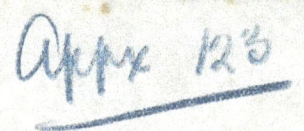

ACCOUNT OF A RAID BY TWO SQUADRONS
CANADIAN CAVALRY BDE.
ON JULY 8TH/9TH, 1917.

A. RECONNAISSANCE.

1. The map attached shows the German trenches and our own front line. This line consists of posts, protected by all round as well as by continuous wire.
It will be seen that "No Man's Land" is from 1500 to 2000 yards broad.

2. By July 2nd. a series of patrol encounters, and a raid previously carried out on ASCENSION WOOD, had already reduced the enemy's patrolling activities to about 1 patrol of 24 men once in three nights. It was therefore decided to plan a raid on his front line.

3. From July 2nd. to 7th. patrols were sent out every night. Their orders were

   (a) To fight any patrol in "No Man's Land".

   (b) To examine the enemy's wire between G.27.a.6.8 and G.20.d.5.10, behind which air photographs indicated the existence of a Headquarters.

   (c) To reconnoitre good routes via G.26.Central to the road junction at G.26.b.7.7.

   (d) To find a good position for assembly of covering party between the road junction above and the German wire.

4. To assist in keeping "No Man's Land" clear of the enemy spasmodic bursts of machine gun fire were kept up on points the enemy used to frequent when our patrols were not out.
The machine guns also fired on the enemy wire during the approach of our patrols and over the enemy parapet while our patrols were close to the wire.

5. The results of the above reconnaissance were:-

   (a) Practically complete command of "No Man's Land" was secured.

   (b) The wire was found to be about 20 feet wide and about 40 yards in front of the trench.
   The information as to wire was confirmed by aeroplane photographs.

6. Observers reported a considerable amount of work going on about the trenches in G.21.c., also confirmed by aeroplane pictures.

B -   P L A N

Reasons for Selection	7.	As the results of the above reconnaissances and of personal observation, it was decided to raid the enemy's trenches, entering at G.21.c.4.1 and coming out at G.20.d.8.8. The chief reasons for choosing this spot were

      (a) A Company Headquarters was suspected, and therefore probably a considerable collection of enemy.

      (b) The two communication trenches afforded easily recognisable marks for entry and exit.

Details.	8.	The detailed plan, equipment etc. is contained in Appendix "A" (Operation Order and Instructions by the acting Brigadier Canadian Cavalry Brigade). Its rough outline is as follows :-

See Map		(a) Entry through the wire by a bangalore torpedo, supplemented by a spare one, and a third in case of wire in front of C. trench.

      (b) One troop (from which the first two torpedo parties were found) blocks A trench North and South and remains there till after withdrawal of collecting post, prisoners and wounded.

      (c) Four troops enter and move East along trench E and then North West along the Banks, and trenches C., B., and A respectively.
Each troop is responsible for the open ground on its right as far as the next trench. Each troop moves in crescent formation with a section or more on each side of the trench.
The Fourth troop opens an exit on reaching G.20.d.8.8 and waits for the other three to pass before withdrawing.
Each troop, on reaching trench D, forms a block and waits for the troops on its right to pass before itself withdrawing down trench D and so out at G.20.d.8.8.

      (d) Collecting Post, 1 troop, moves to end of trench E, passes back wounded and prisoners to the point of entry at G.21.c.4.1, eventually itself withdrawing by the same route. Half this troop was detailed as a cleaning-up party behind the Banks troop.

Protection	9.	(a) Covering Party, 1 troop at G.26.b.7.8.

      (b) Right Flank Guard, 2 troops at G.32.a., with a detachment in G.26.d.

      (c) Left Flank Guard, 1 troop at N.W. edge of ASCENSION WOOD with a detachment towards LITTLE BILL.

Strength	10.	(a) The total strength passing through the wire (para 8) was

            6 officers
           147 other ranks

      (b) Strength of protective detachments (para 9 ~~10~~)

           5 officers
           98 other ranks.

.........11.

Training 11. (a) The hour of Zero (i.e., the explosion of the torpedo) was indicated by Green and Red Very lights fired by the leader of the raid, and repeated from No. 4 Post. It was to be as near as possible 11.30 p.m., the factors deciding this being the moon, which rose at 10.47 and the fact that the party could not cross the ASCENSION Ridge before 10.0 p.m.

(b) The raiders were to withdraw by Zero plus 45, which time was indicated, as a reminder, by a Green rocket fired from our front line. The covering troop remained till Zero plus 55.

Position of Assembly. 12. The position of assembly was Sunken road S.26.b.6.9. Protective detachments to be in position 10 p.m.

Artillery Barrage 13. (a) The artillery taking part were

32 - 13 prs.
12 - 18 "
 3 - 4.5" Hows.
 4 - 6" Hows.
 4 - 60 prs.

(b) Their action consisted of two minutes bombardment from Zero at 6 rounds per gun per minute (Field Guns). The barrage was then lifted gradually, commencing from the right at the point of entry, till at Zero plus 5 it formed a "box" round the area of the raid. The rate of fire from Zero plus 5 to Zero plus 45 was alternately 2 and 6 rounds per minute, for 10 and 5 minutes respectively.

(c) After Zero plus 45 the barrage was brought back on to the German front trenches outside the raided area.

Machine Guns. 14. 20 machine guns co-operated in three groups (see Appx. B).

(a) A Group (6 guns) S. of ASCENSION FARM first barraged the front to be attacked and then lifted to the flanks and rear.

(b) B. Group (10 guns) S.W. of GRAND PRIEL WOOD protected the left flank by fire on BUISSON GAULAINE and S.W. of that place.

(c) C. Group (4 guns) E. of GRAND PRIEL FARM fired on BUISSON GAULAINE.

C. - TRAINING AND ORGANISATION.

15. The whole of the raiding party practised once by day and twice by night for four nights. Every man was taught his particular role and was encouraged to make suggestions regarding it. Particular attention was paid to the importance of every man knowing the exact position of the commander of his detachment.
The evacuation of casualties and prisoners was practised. Touch was kept by means of whistles and electric torches. Officers not taking part were detailed to watch and criticise the action of every party.

16. Special measures were taken to check numbers going in and out of the hostile trenches, as it was particularly desired to leave no one behind.

17. The trenches were taped from aeroplane photographs. Flags were used to show the successive barrages, and whistles to denote the lifting of the barrage. Very lights were fired in order to accustom the men to lie flat and perfectly still under them.

18. The torpedo parties received special training in crawling, inserting the torpedoes under the wire, fusing them, and in cutting away any wire which might remain. They practised both by night and day. Torpedoes were actually fired at each general practice.

19. Sections were divided into bayonet-men and bombers, and worked under their own commander as a group. The sections were also subdivided into pairs of men who always worked together.

D.- PRELIMINARY MEASURES.

20. The torpedo parties were on several occasions led up to the hostile wire by officers.
In order to assist in guiding them, and also to keep the enemy's sentries away from the selected point of entry, one round from a 4.5" was fired at the junction of trenches A and E at irregular intervals and at prearranged times. This was done on the night of the raid as well as previously.

21. As it had been ascertained that the enemy were in the habit of visiting the road junction in G.26.b., which was the position of assembly, one troop was sent into BIG BILL on the night 7th/8th. It had orders to lie up all day and occupy the road junction as soon as it was dusk.

NARRATIVE

22. On the evening of July 8th/9th, the moon rose about 10.45 p.m. A few clouds drifted across it, but the sky was, generally speaking, clear.

23. The troop which had gone out overnight (see para 21) to BIG BILL reached its objective, the road junction in G.26.b., at 10.15 p.m. Soon after a hostile patrol of 15 approached to within 25 yards when fire was opened on it. Three of the enemy fled - the rest were apparently hit. Soon after touch was obtained with the raiding party by means of 2 men sent back to meet them.

24. The raiding party reached the position of assembly without incident. The torpedo parties crawled the last 150 yards to the wire and the torpedo was successfully inserted and exploded at 11.31 p.m. The Red and Green Very lights were fired according to plan and the artillery barrage came down instantly. A second band of wire was found at the point of entry and this was blown up by the second torpedo, the party creeping up in our barrage. Of the 6 men with these two torpedoes, 5 were wounded, 2 by our barrage and 3 by an enemy bomb.

..........25.

25. The six raiding troops then advanced according to the plan, which was successfully adhered to throughout.

(a) The leading troop duly established blocks and bombed some dugouts. "A" trench was found to be very deep and wide.

(b) The Banks troop had its officer and sergeant wounded near the wire and a Corporal commanded it throughout. It was met by a certain amount of machine gun and rifle grenade fire from its right. It killed several of the enemy, took 22 prisoners and bombed 16 small dugouts with Mills and "P" bombs.
The third torpedo was exploded in the largest dugout, an opening having been found in the wire in front of C. trench.

(c) The C. trench troop was met by some wild rifle grenade and a little shrapnel fire. It bayonetted several of the enemy and bombed 4 dugouts and a small work on its right.

(d) The B. trench troop was fired on by three machine guns from the right of the gap. Two were silenced by our heavy artillery, and the third by two bombers and two bayonet men. This troop bayonetted several Germans, fired at some running away who were seen to drop, and took 4 prisoners.

(e) The A. trench troop captured 7 or 8 Germans, killed several and bombed 19 large dugouts. This troop captured a machine gun in an offshoot of D trench. The emplacement was well wired in, but the crew had run away.
The right flanking party of this troop killed 3 and captured 1 prisoner in the open.

(f) The Collecting troop reached the end of E. trench, established a block in C. trench, and accomplished its mission successfully.

26. The exit gap had meanwhile been cut by the covering troop and the raiders withdrew by it according to plan. Their numbers were carefully checked by the O.C. and it was ascertained that none had been left behind.
All German cables were cut, and all dugouts left in flames.

27. The whole party withdrew to the assembly point, guided by tapes laid by the covering troop, and thence to GRAHAM'S POST without further incident, except that an officer of Royal Canadian Horse Artillery was killed by a stray bullet. This officer had gone forward with a gunner party and a team, as a soundranging section had located a 77 mm gun behind the Banks. The emplacement was found, but the gun was unfortunately not there.

28. Communication was kept throughout with Brigade Headquarters by a cable laid to the point of entry. An extra 5 minutes barrage was asked for and obtained by this means, and frequent information of progress was sent back. It was found possible also to direct the machine gun barrage.

............29.

R E S U L T S

29. 1 officer and 35 other ranks were captured, and 1 machine gun: 3 other machine guns were knocked out, but could not be rescued owing to our own barrage.
The area raided was garrisoned by a Company (180 strong) of which the great majority must have been either captured, bombed in dugouts, or killed by bayonet, rifle or artillery fire.
60 are known to have been bayonetted.

30. Our casualties were

        1 officer killed.
        3   "   s wounded (2 at duty).
      23 other ranks (only 3 seriously).

R E M A R K S

31. The success of the operation was due to

(a) Complete command of "No Man's Land". Patrols were instructed to attack instantaneously on all occasions with the bayonet.

(b) Thorough reconnaissance, including study of aeroplane photographs.

(c) Carefully thought out preparations, including training.

(d) All ranks knowing the plan thoroughly, so that casualties among commanders caused no disorganisation.

(e) The element of surprise contained in a raid over such a wide extent of "No Man's Land".

(f) Every one connected being convinced of success from the beginning. Even if the torpedoes had failed, it was intended to carry through the raid.

(g) Adequate Flank and Advanced Guards, the latter of which had to lie out in a concealed position from the previous night.

32. The artillery and machine gun co-operation was reported to be accurate and effective.

33. The use of a H.E. shell to direct parties in the dark is worthy of notice.

34. Coloured Very Lights were found to be much more reliable than rockets.

35. The hostile artillery reply was feeble, as it has been in all raids undertaken on the Divisional front.

36. The resistance put up by the enemy was, on the whole, slight. This is attributed to the moral effect of overhead machine gun fire, the accurate artillery barrage, and surprise.

------ -:-oOo-:- ------

APPENDIX "A".

CANADIAN CAVALRY BRIGADE.

OPERATION ORDER NO.39.

Copy No.12.

Reference Map 1/10,000　　　　　　　　　　　　　　　　July 4th., 1917.
Corps Topo.Sect. No.14.

1. (a) A Raid will be carried out by the Canadian Cavalry Brigade on the night of July 8th/9th, against the enemy's trench line from G.27.a.5.10 to G.20.d.8.8 and the enemy's Strong Points in G.21.c.

   (b) Map of German trenches attached.

2. (a) ZERO Hour, approximately 11.30 p.m. will be indicated by the firing of a Bangalore torpedo in the German wire at G.27.a.4.10.

   (b) The successful firing of this torpedo will be denoted by Green and Red Very Lights fired by the leader of raiding party and a Green and Red Rocket fired from No. 4 Post.

3. (a) The raid will be carried out by one squadron F.G.H. and three troops of L.S. Horse, one of the latter being a covering party.

   (b) R.C. Dragoons will find a Right Flank Guard of 2 troops.

   (c) L.S. Horse will find a Left Flank Guard of 1 Troop.

   Times and dispositions for the above are given in the attached instructions.

4. The password will be communicated later and must be notified to all ranks.

5. (a) The Raiding Party will leave the enemy's trenches at Zero plus 45.

   (b) The covering Party will return at Zero plus 55.

   (c) At Zero plus 40 a Green Rocket will be fired from No. 4 Post to warn the raiding party that the artillery barrage will cease in five minutes. Other Green Rockets will be fired at intervals later to guide any men who might be left behind.

6. The return routes through No Man's Land will be left to the discretion of leaders.

7. An Advanced Dressing Station will be established at GRAHAM POST.

8. Prisoners will be brought back to the Left Regt. H.Q. thence to MONTIGNY FARM.

9. Watches will be synchronised at Brigade H.Q. at 6.30 p.m. July 8th., for the following:-

   　　　　　　　　　Representative of L.S. Horse.
   　　　　　　　　　F.G.H.
   　　　　　　　　　R.C.Dragoons.
   　　　　　　　　　Can. M.G. Squadron.
   　　　　　　　　　C.R.H.A.

10. Machine Gun and Artillery barrages are attached.
11. ACKNOWLEDGE.

　　　　　　　　　　　　　　　　　　　　　　　　　　Captain,
　　　　　　　　　　　Brigade Major, Can. Cav. Bde.

INSTRUCTIONS.

(a) F.G. Horse.   B. Squadron)
    L.S. Horse.   3 Troops.   ) Dispositions.

at 11 p.m.   The SUNKEN ROAD   Bangalore Torpedo party from
               about G.26.b.0.6   1st. Troop F.G.H. work forward
                                       and fire torpedo in the wire
                                           at G.27.a.4.10. If successful
                                           the leader of the raiding party
                                           will signal by a Red and Green
                                           Very light. This signal will
                                           be repeated by RED and GREEN
                                           Rockets fired from No. 4 Post.
                                           This signal will denote Zero
                                           hour.

                                           The explosion of the torpedo
                                           will also be confirmed by
                                           telephone to No. 4 Post.

(b) At Zero Hour plus 2.

F.G. Horse.   1st. Troop will pass through the wire at G.27.a.4.10
                     establish two blocks for the remainder of the
                     squadron to pass through. The left block to be at
                     the junction of "A" Trench with communication
                     trench "E". This passage will be maintained
                     till Zero plus 40.
                     The troop will be prepared to take over any
                     prisoners. They will retire by the L.S.Horse
                     covering party at G.26.b.7.8 and will check all
                     men coming out through their passage.

                     (2nd. Troop in rear of 1st. Troop.
                     (Objective, the banks and dugouts G.21.c.4.6 -
                     (G.21.c.3.8.
                     (Prisoners will be passed back through passage in
                     (G.27.a.4.10.
Under   (This troop will return by "D" trench getting
Squadron   (touch with 3rd. Troop working down "C" Trench.
Commander

                     (3rd. Troop in rear of 2nd. troop.
                     (Objective, "C" Trench returning by "D" Trench and
                     (getting touch with 4th. Troop working down "B"
                     (trench.
                     (Prisoners to be passed back through the passage
                     (in G.27.a.4.10.

                     4th. Troop. In rear of 3rd. Troop.
                     Objective "B" Trench and to be prepared to support
                     parties in either "C" or "A" trench, returning by
                     "D" trench and getting touch with L.S.Horse troops
                     at the junction of "A" and "D" trenches.
                     The latter will open and maintain a passage of
                     exit at G.20.d.7.8.

(c) L.S.Horse at Zero plus 2.

                     1st. Troop will pass through the gap at G.27.a.4.10
                     in rear of 4th. Troop F.G.Horse and will work
                       down the communication trench "E" to the end of
                     the trench. They will wait in trench and be
                     prepared to assist F.G.Horse in "C" trench and pass
                     back prisoners. They will leave the trench at
                     Zero plus 35 via the gap at G.27.a.4.10.

                                                     2nd. Troop......

2nd. Troop, in rear of 1st. Troop L.S.H. will work down "A" trench to G.20.d.8.8, and will open a return exit for the raiding party at G.20.d.7.7.
They will hold this gap open till the three troops of F.G.Horse are through, and will keep a check on the numbers passing through. They will pass on prisoners to 3rd. Troop of L.S. Horse at G.26.b.7.8.

3rd. Troop, will remain as a covering party at the road junction at G.26.b.7.8 and will get touch with F.G.H. party at the entrance gap and L.S.H. party at the exit gap.

They will be prepared to take over any prisoners from either gap and will withdraw at Zero plus 55.

2. FLANK GUARDS.

(a) Right Flank Guard R.C. Dragoons- 2 Troops to reach the banks in G.32.a. by 10 p.m. thence pushing a strong patrol onto the spur in G.26.d.

The role of the Right Flank Guard is to prevent enemy patrols coming West of the road running from G.26.b.6.8 to G.32.b.4.0.

(b) Left Flank Guard L.S.Horse 1 Troop to reach North Western edge of ASCENSION WOOD 10 p.m. to prevent any hostile patrol entering the Sunken Road South of ASCENSION WOOD or crossing East of the Road from ASCENSION WOOD to LITTLEHILL.

(c) Flank Guards will be withdrawn at Zero plus 70.

FURTHER INSTRUCTIONS IN CONTINUATION OF THOSE ISSUED WITH OPERATION ORDER NO. 39.

July 5th, 1917.

1. Equipment.

    (a) P.H. Helmets will be carried by all ranks.

    (b) Rifles, magazines charged, 4 charges in the pocket, chamber empty.

    (c) Bayonets to be fixed - no scabbard or bandolier.

    (d) 80% to carry 6 No. 5 Mills Grenades in the haversack.

    (e) 20% to carry "P" bombs in haversack.

    (f) All ranks will carry wire-cutters.

    (g) Men to carry torpedoes for first wire will be armed with revolvers.

    (h) At least 3 compasses and 3 electric torches to be carried by each troop of the raiding party.

    (i) Troop leaders will carry whistles.

2. Distinctive Marks.

    White strips in the right hand breast pocket and attached to the button.
    These will be pulled out and passed through the right shoulder lapelet at Zero Hour.

3. S.A.A. Dumps.

    Officer Commanding Machine Gun Squadron will arrange for necessary ammunition dumps.

4. Very Pistols.

    L.S.Horse party will take two Very pistols, 2 Red and 2 Green lights to give the signal that the torpedo has been successfully exploded.

5. Rockets.

    Staff Captain will have 4 Red and 4 Green rockets ready to be fired at Zero hour from No. 4 Post.
    4 Green Rockets to fire at Zero plus 40 from the same post.
    An occasional rocket will be fired from Zero plus 50 onwards from No. 4 Post to guide any men that may still be out.

6. Communication.

    Officer Commanding Signals will arrange for a line to be run out from No. 4 Post to L.S.Horse covering party at G.26.b.7.7.

7. Rendezvous for all troops on return will be GRAHAM POST where Officers Commanding Regiments will make a check of the numbers.

8. 10 stretcher-bearers per squadron (additional) to take 3 normal stretchers per squadron.
Remaining stretcher-bearers to carry rifle, which can be made into stretchers with two coats if required.

(sd) G.H.H. Brooke, Captain,
Brigade Major,
Canadian Cavalry Brigade.

Map to illustrate Raid of Canadian Cavalry Brigade: 8/9:7:17: Scale 1/10000

app*124

5TH. CAVALRY DIVISION.

OPERATION ORDER NO. 35.

Copy No. 19.

Reference Map
$\frac{1}{40,000}$ or $\frac{1}{100,000}$.

4-7-17.

1. (a) 3rd. Corps is taking over the front of Cavalry Corps.
   34th. Division relieves 4th. and 5th. Cavalry Divisions.
   35th. Division relieves 2nd. Cavalry Division.

   (b) 101st. Inf. Brigade and attached troops on arrival in the area FLECHIN-POEUILLY-VRAIGNES come temporarily under the orders of G.O.C. 5th. Cavalry Division.

2. 101st. Inf. Bde. and attached troops will relieve 5th. Cavalry Division (less artillery) in accordance with the attached table.

Protection. 3. The relief will be protected by patrols pushed well out. These patrols will not be withdrawn till the relief is complete, or they have been replaced.

Move on Relief. 4. On relief

   (a) Units of 5th. Cavalry Division will withdraw to their bivouacs in the OMIGNON VALLEY.

   (b) Divisional Headquarters and Signal Squadron will move to BOUVINCOURT.

Movement. 5. (a) Horses will not be taken by day East of the line halfway between POEUILLY and VERMAND - SOYECOURT - VENDELLES - JEANCOURT. By night they will not be taken East of the line VADENCOURT - LEVERGUIER.

   (b) All movement East of the line halfway between POEUILLY and VERMAND - SOYECOURT - VENDELLES - JEANCOURT will be conducted in small parties equivalent in size to a troop or platoon, 200 yards distance being maintained between parties.

   (c) Units West of the line VADENCOURT - LEVERGUIER may, subject to sub-paras (a) and (b) above, be relieved by day.

Advanced Parties. 6. Advanced Parties of at least one officer per company and one N.C.O. per platoon will be sent forward

   (a) For front line units, on the evening previous to that of relief.

   (b) For other units, on the morning of the relief.

Guides. 7. Guides will be provided by the outgoing unit for each Company, platoon or post.

Handing over. 8. (a) All maps, plans and schemes will be handed over.

   (b) Lists will be prepared in duplicate of ammunition, tools, and other stores in all dumps, trenches, and posts, and receipts obtained. This part of the handing over should be done, whenever possible, previously in daylight.

........9.

Artillery.	9.	The artillery of the Division, plus batteries attached from 59th. Division, (A/295 and D/298) will remain in the line for the present as a group under Lieut-Colonel W. STIRLING, D.S.O., R.H.A., and will be relieved two or three days later by part of the artillery of 34th. Division.

        Lt. Colonel STIRLING will move his Headquarters to MONTIGNY FARM at 9.0 a.m. on July 10th.

Command.   10.   Command passes from G.O's C. Cavalry Brigades to O's C. Battalions, and from G.O.C. 5th. Cavalry Division to G.O.C. 101st. Inf. Bde. at 9.0 a.m. July 10th. At the same hour G.O.C. 34th. Division assumes command of the sectors of 4th. and 5th. Cavalry Divisions.

Code Word.   11.   Completion of relief will be reported by the code word "PERONNE". Arrival in the back area will also be reported.

Reports.   12.   Reports after 9.0 a.m. [10½] to BOUVINCOURT.

        13.   Acknowledge.

                                                  R. Howard Vyse

                                                Lieut-Colonel, G.S.

No. 1 - 25   O.O. Distribution.
       26   Dismounted Reinforcements.   5th. Cavalry Division.
       27   Cavalry Corps.
       28   22nd. French Division.
       29   4th. Cavalry Division.
       30   34th. Division.

5TH CAVALRY DIVISION
RELIEF TABLE (issued with Operation Order No.35)

4-7-17.

Date	Outgoing Unit	Incoming Unit	Responsibility for Arrangements	Remarks
July 9th.	5th.Field Sqdn. R.E.	1 Field Coy 34th. Div.	C.R.E's concerned.	Dumps to be handed over, also control of the Tunnelling Section.
" "	Cavalry Field Ambulances	1 Field Ambce. 34th.Div.	A.D's M.S. concerned.	
" "	Dismounted Reinforcements Ambala Cavalry Brigade. (VERDRIES).	1 Bn. 101st. Inf. Bde.	Brigadier and O.C. Dismounted Reinforcements.	To be complete by 5 pm.Btn. comes into Div. Res, and eventually into 101st Inf.Bde.Res.
Night July 9/10th.	Secunderabad Cav.Bde.	1 Bn. 101st. Inf. Bde.	Brigadiers concerned.	
" "	Canadian Cav. Bde. (less Reserve Regt).	1 Bn. 101st. Inf. Bde.	"	
" "	Reserve Regt. Can.Cav. Bde. and Garrison of LEVERGUIER.	1 Bn. 101st. Inf. Bde.	"	
" "	Machine gun Sqdns.	101st. M.G. Company	"	
July 10th.	H.Q. Canadian Cav.Bde. (MONTIGNY FARM).	H.Q. 101st. Inf. Bde.	"	Command to pass at 9 a.m.

No. G. 552/15.

SECRET

Headquarters, 5th. Cavalry Division.
Dated 5th. July, 1917.

To/
Normal O.O. Distribution.

In continuation of Operation Order No. 35, para 9.

1. 17th. Bde. R.H.A. and R.C.H.A. Bde. will be relieved by part of the 34th. Divisional Artillery and 16th. R.H.A. Bde. on the nights of July 10th/11th. and 11th/12th.

2. A/295 and D/298 remain in the line.

3. All arrangements for the above will be made between C.R.H.A. and G.O.C. R.A. 34th. Division, acting under instructions issued by G.O.C. R.A. Cavalry Corps.

4. On relief the batteries will withdraw to their present bivouacs in the OMIGNON Valley and are to remain under the orders of C.R.H.A.

5. Acknowledge.

R.E. Howard Vyse
Lieut-Colonel, G.S.
5th. Cavalry Division.

Copy to:-
Dismounted Reinforcements.
Cavalry Corps.
22nd. French Divn.
4th. Cav. Div.
34th. Division.
101st. Inf. Bde.

SECRET   No. G. 552/18.

Headquarters, 5th. Cavalry Division.
Dated 7th. July, 1917.

To/
   Secunderabad Cavalry Brigade.
   Canadian Cavalry Brigade.
   101st. Infantry Brigade.

Reference 5th. Cavalry Division Operation No. 35.

1. Para 3. 101st. Infantry Brigade will arrange to send forward early on July 9th. protective detachments similar in composition to the patrols which will be sent out by the cavalry.
   These detachments will accompany the cavalry patrols when they move out at dusk, and will remain out when the latter withdraw on relief.

2. Battalions of 101st. Inf. Bde. going into Front Line or Support should move up to the line VADENCOURT-VENDELLES after the midday meal on July 9th, so as to have a rest before going into the trenches.

3. The Reserve Regiment Secunderabad Cavalry Brigade (now at VADENCOURT) will withdraw as soon as the forward movement of the infantry mentioned in para 2 above is complete.

4. The following will be substituted for para 10 of the Operation Order:-

10. (a) Command passes from G.O's C. Cavalry Brigades to O's C.
Command.   Battalions, and from G.O.C. 5th. Cavalry Division to G.O.C. 101st. Inf. Bde. (so far as the infantry are concerned) on completion of relief.

     (b) G.O.C. 34th. Division assumes command of the sectors of 4th. and 5th. Cavalry Divisions at 9 a.m. July 10th.

M. Docherty Major for,
Lieut-Colonel, G.S.
5th. Cavalry Division.

Copy to:-
   Cavalry Corps.
   34th. Division.
   22nd. French Division.
   4th. Cavalry Division.
   C.R.H.A.
   Q.
   C.R.E.
   Signals.
   A.D.M.S.

GENERAL STAFF,
84TH
DIVISION.
No. 41 228/15
Date 2-7-17

Appx 125

Secret

5TH. CAVALRY DIVISION.   Copy No. 22

OPERATION ORDER NO. 36.

Reference Map   10th. July, 1917.
      1
   ‾‾‾‾‾‾‾
   100,000
ST. QUENTIN-AMIENS-
LENS.

                                    Northwards
          1. The Division will move   between July 13th.
          and 18th. in accordance with the attached March Table.

GROUPING 2. (a) Divisional Troops will march and billet under the
                  orders of G.O.C. the Brigade to which they are shown
                  as attached.

              (b) Divisional Headquarters and Signal Squadron
                  (less motors) will march under the orders of an
                  officer to be detailed by O.C. Signal Squadron.

              (c) 1 Squadron Inniskilling Dragoons detailed as
                  escort to the Corps Commander, will march under the
                  orders of G.O.C. Canadian Cavalry Brigade.

MARCH CONTROL. 3. (a) Heads of groups should leave billeting areas
                      about 6.0 a.m. each day. This does not apply to the
                      marches of Ambala and Secunderabad Cavalry Brigades
                      on July 13th. and 14th. respectively, which will be
                      carried out after midday.

                  (b) A distance of 500 yards will be maintained between
                      each Regiment, battery, field squadron etc.

                  (c) Attention is directed to the orders regarding
                      cyclists contained in Organisation Tables E, para 5.
                      All cyclists must march in groups under proper control.

BILLETS. 4. (a) Accommodation Table for the ORVILLE area is
                  attached (Brigades, C.R.H.A. and A.A. & Q.M.G. only).

              (b) Information regarding billets in the SUZANNE
                  and HEILLY areas will be forwarded by A.A. & Q.M.G.,
                  who will also issue instructions regarding dispositions
                  in the final (ST. POL) area.

HORSE-
ARTILLERY. 5. Batteries come under the orders of G.O's C. Cavalry
          Brigades on arrival in the ST.POL area. Brigades will
          notify C.R.H.A. where these batteries are to billet.

WATERING 6. On the last day of the march groups will halt to water
          in the CANCHE Valley under arrangements to be made by
          A.A. & Q.M.G.

MOTOR
TRANSPORT. 7. (a) Motors of Divisional Headquarters and Signal
                  Squadron and No. 9 L.A.M. Battery will move on July
                  16th. direct from BOUVINCOURT to ST.POL.

              (b) Motor Ambulances will move under orders of
                  A.D.M.S.

              (c) Supply Column and Reserve Park will move under
                  orders of A.A. & Q.M.G.

                                    .... 8.

8. **Dismounted Reinforcements**

Orders regarding Dismounted Reinforcements will be issued later.

9. **Reports.**

(a) Till 12 noon July 15th.   BOUVINCOURT.

(b) 12 noon July 15th. to 8 a.m. July 17th., KEILLY, where an Intermediate Report Centre will be established.

(c) After 8.0 a.m. July 17th., ST. POL (exact position will be notified later)

10. **ACKNOWLEDGE.**

R.P. Howard Vyse

Lieut-Colonel, G.S.

5th. Cavalry Division.

To/
```
        Normal O.O.    1 - 23.
Cavalry Corps            24.
2nd. Cav. Division       25.
4th. Cav. Division       26.
Mhow Cav. Brigade        27.
```

5TH. CAVALRY DIVISION.

MARCH TABLE, JULY 13TH - 17. (Issued with O.O. No. 36).

Group	Routes	Destinations July 13th.	July 14th.	July 15th.	July 16th.	July 17th.	July 18th.
G.O.C. Ambala Cav.Bde. Amb.Bde (less X-RHA) 5th.Reserve Park Amb Cav.Fd.Ambns. (less Motors).	E. of LONGUE EN CHAUSEE – PROYART – MORCOURT-SUZANNE BRAY – MORLANCOURT thence any Rd. E. of TREUX – RIDEMONT – BUZEUX – MAIEUX – LUCHEUX – IVERGNY – DOUEVILLE – ST. MICHEL, all inclusive.		CATIGNY – BUIRE – COUCELLES	VAUX – SUZANNE	TREUX – BUIRE – RIDEMONT	VAUCHELLES – AUTHIE – THIEVRES – SARTON – MARIEUX	ROLLENCOURT – ORLENCOURT – BRYAS – (approximately)
G.O.C. Sec'bad Cav.Bde. (less X.R.H.A.) Sec'bad Bde. 5th.Fd.Sqn.R.E. Sec. Cav.Fd.Ambs (less motors)	as for Ambala Bde. as far as DUREVILLE, thence optional			CATIGNY – BUIRE – COUCELLES	VAUX – SUZANNE	TREUX – BUIRE – RIDEMONT	VAUCHELLES – AUTHIE – THIEVRES – SARTON – BARLEUX	ST NICHEL – TROIS – VAUX – RAMECOURT – (appx. only).
G.O.C. Canadian Cav.Bde. Can.Bde (Less R.C.H.A. Brigade). Div.H.Q. & Sig Sqdn. (less motors) 1 Sqn Inniskilling Dragoons. 5th Cav Aux H.T.Coy. Can Cav Fld Amb (less Motors).	BRIE – ESREES DENIECOURT – CAPPY – S of SOMME – SAILLY LAURETTE – MERI – COURT – HEILLY – BEAU – QUESNE – DOULLENS – FREVENT – HERLIN LE SEC.		ECLUSIER – CAPPY.	MERICOURT – HEILLY – BONNAY.	ORVILLE – AMPLIER – AUTHIEULE.	GAUCHIN – HERNICOURT – CROIX. (approx. only).
C.R.H.A. 17th Bde R.H.A. R.C.H.A. Brigade.	MONS-en-CHAUSSEE – thence as for Can Brigade.		CAPPY.	MERICOURT – HEILLY – BONNAY.	ORVILLE – AMPLIER – AUTHIEULE.	17th Brigade Areas.

App_x 126

SECRET.   No G.636.

Headquarters, 5th Cavalry Division.
19th July 1917.

To /
Operation Order Distribution.

1. The following reallotment of billeting areas is made.:-

(a) Sec'bad Cav. Bde. (including Sec'bad Field Ambulance)
SAUTRECOURT-HERBEVAL-EPS-ANVIN (exclusive of billets already occupied)-MONCHY CAYEUX.

(b) Ambala Cavalry Brigade.
ROELLECOURT-OSTREVILLE-BRYAS-ROSEMONT (now occupied by Sec'bad Field Ambulance)-ST MICHEL.

(c) Ammunition Column.
The whole of LA THIEULOYE.

(d) 5th Field Squadron.
TROISVAUX.

(e) 5th Cavalry Reserve Park and A.H.T. Company.
RAMECOURT.
Billets to be allotted by O.C., A.S.C.

2. (a) Troops of Sec'bad Cavalry Brigade moving in consequence of the above will be clear of their present area by 5 p.m., tomorrow, July 20th.

(b) Other troops will not enter their new area before 5 p.m.

3. Completion of moves will be reported to this office.

4. Acknowledge.

R. Howard Vyse
Lieut. Col. G.S.
5th Cavalry Division.

Copy to :-
Cavalry Corps.

Secret   Apx 12

CONCENTRATION ORDERS.- July 1917.   No G.S.649.

                                    Headquarters,5th Cavalry Division.
                                              17th July 1917.
To
     Operation Order Distribution.

   1. Concentration Orders for moves in various directions are forwarded herewith.

   2. Brigades will report to this office where their Report Centre will be at the various concentration points.

   3. The term "Brigades" includes Batteries and Field Ambulances, but not "B" Echelons.

   4. (a) On receipt of the orders for the Brigade to concentrate, "B" Echelons will assemble at some point in the Brigade Area to be decided upon by Brigades. The place selected, and the name of the officer appointed to command, will be notified to this office.

   (b) "B" Echelon of Field Squadron will, in all cases, stand fast ready to move. O.C., Field Squadron will appoint an officer to command it, who will also command "B" Echelons of Divisional Headquarters, Signal Squadron and H.Q. 17th Brigade R.H.A.

   5. Reserve Park and A.H.T. Company will harness up, but not hook in, on being notified that the Division is concentrating.

   6. All formations and units will notify this office as soon as it is possible to forecast accurately the time at which they will be able to move off. They will do this without waiting for all units actually to have arrived. E.G.,-"Brigade will be ready to move from concentration point 2 p.m.,"
   It should be noted that the Brigade can move off as soon as the distance between the starting point and the rear unit is less than the length of the column on the march.

   7. Divisional Headquarters and Signal Squadron will stand fast until further orders are received.

   8 Acknowledge

                                              R.J. Howard de Vype
                                              Lieut.Col., G.S.
Copy to :-   5th Cavalry Division.
    Cavalry Corps.

5 T H C A V A L R Y D I V I S I O N.

Concentration Orders. July 1917.

Direction of Move.	Concentration Point (Heads of Column).					Roads Allotment for which planned.
	Ambala Cav. Bde.	Canadian Cav. Bde.	Sec'bad Cav. Bde.	Ammn. Column.	Field Squadron.	
SOUTH	Railway Crossing ROELLECOURT	X roads North of HERLIN LE SEC (via S. side of ST POL)	MORIOCOURT	OSTREVILLE	ROSEMONT	(a) ST POL–FREVENT (b) ROELLECOURT – ETREE WAMIN
EAST	LA BELLE EPINE	Ditto.	Ditto.	X roads 1 mile S.E. of MONCHY BRETON	Ditto.	Any between HERLIN LE SEC – ETREE WAMIN – AVESNES LE COMTE and TINGUES–SAVY
NORTH EAST	OSTREVILLE (Troops at BRYAS do not move)	GAUCHIN VERLOINGT	VALHUON (via HESTRUS)	LA THIEULOYE	X roads S.W. of BRYAS	Any between TINQUES – AUBIGNY – GAMBLAIN L'ABBE and DIEVAL – BRUAY
NORTH	BRYAS	HESTRUS	HEUCHIN	S.E. end of VALHUON	Ditto.	Any between PERNES – LILLERS and BERGUENEUSE – WESTREHEM – ST HILAIRE

SECRET.

Instructions regarding War Diaries and Intelligence Summaries are contained in F.S. Regs., Part II. and the Staff Manual respectively. Title pages will be prepared in manuscript.

WAR DIARY
or
INTELLIGENCE/SUMMARY
(Erase heading not required.)

General Staff, 5th Cavalry Division.

Army Form C. 2118.

Place	Date	Hour	Summary of Events and Information	Remarks and references to Appendices
HEUCHIN.	1917 1st August.		Lt.-Colonel W.T. HODGSON, M.C., 1st Royal Dragoons, assumed duties of G.S.O.1 vice Lt-Col. HOWARD-VYSE appointed B.G.G.S. to troops in Egypt. Canadian Cavalry Brigade Headquarters moved to SAUTRECOURT.	Appx.No. 28
do.	2nd August.		III Corps Commander congratulated Division on state of defences in area recently held by the Division. (Copy attached).	
do.	4th August.		No. 9 L.A.M. Battery moved from ST. POL to HEUCHIN.	
do.	5th August.		Headquarters and No.2 Section Reserve Park moved to BRYAS.	
do.	6th August.		No.1 Section Reserve Park moved to BRYAS. 13th Machine Gun Squadron moved to FLEURY.	
do.	8th August.		Divisional Commander visited Indian Training Depot at ROUEN.	
do.	13th August.		Divisional Commander visited the wagon-lines of 17th Brigade R.H.A. and R.C.H.A. Brigade.	
do.	15th August.		Divisional Horse Show at BRYAS.	
do.	18th August.		The Corps Commander inspected the Canadian Cavalry Brigade in Marching Order.	
do.	20th August.		The Divisional Commander inspected the Sec'bed Cavalry Brigade in Marching Order.	
do.	21st August.		The Divisional Commander inspected the Ambala Cavalry Brigade in Marching Order.	
do.	23rd August.		The Divisional Commander and G.S.O.1 attended a Conference at Corps Headquarters.	

Moberly

Major,
for General Staff, 5th Cavalry Division.

No. G.S. 657.

Appx 128

Headquarters, 5th. Cavalry Division.
Dated 2nd. August, 1917.

To/
Canadian Cavalry Brigade.	6
Sialkot Cavalry Brigade.	6
Ambala Cavalry Brigade.	6
17th. Bde. R.H.A.	4
R.C.H.A. Bde.	3
Field Squadron.	1
Signal Squadron.	1
A.A. & Q.M.G.	1
A.D.M.S.	1
No. 9 L.A.C. Battery.	1

Copy of correspondence received with Cavalry Corps letter No. G. 511, dated 1-8-17.

Third Army No. G.9/99
Cav. Corps No. G.511
30/7/17.

Third Army.
G.O. 4749.

I wish to put on record the excellent state of the defences in the area previously held by the Cavalry Corps and recently taken over by 34th. and 35th. Divisions.

If it is possible to pick out one formation where the work of all was so good, I should mention the 5th. Cavalry Division. The obstacles put up by this Division are quite the best I have seen in this country.

I should be much obliged if this fact is conveyed to O.C. Cavalry Corps.

(Sd) W.P. PULTENEY
Lieut-General,
Commanding III Corps.

(2)

Cavalry Corps.

Forwarded.

A copy is being sent to G.H.Q.

(Sd) J. BYNG, General,
Commanding Third Army.

29th. July, 1917.

Copy to Adv.G.H.Q.

(3)

2nd. Cavalry Division.
3rd. Cavalry Division.
4th. Cavalry Division.
5th. Cavalry Division.
C.R.E.

For information.   (Sd) G. CRASTER, Maj. for
Cav. Corps HQ 1st. Aug. 1917.   B.G.G.S. Cav. Corps.

1. The Major-General Commanding congratulates the Division on this very satisfactory report and wishes the remarks of the III Corps Commander communicated to all ranks.

N. T. Hodgson
Lieut-Colonel, G.
5th. Cavalry Division.

Serial No. 244.

Army Form C. 2118.

SECRET

Instructions regarding War Diaries and Intelligence Summaries are contained in F.S. Regs., Part II. and the Staff Manual respectively. Title pages will be prepared in manuscript.

WAR DIARY
or
INTELLIGENCE SUMMARY

General Staff, 5th Cavalry Division.

(Erase heading not required.)

SEPTEMBER. 1917.

Place	Date	Hour	Summary of Events and Information	Remarks and references to Appendices
ST. POL Billeting Area.	1st.		Cavalry Corps Horse Show.	
	8th		The four Indian Regiments and Mhow and Secunderabad Cavalry Field Ambulances were inspected by Lieut-General Sir H.V. COX, K.C.M.G., C.B., C.S.I., Military Secretary, India Office.	
	9th		17th Brigade R.H.A. and R.C.H.A. Brigade rejoined Division from Canadian Corps.	
	10th		Captain J.W.M. O'RORKE resumed duties of G.S.O. (2).	

W.T. Morgan

Lieut-Colonel, G.S.,
5th Cavalry Division.

Army Form C. 2118.

WAR DIARY
or
INTELLIGENCE SUMMARY.

S E C R E T.

(Erase heading not required.)

1917

Place	Date	Hour	Summary of Events and Information	Remarks and references to Appendices
HEUCHIN	OCTOBER 1st		Orders received for X.Battery and its Section of Ammunition Column to be prepared to entrain by 6th instant for service overseas - Warning Order issued.	
	3rd		Orders received for 5th Field Squadron to move on the 4th instant to ST VENANT area - March orders issued - G.S.690 dated 3rd October 1917.	Appx: 129
	4th		Orders received from Cavalry Corps for the Division to move North to an area W.of POPERINGHE, 5th Field Squadron to rejoin the Division in that area.	
	5th		Orders issued for the movement of the Division (less X Battery R.H.A.and its Section of Ammunition Column and 5th Field Squadron) to the area W.of POPERINGHE.(O.O.37)	Appx:130.
	6th		Orders received that X Battery R.H.A.and its Section of Ammunition Column will entrain at ST POL for MARSEILLES on the 8th instant and will be struck off the strength of the Division from that date.	
	7th		Divisional H.Q.opened at POPERINGHE at 10 a.m., Canadian and Secunderabad Cavalry Brigades arrived in the WATOU area. Ambala Cavalry Brigade ,Reserve Park and 17th Bde and R.C.H.A. Bde Ammunition Columns arrived in THIENNES area. Weather very wet. Orders received about 10 p.m, for Division to remain halted as at present distributed until further orders- Orders issued accordingly by wire.	
	8th		X Battery and its Section of Ammunition Column entrained at ST POL for MARSEILLES and struck off strength of Division. Weather wet and windy.	
	9th		Weather wet and some showers. Divisional Commander attended a Cavalry Corps conference regarding future operations,at AIRE.	
	10th		Orders received from Cavalry Corps for troops in the STEENBECQUE area to complete their march to the WATOU area on the 11th instant. Orders issued accordingly ((G735 dated 10th inst.) Dismounted men of the Division,who were concentrated at GAUCHIN-VERLOINGT near ST POL on the departure of the Division from that area,arrived at BAILLEUL by rail.	Appx:131.
	11th			

Army Form C. 2118.

WAR DIARY
or
INTELLIGENCE SUMMARY.
(Erase heading not required.)

Instructions regarding War Diaries and Intelligence Summaries are contained in F.S. Regs., Part II. and the Staff Manual respectively. Title pages will be prepared in manuscript.

Place	Date	Hour	Summary of Events and Information	Remarks and references to Appendices
	11th		Orders issued for the concentration of "B" Echelon (Divisionalised) Reserve Park (less Light Section) and A.H.T.Company in the event of a forward move by Division.(G.728/2 dated 11th) Ambala Cavalry Brigade and attached troops, Reserve Park, 17th Bde R.H.A.Ammunition Column and R.C.H.A.Bde Ammunition Column arrive in WATOU area. Stormy weather with some showers.	Appx:132.
	12th		Division is located as in Q/213/8. Weather wet and stormy.	Appx:133.
	13th		Orders are received for the movement of the Division to the S.W. — O.O.38 issued in consequence.	Appx:134.
	14th		Divisional H.Q. arrived at RENESCURE. Ambala Cav.Bde., Divnl.Ammn.Col. and Reserve Park arrived in RENESCURE Area. Weather fine.	
	15th		Final destination of the Division in the Cavalry Corps area having been received O.O.39 is issued for completion of the March. Weather fine.	Appx:135.
	16th		Divnl.H.Q. arrived at FRESSIN - Ambala Cavalry Brigade and attached troops arrive in the new area. Orders are issued for the formation of a Cavalry Dismounted Regiment at BAILLEUL for work under Second Army (G.S.698)	Appx:136.
	19th		The Cavalry Battalion was formed at BAILLEUL and ready to move on 20th. The reinforcements sent up from the Base arrived in the evening of the 17th - 244 strong - and equipped as Infantry. Ranks from 5th Cavalry Division arrived on 18th to complete establishment.	
	20th		5th Cavalry Battalion is inspected at BAILLEUL by G.O.C.5th Cavalry Division. The Battalion comes under orders of Second Army from this date. The Battalion is ordered to move into Canadian Corps area for Pioneer work on 22nd instant.	
	22nd		Orders are received for No 9 L.A.M.Battery to be withdrawn to G.H.Q.Troopsarea and to billet at MARCONNE near HESDIN - Wire sent ordering No 9 L.A.M.Battery to move as required on 23rd inst.	
	23rd		No 9 L.A.M.Battery moved to G.H.Q.Troops area and billeted at MARCONNE.	
	28th			

Army Form C. 2118.

WAR DIARY
or
INTELLIGENCE SUMMARY.
(Erase heading not required.)

Instructions regarding War Diaries and Intelligence Summaries are contained in F. S. Regs., Part II. and the Staff Manual respectively. Title pages will be prepared in manuscript.

Place	Date	Hour	Summary of Events and Information	Remarks and references to Appendices
	28th		2nd Anzac Corps Cavalry Regiment and Cyclist Battalion came under the Administration of 5th Cavalry Division and were billeted in the vicinity of RUISSEAUVILLE.	

Captain, G.S.

for G.O.C., 5th Cavalry Division.

SECRET.   Appx 129   No. G.S.690.

Headquarters, 5th Cavalry Division,
3rd October, 1917.

To/
    5th Field Squadron, R.E.

1.   The 5th Field Squadron R.E. (less Troop detached in Third Army area) will proceed to ST. FLORIS, near ST. VENANT, tomorrow, October 4th, in accordance with the following March Table :-

Starting Point.	Time.	Route.	Destination.	Remarks.
TROISVAUX	9 a.m.	PERNES - LILLERS - BUSNES.	ST. FLORIS	Move to be completed by 4 p.m.

2.   On the following day, October 5th, the march will be continued under orders to be issued by Second Army.

3.   The Squadron will be rationed up to and for 5th October.

4.   Billeting Party will report to Town Major ST. VENANT.

5.   Acknowledge. (Field Squadron only).

                      N. T. Hodgson
                      Lt-Colonel, G.S.,
                  5th Cavalry Division.

Copies to :-
    "Q".
    O.C., A.S.C.
    D.A.D.O.S.
    A.D.M.S.
    A.D.V.S.
    Cavalry Corps.

- SECRET -

Appx 130

5TH CAVALRY DIVISION.

OPERATION ORDER No. 37.   COPY No. 22

Reference Maps   Dated 5th October, 1917.
$\frac{1}{100,000}$
LENS and HAZEBROUCK.

1. The Division (less "X" Battery R.H.A. and one gun section Ammunition Column and 5th Field Squadron R.E.) will march North on 6th, 7th and 8th October in accordance with the attached March Table.

    5th Field Squadron R.E. will rejoin the Division on arrival of the Division at POPERINGHE.

2. (a) Where Divisional Troops are shewn as attached to a Brigade they will march and billet under the orders of that Brigade.

    (b) Divisional Headquarters and the 5th Signal Squadron (less Motors) will march under the orders of an officer to be detailed by O.C., 5th Signal Squadron.

    (c) Motor Ambulances and Snaitary Section will move under orders of A.D.M.S.

3. During the 1st day's march a distance of 500 yards will be maintained in rear of Regiments, Batteries and similar units.

    During the 2nd day's march a distance of 200 yards is to be maintained between Squadrons and groups of 10 Transport Vehicles.

4. "B" Echelons will march with Brigades and Units of Divisional Troops.

5. Dismounted Reinforcements will be concentrated at GAUCHIN VERLOINGT by 4 p.m. on 7th October under orders to be issued by Brigades.

    Lt-Colonel YOUNG, Royal Canadian Dragoons, will command the Dismounted Reinforcements of the Division.

6. Railhead on 7th inst. and 8th inst will be at THIENNES.
    Railhead for and after 9th inst. will be notified later.

7. Report Centre closes at HEUCHIN at 10 a.m. on October 7th and opens at POPERINGHE at the same hour.

    An Advanced Report Centre will be opened at STEENBECQUE at 12.30 p.m. on October 6th and closes at 10 a.m. on October 8th.

8. ACKNOWLEDGE.

W. T. Hodgson
Lt-Colonel, G.S.,
5th Cavalry Division.

Issued by D.R. at 3 p.m.

To/
    Normal O.O. Distribution   1 - 23
    Cavalry Corps   No.   24
    First Army   "   25
    Second Army   "   26

5th Cavalry Divn:— March Table — (Issued with Operation Order No. 37).

FORMATION OR UNIT.	STARTING POINT.	TIME & DATE	ROUTE	DESTINATION.	REMARKS.
I. Canadian Cav Bde. R.C.H.A.Bde.(less Ammn. Column). Canadian Fld.Amb.	VALHUON.	9 a.m. 6th Oct.	PERNES – LILLERS – ST.VENANT.	STEENBECQUE(LE BAS, LE HAUT)(less accomodation now occupied by Field Coy,R.E. of 59th Division). THIENNES, TANNAY, HOULERON.	Billets from Area Comdt. & Town Maj. THIENNES. ———— Not to be N. of the line LAMBRES –GUARBECQUE before 12.15 p.m.
II. Serial No.I.	Junction of ST.VENANT –HAZEBROUCK Road and the AIRE–HAZEBROUCK Road.	10 a.m. 7th Oct.	HAZEBROUCK– STEENVOORDE.	WAROU Area. ———— Billets as detailed by A.A.& Q.M.G.	Not to pass ST. SYLVESTRE CAPPEL before 12 noon.
III. Sec'bad Cav Bde. Divnl.Hqrs. Signal Sqdn. Hqrs.17th Bde RHA. "N" Bty.R.H.A. Sec'bad Fld.Amb.	HEUCHIN Church. (N.east of HEUCHIN)	9 a.m. 6th Oct.	ST.HILAIRE– AIRE.	PECQUEUR, BOESEGHEM, LES CISEAUX, WITTES, GUARLINGHEM, ST. MARTIN, NEUFPRE.	Billets from Town Major BOESEGHEM. ———— Not to be N. of the line LAMBRES –GUARBECQUE before 12.15 p.m. T'v.Hqr.& Sig. Sqn.,H.Q.17th Bde RHA to billet at STEENBECQUE. Billets to be allotted by Canadian Cav Bde.
IV. Serial No. III.	Junction of ST.VENANT –HAZEBROUCK Road and the AIRE–HAZEBROUCK Road.	11.15 a.m. 7th Oct.	HAZEBROUCK– STEENVOORDE.	WAROU Area. ———— Billets as detailed by A.A.& Q.M.G.	
V. Ambala Cav Bde. Mhow Fld.Amb.	VALHUON.	8 a.m. 7th Oct.	PERNES–LILLERS –ST.VENANT.	STEENBECQUE(LE BAS, LE HAUT)(less accomodation now occupied by Fld.Coy. R.E.59th Div). THIENNES, TANNAY, HOULERON.	Billets from Area Comdt. & Town Major THIENNES. ———— Not to be N.of the line LAMBRES-GUARBECQUE before 12.15 p.m.

FORMATION OR UNIT.	STARTING POINT.	TIME & DATE.	ROUTE.	DESTINATION.	REMARKS.
VI. Serial No.V.	Junction of ST.VENANT "HAZEBROUCK" Road and the AIRE-HAZEBROUCK Road.	10 a.m. 8th Oct.	HAZEBROUCK-STEENVOORDE.	WATOU Area. --- Billets as detailed by A.A.& Q.M.G.	Not to pass ST. SYLVESTRE CAPPEL before 12 noon.
VII. 17th Bde Am.Col. R.C.H.A.Am.Col.	VALHUON.	9 a.m. 7th Oct.	PERNES-FERFAY BOESEGHEM. -ST.HILAIRE-AIRE.		
VIII. Serial No.VII.	Junction of ST.VENANT-HAZEBROUCK Road and the AIRE-HAZEBROUCK Road.	11.15 a.m. 8th Oct.	HAZEBROUCK-STEENVOORDE.	WATOU Area. --- Billets as detailed by A.A.& Q.M.G.	
IX. Reserve Park. Hqrs.A.H.T.Coy.	VALHUON.	9.15 a.m. 7th Oct.	PERNES-FERFAY -ST.HILAIRE-AIRE.	WITTES.	
X. Serial No.IX.	STEENBECQUE.	11.15 a.m. 8th Oct.	HAZEBROUCK-STEENVOORDE.	WATOU Area. --- Billets as detailed by A.A.& Q.M.G.	
XI. Divnl.Hqrs. & Sig.Sqn. motors. 9th L.A.C. Battery.	HEUCHIN.	7th Oct.	ST.HILAIRE-AIRE. HAZEBROUCK-STEENVOORDE.	POPERINGHE.	

NOTE I. Fighting Troops and "A" Echelon may pass "B" Echelons on the march but the distances ordered between Units and Squadrons are to be strictly adhered to.

NOTE II. Watering arrangements for the march will be issued later.

App & 131   *War Diary*

SECRET.   No. G.735.

                                    Headquarters, 5th Cavalry Division,
                                              10th October, 1917.

1.   The Ambala Cavalry Brigade and Divisional Troops, now in the STEENBECQUE Area, will complete the march to the WATOU Area on the 11th inst., in accordance with the attached March Table.

2.   The Divisional Troops will march under orders of the G.O.C., Ambala Cavalry Brigade.

3.   A distance of 200 yards will be maintained between Squadrons and groups of ten transport vehicles.

4.   ACKNOWLEDGE.
        (AMBALA. BDE. ONLY)
                                        J. O'Rorke
                                              Captain, G.S.,
                                              5th Cavalry Division.

To/   Normal Operation Order Distribution.

Copies to :-
        Cavalry Corps.
        Second Army.
        First Army.

5TH CAVALRY DIVISION.

MARCH TABLE - (Issued with No.G.735 dated 10th October, 1917.)

FORMATION OR UNIT.	STARTING POINT.	TIME.	ROUTE.	DESTINATION.	REMARKS.
AMBALA CAVALRY BDE. Mhow Field Amblce, 17th Bde, R.H.A., Ammunition Col, R,C.H.A. Ammn. Col. Reserve Park.	Junction of ST VENANT - HAZEBROUCK and the AIRE - HAZEBROUCK Roads.	—	HAZEBROUCK STEENVOORDE.	WATOU AREA. Billets as detailed by A.A.& Q.M.G.	Head of the Column not to pass Cross-roads LE BREARDE before 10 a.m. Tail of the Column to be clear of HAZEBROUCK by 12 noon.

****
****
****

--C O P Y.--

S E C R E T.

akh 132

No. G.728/2.

Headquarters, 5th Cavalry Division.

11th Ocotber, 1917.

To /
O.O.Distribution.

In continuation of my G.728 dated 9th instant.

Reference Sheet 27, 1/40,000.

In the event of a forward move)-

    "B" Echelon Divisionalised.
    Reserve Park.(less Light Section).
    Aux. Horse Transport Company.

will concentrate about L.9.d. under Captain ALDERCRON, 8th Hussars.

2.   Officer Commanding B.Echelon of Brigades.
    -:-   -:-   Reserve Park (Heavy Section).
    -:-   -:-   Aux.H.T.Company.

will meet Captain ALDERCRON at 4 p.m., on the 12th instant on the road at L.9.central, when ground will be allotted.

            (sd) J.O.Rorke.Capt.G.S.

        5th Cavalry Division.

Copy to :-
    Captain ALDERCRON., 8th Hussars.

SECRET

LIST OF BIVOUACS – 5TH CAVALRY DIVISION.

Reference Sheet 27 – 1/40,000.

Divisional Headquarters	POPERINGHE.
Field Cashier	WATOU.
Signal Squadron	POPERINGHE.
Field Squadron	K.24.a.9.8.
C.R.H.A.	POPERINGHE.
Ammunition Column	K.10.d.5.2.
Ammunition Park	WINNEZEELE.
Supply Column	WATOU.
Sanitary Section	WATOU.
9th L.A.C. Battery	POPERINGHE.
A.H.T. Coy.	L.16.c.3.3.
Reserve Park	L.17.a.9.6.
Dismounted Reinforcements	BAILLEUL.
Railhead (Supplies)	WIPPENHOEK.

CANADIAN CAVALRY BRIGADE.

Brigade Headquarters	L.9.b.6.4.
R.C.Dragoons	L.9.b.5.8. & L.9.c.6.6.
L.S.Horse	L.15.b.3.7.
R.C.H.A. Brigade	L.15.b.7.3.
F.G.Horse	L.9.b.3.7.
Canadian M.G. Squadron	L.15.b.9.5.
Canadian C.F.A.	L.10.c.8.1.
Canadian M.V. Section	L.8.d.6.5.

SEC'BAD CAVALRY BRIGADE.

Brigade Headquarters	WATOU.
7th Dragoon Guards	K.3.d.6.6.
20th Horse	K.4.d.6.5. & K.4.d.4.4. (SCOTS FARM).
34th Horse	K.3.d.7.2.
"N" Battery R.H.A.	K.3.c.2.2.
No. 13 M.G. Squadron	K.3.d.5.1.
Sec'bad I.C.F.A.	K.4.c.4.4.
M.V. Section	K.5.d.8.7.

AMBALA CAVALRY BRIGADE.

Brigade Headquarters	K.10.d.7.2.
8th Hussars	K.17.b.2.1.
9th Horse	K.9.a.6.4.
18th Lancers	K.15.b.3.8.
No. 14 M.G. Squadron	K.9.b.7.5.
Mhow I.C.F.A.	K.16.d.9.7.
M.V. Section	K.10.d.7.2.

No.Q/213/8.

Headquarters, 5th Cavalry Division.
12th October 1917.

To/ Second Army "Q".

Forwarded.

for Lieut-Colonel,
for G.O.C., 5th Cavalry Division.

Copies to :-
    Cavalry Corps "Q".
    Usual Billeting List Distribution.
    1st, 2nd, 3rd and 4th Cavalry Divisions "Q".
    Area Commandant, WATOU.
    O.C., Dismounted Reinforcements, 5th Cavalry Division.

Appx 134

SECRET.   Copy No. 20

5TH CAVALRY DIVISION.

OPERATION ORDER NO. 38.

Ref. Map 1/100,000.   Dated 13th October, 1917.

1.   The Division will march to an area South of MONTREUIL in accordance with attached March Table.

   Orders for the march from the BLEQUIN area to the MONTREUIL area will be issued later.

2.   (a)   Where Divisional Troops are shown as grouped with a Brigade they will march and billet under orders of that Brigade.

   (b)   Divisional Headquarters and 5th Signal Squadron (less motors) will march under the orders of an officer to be detailed by the O.C., Signal Squadron.

   (c)   Motor Ambulances and Sanitary Section will move under orders of A.D.M.S.

   (d)   "B" Echelon will march with Brigades and Units of Divisional Troops.

3.   A distance of 200 yards between Squadrons and groups of 10 transport vehicles is to be maintained.

   Railhead October 14th - 15th at WIPPENHOEK.

         October 16th   at LUMBRES.

         October 17th   at HESDIN.

5.   A Divisional Staff Officer will meet representatives from Ambala Brigade, Reserve Park, Ammunition Column and Signal Squadron at the E of LA CROSSE (1 mile North of RENESCURE) at 10 a.m. on 14th inst., and allot billets.

6.   Divisional Report Centre will close at POPERINGHE at 11 a.m. on the 14th inst. and open at RENESCURE at the same hour.

7.   ACKNOWLEDGE.

                                                   H. T. Hodgson
                                                   Lt-Colonel, G.S.
                                                   5th Cavalry Division.

Issued by D.R. at 9-45 p.m.

To/
   Normal O.O. Distribution Nos. 1 - 23.
       Second Army .... No. 25.
       Cavalry Corps .... No. 26.

5TH CAVALRY DIVISION.

March Table. (Issued with Operation Order No.38).

FORMATION OR UNIT.	STARTING POINT.	TIME.	ROUTE.	DESTINATION.	REMARKS.
Ambala Cav Bde. Mhow Field Ambulance. 17th Bde Ammn.Col. R.C.H.A. Ammn.Col.	Road Junction on ABEELE-STEENVOORDE Road ½ mile E. of STEENVOORDE Church.	9.30 a.m. Oct 14th.	STEENVOORDE - CASSEL.	RENESCURE Area.	
---do---	ARQUES Church.	9 a.m. Oct 15th.	ARQUES - WIZERNES.	Southern portion of BLEQUIN Area.	Billets from Area Commandant, THIEMBRONNE.
Signal Sqdn(less Motors) Divnl.Hqrs.(" ") Hqrs 17th Bde R.H.A.	K of HILLEHOEK.	11 a.m. Oct 14th.	STEENVOORDE - CASSEL.	RENESCURE AREA.	
---do---	ARQUES Church.	11 a.m. Oct 15th.	ARQUES - WIZERNES.	Southern portion of BLEQUIN Area.	Billets from Area Commandant, THIEMBRONNE.
Reserve Park.	K of HILLEHOEK.	11.15 a.m. Oct 14th.	STEENVOORDE-CASSEL	RENESCURE Area.	
---do---	ARQUES Church.	11.15 a.m. Oct 15th.	ARQUES - WIZERNES.	Southern portion of BLEQUIN Area.	Billets from Area Commandant, THIEMBRONNE.
Sec'bad Cav Bde. "N" Battery R.H.A. Sec'bad Field Ambulance.	Road Junction on ABEELE-STEENVOORDE Road ½ mile E. of STEENVOORDE Church.	10 a.m. Oct 15th.	STEENVOORDE - CASSEL.	RENESCURE Area.	Billets from Area Commandant, RENESCURE at ARQUES.
---do---	ARQUES Church.	9 a.m. Oct 16th.	ARQUES - WIZERNES.	Southern portion of BLEQUIN Area.	Billets from Area Commandant, THIEMBRONNE.
Canadian Cav Bde. Canadian Field Amb. R.C.H.A.Bde(less Am.Col) 5th Field Sqdn R.E. Hqrs A.H.T. Company.	Road Junction on ABEELE-STEENVOORDE Road ½ mile E. of STEENVOORDE Church.	10 a.m. Oct 16th.	STEENVOORDE -CASSEL.	RENESCURE Area.	Billets from Area Commandant, RENESCURE at ARQUES.

FORMATION OR UNIT.	STARTING POINT.	TIME.	ROUTE.	DESTINATION.	REMARKS.
Canadian Cav Bde. Canadian Field Amb. R.C.H.A.Bde(less Amn Col) 5th Field Sqdn R.E. Hqrs A.H.T.Company.	ARQUES Church.	9 a.m. Oct 17th.	ARQUES - WIZERNES.	Southern portion of BLEQUIN Area.	Billets from Area Commandant, THIEMBRONNE.
Motors of Divnl Hdqrs. No. 9 L.A.C. Battery.	POPERINGHE.	Oct 14th.	STEENVOORDE - CASSEL.	RENESCURE.	
----- do -----	RENESCURE.	Oct 15th.	ARQUES - WIZERNES.	THIEMBRONNE.	

Appx 135   War Diary

SECRET.   Copy No. 21

5TH CAVALRY DIVISION.

OPERATION ORDER NO. 39.

Ref. Map 1/100,000.   Dated 15th October, 1917.

1.   The Division will march to the FRUGES area from the Southern portion of the BLEQUIN area in accordance with attached March Table.

2.   The Division comes under the administration of Cavalry Corps at Noon on the 17th inst.

3.   Divisional Report Centre closes at RENESCURE at 11 a.m. on the 16th inst and opens at FRESSIN at the same hour.

4.   ACKNOWLEDGE.

W. T. Hodgson Lt-Colonel, G.S.,
5th Cavalry Division.

Issued by D.R. at 11.30 a.m.

To/
    Normal O.O. Distribution Nos. 1 - 23.
    Cavalry Corps ....No. 24.

5TH CAVALRY DIVISION.

MARCH TABLE - (Issued with Operation Order No.39).

FORMATION OR UNIT.	STARTING POINT.	DATE & TIME.	ROUTE.	DESTINATION.	REMARKS.
Ambala Cav Brigade. Mhow Field Ambulance.	FAUQUEMBERGUES.	9 a.m. 16th October.	No restrict'ns.	BOUIN-AUBIN ST. VAAST-FOQUEMICOURT -MARESQUEL-AVRON) ST.MARTIN-CONTES-) WAMBERCOURT-SAINS LEZ FRESSIN.	
Signal Sqdn(less motors) Div.Hqrs. ( ) Hqrs 17th Bde R.H.A.	FAUQUEMBERGUES.	9.45 a.m. 16th October.	FAUQUEMBERGUES-FRUGES-PLANQUES.	FRESSIN - PLANQUES.	
Reserve Park.	FAUQUEMBERGUES.	11 a.m. 16th October.	No restrictions.	RUMILLY.	
17th Bde Ammn Column. R.C.H.A.Bde Ammn Col.	FAUQUEMBERGUES.	11.30 a.m. 16th October.	No restrictions.	VERCHOCQ.	
Motors Divnl.Hqrs. 9th L A.C.Battery		16th October.		FRESSIN - PLANQUES.	
Sec'bed Cav Brigade. "K" Battery R.H.A. Sec'bed Field Amb.	Brigade arrangements.	17th October.	No restrictions.	BEAURAINVILLE(N. of river)-LOISON-OFFIN-HESMOND-LEBIEZ-ROYON-TORCY-CREQUY-FRUGES.	
Canadian Cav Brigade. R.C.H.A. Brigade. Hqrs A.H.T.Company.	Brigade arrangements.	18th October.	No restrictions.	BEAURAINVILLE(S.of river)-LESPINOY-LE PETIT BRIMEUX-MAREMLA -MARLES SUR CANCHE-MARANT-AIX EN ISSART-ST.DENOEUX-BOUBERS LES HESMOND-EMBRY-RIMBOVAL.	A.H.T.Coy.will billet at PIT BEAURAIN.

SECRET.

appx 136

No. G.S.698.

Headquarters, 5th Cavalry Division,

16th October, 1917.

To/
    Canadian Cavalry Brigade.
    Sec'bad   "   "
    Ambala   "   "
    5th Signal Squadron.
    A.A.& Q.M.G.
    O.C., A.S.C.
    A.D.M.S.
    D.A.D.O.S.
    Gas Officer.
    Officer Interpreter.

1.   A Cavalry "Battalion" will be formed at BAILLEUL forthwith from the 5th Cavalry Division for work in Second Army area.

2.   250 reinforcements are being sent up to BAILLEUL from the Base to assist in forming the Battalion.

3.   The Battalion will be ready to move from BAILLEUL two days after arrival of reinforcements there from the Base.

4.   War Establishment of the Battalion is attached and the Headquarters and Companies will be found as below :-

(a) HEADQUARTERS.

Commanding Officer .... Lt-Col. D.L. YOUNG
                                                        R.C.Ds.

Adjutant	To be detailed by	Sec'bad Cav. Bde.(Ind.Regt)
Quartermaster	" " " "	Ambala Cav.Bde.(Indian Regt.)
Sergt.Major......	" " " "	Canadian Cav. Bde.
Orderly Room Sergt.) " " " "	Clerk.)	Canadian Cav. Bde.
Transport Sergt...	" " " "	O.C., A.S.C.
Saddler	" " " "	Sec'bad Cav.Bde.(Brit.Regt)
Farrier Sergt. ...	" " " "	Ambala Cav.Bde.(Brit.Regt.)
Shoeing Smiths ...	To be detailed	(1 from Ambala Bde (Indian) (1 from Canadian Bde.
Salutri	To be detailed by	Sec'bad Cav. Bde.
Drivers	" " " "	O.C., A.S.C.
Batmen.	(2 for C.O., 1 for each of Adjutant, Quartermaster (and Medical Officer to be taken by Officers concerned.	
Cook	To be detailed by	Canadian Cav. Bde.
Signallers	" " " "	O.C., Signal Squadron.
Orderlies for M.O.	" " " "	A.D.M.S.

ATTACHED.

First six items of) Medical personnel)	To be detailed by	A.D.M.S.
Gas Duties	" " " "	Divn'l Gas Officer.
Armourer Sergeant ...	" " " "	Canadian Cav. Bde.
Interpreter	" " " "	Divn'l Officer Interpreter.
Bootmakers	To be detailed	(1 from Canadian Cav.Bde. (1 from Sec'bad Cav. Bde.

(b) COMPANIES. ....

(b) COMPANIES.

    (i)   1 Company will be detailed by Canadian Cavalry Brigade.

    (ii)   1 INDIAN Company of 4 Platoons :-

        2 Platoons to be detailed from Sec'bad Cav. Bde.
        2   "   " "   "   "   Ambala Cav. Bde.

Company Headquarters of this Company will be found as follows :-

Capt. or Major - O.C. to be detailed by Ambala Cav. Bde.
1 Subaltern (2nd in Cmd) To be detailed by Sec'bad Cav. Bde.
2 Subalterns .... " " " (1 from Sec'bad Bde.
                                      (1 from Ambala Bde.
Indian Officers .... To be detailed :-
        3 (including 1 as Woodie Major) from Sec'bad Bde.
        2 from Ambala Cav. Bde.
Kot-Dafadar .... To be detailed from Ambala Cav. Bde.
Q.M. Dafadar .... " " " " Sec'bad Cav. Bde.

NOTE.- Sec'bad Cav. Bde. will detail 93 privates.
       Ambala Cav. Bde. will detail 92 privates.
       All other personnel of this Company, not noted above,
         will be found half , each by Sec'bad and Ambala
         Cav. Bdes., except Drivers for whom see para.4(c)
         below.

    (iii)   1 British Company to be formed out of the 250 reinforcements going to BAILLEUL from the Base.
        The Officers and N.C.O's of this Company will be found as under :-

Captain by Ambala Cavalry Brigade.
1 Subaltern (2nd in Command) by Sec'bad Cavalry Brigade.
2 Subalterns (Platoon Leaders) by Ambala Cavalry Brigade.
2 Subalterns by Sec'bad Cavalry Brigade. (Platoon Leaders)
1 Coy.Sergt.Major by Ambala Cavalry Brigade.
1 Coy.Q.M.S. by Sec'bad Cavalry Brigade.
4 Sergeants by Ambala Cavalry Brigade.
4 Sergeants by Sec'bad Cavalry Brigade.

All the above will be found by the British Regiments.

(c) TRANSPORT.

    All Transport, including personnel, for Headquarters of Battalion and for each Company will be detailed by O.C., A.S.C.

5.   Brigades will forward by 6 p.m. to-morrow (17th) as follows :-

    (a)   The numbers (Officers and O.R's) of details required to be sent to BAILLEUL to complete their respective Companies to Establishment.

    (b)   The numbers (Officers and O.R's) of dismounted reinforcements now at BAILLEUL who will be surplus to establishments of their respective Companies.

    (c)   A nominal roll of Officers detailed for :-
      (i)   Headquarters of Battalion.
     (ii)   Canadian Company.
    (iii)   Indian Company.
    (iv)   "Reinforcement" Company.

6.   ACKNOWLEDGE.

N. T. Hodgson
Lt-Colonel, G.S.,
5th Cavalry Division.

WAR ESTABLISHMENT.
INDIAN CAVALRY PIONEER BATTALION.

DETAIL.	Personnel.							Horses.			BICYCLES.
	OFFICERS	W.O.S.	CLERKS	S/SGTS AND SERGEANTS	ARTIFICERS	RANK AND FILE	TOTAL	RIDING	DRAUGHT	TOTAL	
H.Q. (excluding attached)	3	1	1	3	5	18	31	4	14	18	6
H.Q. attached.	2			2		23	27				
3 Coys.(2 Br.& 1 Ind.)	21	3		27		646	697		36	36	
TOTAL BATTALION.	26	4	1	32	5	687	755	4	50	54	6

Composition in Detail.

Detail	OFFICERS	W.O.S.	CLERKS	S/SGTS AND SERGEANTS	ARTIFICERS	RANK AND FILE	TOTAL	RIDING	DRAUGHT	TOTAL	BICYCLES
Headquarters.											
Lt.Col. or Major - C.O.	1						1	1		1	
Adjutant.	1						1	1		1	
Quartermaster.	1						1	1		1	
Sergeant Major.		1					1				
Quartermaster Serjeant.				1			1				
Orderly Room Sergt.				1			1				
Orderly Room Clerk.			1				1				
Transport Sergeant.				1			1	1		1	
Saddler.					1		1				
Farrier Corporal.					1		1				
Shoeing Smiths.					2		2				
Salutri.					1		1				
Drivers (Tpt.for vehicles)						7	7				
Batmen.						5	5				
Cook.						1	1				
Signallers.											
Corporal.						1	1				
Privates.						2	2				
Orderlies for M.O.						2	2				
Attached.											
R.A.M.C. - M.O.	1						1				
Sub.Assistant Surgeon.	1						1				
R.A.M.C.						2	2				
Ward Orderly (Indian).						1	1				
Sanitary Section.				1		4	5				
Stretcher Bearers.						12	12				
Gas Duties.						1	1				
Armourer Sergeant.				1			1				
Interpreter.						1	1				
Bootmakers.						2	2				
TOTAL.	5	1	1	5	5	41	58	4	14	18	6

DETAIL.	OFFICERS.	Personnel.				Horses.	
		W.O.s.	S/Sgts. & Sgts.	RANK AND FILE	TOTAL	DRAUGHT HORSES	TOTAL.
COMPANY – British or Canadian of 4 Platoons.							
Captain. – O.C.	1				1		
Subalterns (1 2nd in Cmd)	5				5		
Company Sergt. Major.		1			1		
Company Qr.Mr.Sergt.			1		1		
Sergeants.			8		8		
Corpls. or L/Cpls.				14	14		
Privates.				185	185		
Drivers (Tpt.for vehicles)				6	6		
Batmen.				3	6		
Cooks.				2	2		
TOTAL.	6	1	9	213	229		
COMPANY – Indian of 4 Platoons.							
Captain. – O.C.	1				1		
Subalterns (1 2nd in Cmd)	3				3		
Indian Officers.	5				5		
Company Sergt.Major.		1			1		
Company Qr.Mr.Sergt.			1		1		
Sergeants.			8		8		
Corporals or L/Cpls.				14	14		
Privates.				185	185		
Drivers (Tpt.for vehicles)				6	6		
Batmen.				9	9		
Cooks.				4	4		
Sweepers.				2	2		
TOTAL.	9	1	9	220	239		

	Transport.					
Headquarters.	Vehicles.		Drivers.			
Limbered G.S. in lieu of Maltese.	1		1		2	2
Carts, Officers Mess.	1		1		2	2
Carts, Water.	1		1		2	2
Wagons, Limbered G.S.	1		2		4	4
Wagons, G.S.	1		2		4	4
3 Coys (Wagons, Limbd.G.S.	6		12		24	24
(Wagons, G.S.	3		6		12	12
TOTAL.	14		25		50	50

Army Form C. 2118.

WAR DIARY
or
INTELLIGENCE SUMMARY

(Erase heading not required.)

Nov 1916

Place	Date	Hour	Summary of Events and Information	Remarks and references to Appendices
CAVILLON	1st.		The Division came under the orders of Cavalry Corps and marched Westwards. Intimation received that a Pioneer Battalion is to be formed from each Cavalry Bde. One Bde. in each Division to be kept intact and two Bde's Btns. to be available for work with Infantry.	(O.O.No.13) (Entry for October) Appx. 88.
"	"	6 p.m.	The Division arrived in new billets as detailed in accompanying list.	
DARGNIES	2nd. to 5th.		Division engaged in training in new area.	
"	6th.		2nd.Ind.Aux.H.T.Coy. rejoined Division, and went into billets at OUST MAREST.	
"	7th. and 8th.		Division engaged in training.	
"	9th.	4 pm.	Headquarters of Divisional School opened at Hotel de France, AULT.	
"	10th. and 11th.		Division engaged in training.	
"	12th.		Dismounted reinforcements rejoined division from work in front area under XIV th. Corps.	
"	13th.		Divisional School opened.	
"	14th.		2nd. Ind. R.H.A.Bde with their sections of Ammn.Col. and Ammn.Park, rejoined Division from XVth. and XIV th. Corps respectively, and went into billets. Revised billeting list attached.	Appx 89.
"	16th.		Orders received that the two pioneer battalions from this Division, i.e. Ambala and Sec'bad Battalions - strength as per W.E. table attached - to be ready to move on or after 20th. inst.	Appx 90.
"	20th.		No. 9 L.A.C. Battery came under orders of 2nd.Ind.R.H.A.Bde.	

Army Form C. 2118.

WAR DIARY
or
INTELLIGENCE SUMMARY
(Erase heading not required.)

Instructions regarding War Diaries and Intelligence Summaries are contained in F.S. Regs., Part II and the Staff Manual respectively. Title Pages will be prepared in manuscript.

Place	Date	Hour	Summary of Events and Information	Remarks and references to Appendices
DARGNIES	21st. Nov.		Ambala Pioneer Battalion left LONGROY GAMACHES at 15.46 by train for attachment to XIVth. Corps.	
"	22nd.		Sec'bad Pioneer Battalion left LONGROY GAMACHES at 16.00 by train, for attachment to XIVth. Corps.	
"	25th.		Title of "2nd. Indian Cavalry Division" changed to "5th. Cavalry Division" and also that of certain Divisional Troops units.	
"	26th. to 30th.		Division engaged in training in Divisional area.	

A.D.Williams Major. G.S.
for G.O.C. 5th Cav Division

No. G.S. 363/1.

Headquarters, 5th. Cavalry Division.
Dated 25th. November, 1916.

Confidential.

Copy of a letter No. O.B. 1385, dated 24-11-16, from G.H.Q. (Received under Cavalry Corps No. G-147, dated 25-11-16.)

In order to avoid confusion in nomenclature now that all Cavalry Divisions form part of one Cavalry Corps, it has been decided to change the titles of the 1st. and 2nd. Indian Cavalry Divisions.

In future these Divisions will be numbered as follows:-

Old Title.	New Title.
1st. Indian Cavalry Division	4th. Cavalry Division.
2nd. Indian " "	5th. " "

2. No change will be made in the titles of the Cavalry Brigades forming these divisions.

3. Consequent on the above, the undermentioned Units of the Divisional Troops of the 4th. and 5th. Cavalry divisions will be re-numbered as follows:-

Old Title.	New Title.
1st. Indian Field Squadron	4th. Field Squadron, R.E.
2nd. Indian Field Squadron	5th. Field Squadron, R.E.
1st. Indian Signal Squadron	4th. Signal Squadron.
2nd. Indian Signal Squadron	5th. Signal Squadron.
H.Q. 1st. Ind.Cav.Div. A.S.C.	H.Q. 4th.Cav.Div. A.S.C.
H.Q. 2nd. Ind.Cav.Div. A.S.C.	H.Q. 5th.Cav.Div. A.S.C.
1st. and 2nd.) Ammunition Park	4th. and 5th. (Ammn. Park.
Indian Cav.) Supply Column	Cavalry (Supply Column.
Divisional) Aux. H.T.Coy.	Divisional (Aux.H.T.Coy.
1st.Ind.Cav.Sanitary Section	No.4 (Cav) Sanitary Section.
2nd. " " " "	No.5 " " "

4. Orders regarding the new title of the R.H.A. Brigades will be issued in due course.

5. No change will be made in the existing titles of the combined Cavalry Field Ambulances.

To/
Ambala Cavalry Brigade — 2nd. Ind. R.H.A. Bde.
Sec'bad " " — R.C.H.A. Bde.
Canadian " " — 2nd. Ind. Field Squadron.
2nd. Ind. Signal Squdn — No. 9 L.A.C. Battery.
A.D.M.S. — O.C. A.S.C.
D.A.D.O.S. — A.D.V.S.
Field Cashier — Divisional Gas Officer.
Ammunition Park. — Supply Column.
Aux. H.T. Coy. — Camp Commandant.
A.P.M. — Liaison Officer.
R.T.O. — A.A. & Q.M.G.
D.A.A. & Q.M.G. — Divisional School.

Forwarded for guidance.

Captain for
5th. Cavalry Division.

No. Q-2798.

Headquarters 2nd Indian Cavalry Division.
1st November 1916.

Appx 88

BILLETING LIST.

UNIT.	WHERE BILLETED.
DIVISIONAL TROOPS.	
Headquarters	DARGNIES.
Signal Squadron	"
A.P.M.	"
A.D.M.S.	"
A.D.V.S.	"
O.C., A.S.C.	"
D.A.D.O.S.	"
No.9 L.A.C. Battery	BEAUCHAMPS.
S.A.A. Section, Amn: Park	OUST MAREST.
Supply Column	WOINCOURT.
Field Cashier	"
S.A.A. Section, Amn: Column	BEAUCHAMPS.
Mhow I.C.F.A.	BOUVAINCOURT.
Canadian C.F.A.	TULLY.
Sanitary Section	BOUVAINCOURT.
Field Squadron	EMBREVILLE.
Divisional School	AULT.
AMBALA BRIGADE.	
Brigade Headquarters	GAMACHES.
8th Hussars	GAMACHES - HELICOURT.
9th Horse	ANSENNE - MONCHAUX - RIEUX - SORENG - MONTIERES.
18th Lancers	BAZINVAL - LONGROY - Ste ADELAIDE - GOUSSEAUVILLE.
M.G. Squadron	TILLOY FLORIVILLE.
M.V. Section	GAMACHES.
Signal Troop	"
Bde. H.Q., A.S.C.	"
SEC'BAD BRIGADE.	
Brigade Headquarters	FEUQUIERES-on-VIMEU.
7th Dragoon Guards	FEUQUIERES - HOCQUELUS.
20th Horse	FRETTEMEULE - MAISNILRES - VISSE - MONCHELLET - HANDRECHY - HARCELAINES.
34th Horse	AIGNEVILLE - COURCELLES - COURTIEUX - CARROY.
M.G. Squadron	BUIGNY les GAMACHES.
M.V. Section	FEUQUIERES-on-VIMEU.
Signal Troop	------do-------
Bde. H.Q., A.S.C.	------do-------
CANADIAN BRIGADE.	
Brigade Headquarters	TULLY.
F.G. Horse	FRIAUCOURT - ALLENAY.
R.C. Dragoons	BOURSEVILLE - WOIGNARUE - MARTAIGNEVILLE - HAUTEBUT.
L.S. Horse	BETHENCOURT - YZENGREMER.
M.G. Squadron	MENESLIES.
M.V. Section	TULLY.
Signal Troop	"
Bde. H.Q., A.S.C.	"

TO/
   Cavalry Corps "Q".

        Forwarded.

                             Lieut-Col.
                   for G.O.C. 2nd Indian Cavalry Divn.

Copies to :-
     Brigades and Divisional Troops.

No.G/3498

Appx 89.

Headquarters 2nd Indian Cavalry Division.
14th. November, 1916.

BILLETING LIST.

UNIT.	WHERE BILLETED.

DIVISIONAL TROOPS.
```
Headquarters................DARGNIES.
Signal Squadron.............    "
A.P.M.......................    "
A.D.M.S.....................    "
A.D.V.S.....................    "
O.C., A.S.C.................    "
D.A.D.O.S...................    "
No.9 L.A.C.Battery..........EMBREVILLE.
Ammunition Park.............MERS.
Supply Column ) 1 Section...MERS.
              ) 1 Section...WOINCOURT.
Field Cashier...............MERS.
2nd Ind.R.H.A.Bde.Hdqrs.....INCHEVILLE.
"X" Battery R.H.A...........    "
"N" Battery R.H.A...........BEAUCHAMPS.
2nd Ind. Amn: Column........OUST HAREST.
R.C.H.A. Brigade............(ST.QUENTIN Lamotte-Croix-au-Bailly,
Canadian Amn: Column........(
Mhow I.C.F.A................BOUVAINCOURT.
Sec'bad I.C.F.A.............    "
Divisional Hospital.........    "
Sanitary Section............    "
Canadian C.F.A..............TULLY.
2nd Ind. Aux: H.T.Coy.......WOINCOURT.
Field Squadron..............EMBREVILLE.
Divisional School...........AULT.
```

AMBALA BRIGADE.
```
Brigade Headquarters........GAMACHES.
8th Hussars.................GAMACHES - ELLICOURT.
9th Horse...................FONTIERES - AUSENNE - MONCHAUX - RIEUX -
                                                        ( SORENG.
18th Lancers................LONGROY - BAZINVAL - Ste ADELAIDE -
                                      LE LIEU DIEU - GOUSSEAUVILLE.
M.G. Squadron...............TILLOY FLORIVILLE.
M.V. Section................L'EPINOY.
Signal Troop................GAMACHES.
Bde. H.Q., A.S.C............    "
```

SEC'BAD BRIGADE.
```
Brigade Headquarters........FEUQUIERES-en-VIMEU.
7th Dragoon Guards..........FEUQUIERES - HOCQUELUS.
20th Horse..................HARCELAINES - FRETTEMEULE - MAISNILRES -
                                      VISSE - MONCHELET - HANDRECHY.
34th Horse..................AIGNEVILLE - COURCELLES - COURTIEUX - CARROY.
M.G. Squadron...............BUIGNY les GAMACHES.
M.V. Section................FEUQUIERES-en-VIMEU.
Signal Troop................--------do--------
Bde. H.Q., A.S.C............--------do--------
```

CANADIAN BRIGADE.
```
Brigade Headquarters........TULLY.
F.G. Horse..................FRIAUCOURT - ALLENAY.
R.C. Dragoons...............BOURSEVILLE - WOIGNARUE - HARTAIGNEVILLE.
L.S. Horse..................BETHENCOURT - YZENGREMER.
M.G. Squadron...............MENESLIES.
M.V. Section................TULLY.
Signal Troop................    "           NOTE.- Headquarters of
Bde. H.Q., A.S.C............    "                  Units underlined.
```

Headquarters 2nd Indian Cavalry Division.
15th November 1915.

BILLETS.

To/ Cavalry Corps "G".

Forwarded.

[signature] H H Corbe
Lieut-Col:
for G.O.C. 2nd Indian Cavalry Division.

Copies to :-

Brigades & Divisional Troops.

DIVISIONAL TROOPS.
Headquarters.............................
Signal Squadron..........................
A.D.M.S..................................
A.D.V.S..................................
A.D.S....................................
C.R.E....................................
D.A.D.O.S................................
"N" Battery, R.H.A.......................BEUVILLE.
Ammunition Park..........................
} Section..............................INGOUVILLE.
Supply Column } Section..............................INGOUVILLE.
Field Cashier............................
2nd Ind.A.M.M.Mob.Vety.Sec...............INGOUVILLE.
"V" Battery R.H.........................
"W" Battery, R.H.A......................
2nd Ind. Amn. Column.....................OUST AMMER.
S.O.R.A. Brigade.........................
Canadian Armd Column.....................ST QUENTIN Lamottes-Croix-au-Bailly.
Sec: I.G.F.A............................BOUVAINCOURT.
Sec/ad I.G.F.A..........................   "
Divisional Hospital......................   "
Sanitary Section.........................   "
Canadian C.F.A..........................OUST.
2nd Indn.Amn.Park(new)..................BEUVAINCOURT.
Field Squadron..........................ERNEVILLE.
Divisional School.......................AULT.
AMBALA BRIGADE.
Brigade Headquarters....................LA KERRE.
8th Hussars.............................LA ACHRIE – HALICOURT.
9th Horse...............................CRIEL – MESNIL – BONCHAUX – MIEUX – SOMIS.
18th Lancers............................TOURHOY – JAINVAL – Ste ADELAIDE –
                                        LA LIEU DIEU – GOUESMAUVILLE.
H.q. Squadron..........................TILLEUX BLONVILLE.
F.V. Section...........................TRIPORT.
Signal Troop...........................PONGY.
Bde. H.Q., A.S.C.......................
SIALKOT BRIGADE.
Brigade Headquarters...................BLARGUIES-EM-VIMEU.
7th Dragoon Guards.....................FOUCAULT – INCQUEVILLE.
20th Horse.............................CRIEVILLE – FRETTEMEULE – MAISNIERES –
                                      VIGEN – FONTALET – HANDBECHT.
34th Horse.............................TREFAUVILLE – COURCELLES – COURTIEUX – CARROY.
H.Q. Squadron..........................MOTTEVILLE Les JAURNES.
F.V. Section...........................ENGUILBEAU-sur-VIMEU.
Signal Troop...........................   "
Bde. H.Q. A.S.C........................   "
CANADIAN BRIGADE.
Brigade Headquarters...................TULLY.
F.G. Horse.............................FATSCOURT – ALIBAY.
R.C. Dragoons..........................MONSUVITZ – NOIBEAUX – CHATAIGNEVILLE.
R.C. Horse.............................FRIUCOURT – FEGRINEUL.
R.C.A. Squadron........................TULLY.
F.V. Section...........................
Signal Troop...........................

NOTE:- Headquarters of Units underlined.
Bde. H.Q., A.S.C.......................

WAR ESTABLISHMENT.
Indian Cavalry Pioneer Battalion.

Detail	Personnel							Horses			Bicycles
	Officers	W.O's.	Clerks	S. Sergts & Sergts.	Artificiers	Rank and File	Total	Riding	Draught	Total	
H.Q. (excluding attached)	4	2	1	3	5	22	37	5	16	21	6
" attached		3		3		51	57	2		2	
3 Cos.(1 Br. & 2 Ind)	24	3		27		720	776		48	48	
Total Battalion	31	5	1	33	5	793	870	7	64	71	6

Composition in detail.

Detail	Officers	W.O's.	Clerks	S. Sergts & Sergts.	Artificiers	Rank and File	Total	Riding	Draught	Total	Bicycles
Headquarters.											
Lt. Col. or Major C.O.	1						1	1		1	
Maj. or Capt. 2nd. in C.	1						1	1		1	
Adjutant	1						1	1		1	
Quartermaster	1						1	1		1	
Sergeant Major		1					1				
Quartermaster Sergt.		1					1				
Orderly room Seggt.				1			1				
" " Clerk.			1				1				
Transport Sergt.				1			1	1		1	
Saddler					1		1				
Farrier Corporal					1		1				
Shoeing Smiths					2		2				
Salutri					1		1				
Drivers (Tpt.for vehicles)						7	7		16	16	
Batmen						5	5				
Cook						1	1				
Signallers-											6
Sergeant				1			1				
Corporal						1	1				
Privates						6	6				
Orderlies for M.O.(a)						2	2				
Attached.											
R.A.M.C. M.O.	1						1				
Sub Assistant Surgeon	1						1				
R.A.M.C.						2	2				
Ward Orderly (Indian)						1	1				
Sanitary Section				1		8	9				
Stretcher Bearers						18	18				
Gas Duties						1	1				
Armourer Sergt.				1			1				
Interpreter						1	1				
Field Squadron.											
Subaltern.	1						1	2		2	
Sergeant				1			1				
Sappers						18	18				
Batmen						2	2				
Total -	7	2	1	6	5	73	94	7	16	23	6

(a) 1 drives maltese cart or L.G.S. for M.O.

WAR ESTABLISHMENT
Indian Cavalry Pioneer Battalion (continued)

Detail	Personnel					Horses	
	Officers	W.O's.	S.Sergts. & Sergts.	Rank and File	Total	Draught Horses	Total
Company-British of 4 Platoons.							
Captain O.C.	1				1		
Subalterns (1 2nd.in C)	5				5		
Co. Sergeant Major		1			1		
Co. Qr.Mr.Sergt.			1		1		
Sergeants			8		8		
Cpls.or L/Cpls.				16	16		
Privates				204	204		
Drivers (Tpt.for veh's)				8	8	16	16
Batmen				6	6		
Cooks				2	2		
Total -	6	1	9	236	252	16	16
Company -Indian, of 4 Platoons.							
Captain O.C.	1				1		
Subalterns (1-2nd.in C)	3				3		
Indian Officers	5				5		
Co. Sergt. Major		1			1		
Co. Qr. Mr. Sergt.			1		1		
Sergeants			8		8		
Corporals or L/Cpls.				16	16		
Privates				204	204		
Drivers (Tpt.for vehicles)				8	8	16	16
Batmen				9	9		
Cooks				4	4		
Sweepers				2	2		
Total -	9	1	9	243	262	16	16

Transport.

	Vehicles.	Drivers.		
Headquarters.				
Limbd.G.S. in lieu of Maltese.	1	1	2	2
Carts Offrs.Mess	1	1	2	2
" Water	2	2	4	4
Wagons Limb.G.S.	1	2	4	4
Wagons G.S.	1	2	4	4
(Wagons limbd GS	6	12	24	24
(Wagons G.S.	3	6	12	12
3 Coys (Trav.Kitchens or				
(Wagons limb.GS	3	6	12	12
Total -	18	32	64	64

SECRET.

NOVEMBER, 1917.   Army Form C. 2118.

General Staff, 5th Cavalry Division.

WAR DIARY
or
INTELLIGENCE SUMMARY.
(Erase heading not required)

Instructions regarding War Diaries and Intelligence Summaries are contained in F. S. Regs., Part II. and the Staff Manual respectively. Title pages will be prepared in manuscript.

244

Place	Date	Hour	Summary of Events and Information	Remarks and references to Appendices
	NOVEMBER, 1917.			
FRESSIN. (LENS Sheet, 1/100,000.)	4th		Warning received by telephone from Cavalry Corps "Q" for Heavy Section, Reserve, 5th Cavalry Division, to be prepared to move South.	
do.	5th		Orders received by "Q" Division for Heavy Section, Reserve Park to move to BRIE, 5 miles South of PERONNE.	
do.	6th		Heavy Section, Reserve Park moves from Divisional Area to WAVRANS, 3 miles East of AUXI-LE-CHATEAU, en route for BRIE.	
do.	7th		Orders received from Cavalry Corps for the Division to move S.E. on 9th, 10th and 11th. Orders issued accordingly with orders for movement of Dismounted Reinforcements. (G.13) dated 7.11.17 and Operation Order 40 dated 7.11.17.	(Appx.137 (Appx.138
do.	8th		Revised Normal Operation Distribution issued (G.S.525/4 dated 8.11.17)	Appx.139
do.	9th		March Table for 11th issued with O.O.No.40 and amendment issued under G.17 are cancelled and G.19 issued - Ambala and Sec'bad Cavalry Brigades march to OUTREBOIS Area - Canadian Cavalry Brigade and Divisional Troops move up into area evacuated by Ambala and Sec'bad Cav. Brigades.	Appx.140 Appx.141
do.	10th		Divisional Report Centre closes at FRESSIN and opens at OCCOCHES. Chateau at 11 a.m. Operation Order No.40 is issued *furnishe* with March Table for completion of the move of Division. Heavy rain during the night 10th/11th. Canadian Cavalry Brigade and Divisional Troops arrive in OUTREBOIS Area. Ambala and Sec'bad Cavalry Brigades arrive in CONTAY - QUERRIEU Area. G.21 shewing revised billeting area, reference O.O.41.	Appx.142. Appx.143.
OCCOCHES	11th.		Divisional Report Centre closes at OCCOCHES and opens at QUERRIEU at 12 noon. Canadian Cav. Bde. and Divisional Troops move to CONTAY - QUERRIEU Area. Ambala and Sec'bad Cavalry Brigades move to Bray area for the evening.	

SECRET.

Army Form C. 2118.

WAR DIARY
INTELLIGENCE SUMMARY

GENERAL STAFF, 5TH CAVALRY DIVISION.

DECEMBER, 1917.

Instructions regarding War Diaries and Intelligence Summaries are contained in F.S. Regs., Part II. and the Staff Manual respectively. Title pages will be prepared in manuscript.

(Erase heading not required.)

Place	Date	Hour	Summary of Events and Information	Remarks and references to Appendices
	DECEMBER, 1917.			
QUERRIEU.	12th		Divisional Report Centre closed at QUERRIEU and opened at BOUVINCOURT at 3 p.m. Ambala and Sec'bad Cavalry Brigades march after dark and arrive in forward area about BOUVINCOURT. Canadian Cavalry Brigade and Divisional Troops leave CONTAY - QUERRIEU after dark and move into BRAY Area. All moves complete by 11 p.m. Weather fine with heavy mist.	
BOUVINCOURT	13th		Canadian Cavalry Brigade and Divisional Troops leave BRAY Area at dusk and march by night to BOUVINCOURT Area. Move is complete by 11 p.m. Heavy damp fog throughout the day.	
do.	14th		Divisional Headquarters, BOUVINCOURT. Ambala Cavalry Brigade, CARTIGNY. Sec'bad Cavalry Brigade, VRAIGNES. Canadian Cavalry Brigade, BOUCLY.	
do.	15th		Instructions regarding a future operation comprising the capture of CAMBRAI and the occupation of the quadrilateral CANAL DE L'ESCAUT - LA SENSEE RIVER - CANAL DU NORD are communicated secretly. A precis of the future operations is given in Appendix 144.	Appx.144
do.	16th		Cavalry Corps Conference for Divisional Commanders. Weather misty. Communication arrangements at and forward of FINS issued under G.S.713/4. Concentration	Appx.145
do.	17th		Divisional Conference for Brigadiers. Reconnaissance of forward area and tracks forward. Orders for move to forward concentration area (less March Table) are issued under 0.0.42. Weather dull and cloudy.	Appx.146
do.	18th		Corps Conference of G.S.O's 1. Operation Order No.43 issued. Reconnaissance of forward area concentration area and route to and in advance of that area. (N.E. of FINS around DESSART WOOD) Maps shewing how this area is allotted and tracks forward are issued to all concerned (G.S.713/14)	Appx.147 Appx.148
do.	19th		G.S.715/14 issued stating that no papers which would be of value to hostile intelligence should be taken forward of our own trench line in the event of a break through. G.S.713/16 issued reporting ZERO hour to be 6.20 a.m. on 20th inst. On the night of 19th/20th the Division marched North from BOUVINCOURT Area to forward concentration area N.E. of FINS.	Appx.149 Appx.150
FINS.	20th & 21st.		An account of the operations on these two dates is given in Appendix 150. The weather throughout was mild but wet and misty.	Appx.151

SECRET.

WAR DIARY or **INTELLIGENCE SUMMARY**

Army Form C. 2118.

GENERAL STAFF, 5TH CAVALRY DIVISION.

DECEMBER, 1917.

(Erase heading not required.)

Instructions regarding War Diaries and Intelligence Summaries are contained in F.S. Regs., Part II and the Staff Manual respectively. Title pages will be prepared in manuscript.

Place	Date	Hour	Summary of Events and Information	Remarks and references to Appendices
FINS EQUANCOURT.	22nd		The Division was withdrawn from the vicinity of MASNIERES and MARCOING and arrived in the area N.W. of FINS, Ambala Cavalry Brigade rejoining the Division from the 1st Cavalry Division at this place. O.O. No.44 issued.	Appx.152
SUZANNE.	23rd		The Division marched to the BRAY Area in accordance with Divisional Operation Order No.44. The Division is put on one hour's notice to move. Divisional Headquarters SUZANNE. The Light Section, Reserve Park remained in FINS Area for duty in connection with Tanks Corps.	
do.	24th			
do.	25th		The Division is taken off one hour's notice to move.	
do.	26th		Telephone warning order received from Cavalry Corps that the Division will move to MONCHY LAGACHE (D.Area) on the 27th. Warning order issued accordingly. O.O. No.45 issued for move of the Division to MONCHY LAGACHE (D.Area)	Appx.153
MONCHY LAGACHE	27th		Rain and sleet during the night 26th/27th. The Division moved to "D" Area. All troops arrived by 4.30 p.m. Divisional Headquarters MONCHY LAGACHE. Windy weather and some showers.	
do.	28th		Warning Order received from Cavalry Corps for the Division to be prepared to take over the line from River OMIGNON to GRAND PRIEL WOOD at an early date. G.S.722 issued accordingly. Orders received accordingly for all personnel and material of R.F.C. with the Division to be handed over. Orders issued accordingly to R.F.C. Liaison Officer.	Appx.154
do.	29th		Conference at Divisional Headquarters 9.20 a.m. regarding taking over the line. Preliminary orders issued as to the formation of the Divisional School at CORBIE. 1st Course to open on December 10th. O.O. No.46 issued with reference to taking over the line. (This order was not carried out on account of the Division going into action elsewhere on the 30th November.)	Appx.155
do.	30th		The Division ordered to move at once about 9 a.m. Divisional Operation Order No.47 issued. An account of the operations of the Division from November 30th to December 3rd is attached as an Appendix to War Diary for the Month of December.	Appx.156

N.T.Holt~
Lt-Colonel, G.S.
5th Cavalry Division.

appx 138

```
-----------
S E C R E T.                                            No. G.13.
-----------
```

Headquarters, 5th Cavalry Division,

7th November, 1917.

To/
    Canadian Cavalry Brigade.
    Sec'bad   "   "
    Ambala   "   "
    17th Brigade, R.H.A.
    R.C.H.A. Brigade.
    17th Brigade R.H.A. Ammunition Column.
    R.C.H.A. Ammunition Column.
    5th Field Squadron, R.E.
    5th Signal Squadron;
    5th Cav. Aux. M.T. Company.
    5th Cav. Reserve Park.
    A.D.M.S.
    O.C., A.S.C.
    A.P.M.
    Camp Commandant.
    A.A.& Q.M.G.
    A.D.C.
----

1.   The Division will move South on November 9th and 10th.

2.   The Ambala and Sec'bad Brigades will move on the 9th inst. to OUTREBOIS Area and on the same day Canadian Cavalry Brigade and Divisional Troops will move to the area vacated by these Brigades.

3.   Further orders follow.

4.   ACKNOWLEDGE.

[signature]

Lt-Colonel, G.S.,

5th Cavalry Division.

SECRET.

App/138

Copy No. 23

5TH CAVALRY DIVISION.

OPERATION ORDER NO. 40.

Reference Map 1/100,000.   Dated 7th November, 1917.

1.   The Division will move SOUTH on November 9th, 10th and 11th in accordance with attached March Table.

Orders for the March of the Division on the 12th inst. will be issued later.

2.   "B" Echelons will march with Brigades and Divisional Troops.

3.   Divisional Troops will march on the 10th and following days under orders to be issued by C.R.H.A. through Divn'l Signals.

4.   Motor Ambulances and Sanitary Section will march under orders to be issued by A.D.M.S.

5.   Divisional Headquarters will close at FRESSIN at 11 a.m. on the 10th inst. and open at OCCOCHES at the same hour.

6.   ACKNOWLEDGE.

H. T. Hodgson
Lt-Colonel, G.S.,
5th Cavalry Division.

Issued by D.R. at 9 p.m.

To/
  Normal O.O. Distribution Nos. 1 to 23.
                              .. No. 24.
  Cavalry Corps ....

5TH CAVALRY DIVISION.

March Table for Nov. 9th - (issued with Operation Order No.40).

FORMATION OR UNIT.	STARTING POINT.	TIME.	ROUTE.	DESTINATION.	REMARKS.
Ambala Cav Bde. Bhow I.C.F.A.	PLUMOISON Church.	9 a.m.	CONCHY SUR CANCHE - BONNIERES.	OUTREBOIS Area, Billets to be allotted by D.A.A. & Q.M.G.	To be East of ABBEVILLE-HESDIN road by 10.30 am
Sec'bad Cav Bde. "N" Battery R.H.A. Sec'bad I.C.F.A.	HESDIN Railway Station.	10.30 a.m.	LABROYE - AUXI LE CHATEAU.	---- do ----	In moving to starting point, troops of Sec'bad Bde will not use HESDIN-MARESQUEL road.
Canadian Cav Bde. R.C.H.A. Bde. Canadian C.F.A.	Brigade arrangements.	10 a.m.	No restrictions.	BOUIN-AUBIN ST.VAAST-CONTES-ECQUEMICOURT-MARESQUEL-BEAURAINVILLE-LOISON.	Canadian M.G. Sqdn. will remain night of 8/9th at LESPINOY.
17th Bde R.H.A. Ammn. Column. R.C.F.A. Ammn. Column.	VERCHOCQ.		FRUGES - RUISSEAU-VILLE - LA LOGE.	CAVRON ST.MARTIN-WAMBERCOURT.	
Reserve Park (less Heavy Section). Hqrs.A.H.T.Coy.	HERLY.	10.30 a.m.	HENOVELLE - EMBRY.	OFFIN-HESMOND-BOUBERS.	
5th Field Squadron.	REMTY.	10 a.m.	COUPELLE VIEILLE - CREQUY.	LEBIEZ.	

5TH CAVALRY DIVISION.

March Table for Nov.10th – (issued with Operation Order No.40).

FORMATION OR UNIT.	STARTING POINT.	TIME.	ROUTE.	DESTINATION.	REMARKS.
Canadian Cav Bde. R.C.H.A. Bde. Canadian C.F.A.	PLUMOISON Church.	9 a.m.	LABROYE – AUXI LE CHATEAU.	OUTREBOIS Area. Billets to be allotted by D.A.A.& Q.M.G.	
Divnl.H.Q.(less motors). Signal Sqn.(" "). Hqrs 17th Bde R.H.A. 5th Field Squadron R.E. 17th Bde R.H.A. Ammn.Col. R.C.H.A. Bde Ammn Col. Reserve Park(less Heavy Section). Hqrs A.H.T. Coy.	X Roads at W of Pt. WAMIN.	9 a.m.	HESDIN–2nd N in MARCONNE–ST.GEORGES– CAUCHY SUR CANCHE– BONNIERES.	---- do ----	
Ambala Cav Bde. Mhow I.C.F.A.	T roads just N. of H in HEM.	9.30 a.m.	–BEAUQUESNE – TOUTENCOURT.	DOULLENS CONTAY Area. Billets to be allotted by D.A.A.& Q.M.G.	
Sec'bad Cav Bde. N.Bty.RHA Sec'bad I.C.F.A.	FIENVILLERS.	9.30 a.m.	– le VAL DE MAISON.	CANDAS – ---- do ----	

5TH CAVALRY DIVISION.

March Table for Nov.11th - (issued with Operation Order No.40).

FORMATION OR UNIT.	STARTING POINT.	TIME.	ROUTE.	DESTINATION.	REMARKS.
Canadian Cav.Bde. R.C.H.A. Bde. Canadian C.F.A.	FIENVILLERS.	9.30 a.m.	CANDAS - le VAL DE MAISON.	CONTAY Area.	Not to enter CONTAY Area before 4.30 p.m.
Divnl.Hors.(less motors). Signal Sqn.("). Hqrs 17th Bde R.H.A. 5th Field Squadron. 17th Bde R.H.A. Ammn.Col. R.C.H.A. Brigade Ammn Col. Hqrs A.H.T. Coy. Reserve Park(less Heavy Section).	T roads just N. of H in HEN.	9.30 a.m.	DOULLENS- BEAUQUESNE- TOUTENCOURT.	-- do --	-- do --

Subject:- OPERATION ORDERS.   APPX 39   No. G.S.525/4.

Headquarters, 5th Cavalry Division,
8th November, 1917.

1. The following revised NORMAL O.O. DISTRIBUTION is issued for guidance :-

	Copy No.
Canadian Cavalry Brigade	1
Secibad " "	2
Ambala " "	3
17th Brigade, R.H.A.	4
R.C.H.A. Brigade	5
17th Bde. R.H.A. Ammunition Col.	6
Field Squadron	7
Signal Squadron	8
A.A.& Q.M.G.	9 and 10
A.D.M.S.	11
O.C., A.S.C.	12 and 13
Aux. H.T. Company	14
Reserve Park	15
A.P.M.	16
Camp Commandant	17
A.D.C.	18
G.S.O.1	19
Office	20
War Diary	21 to 23.

NOTE.-
(1) A.D.V.S. will see and initial A.D.M.S's copy.
(2) Officer Interpreter will see and initial A.P.M's copy.
(3) A separate copy will not normally be issued to R.C.H.A. Brigade Ammunition Column.

2. All earlier correspondence on above may now be destroyed.

3. When units or details are grouped with Brigades for the March they will be billeted by Brigades concerned unless orders to the contrary are issued.

[signature]

Lt-Colonel, G.S,
5th Cavalry Division.

To/
O.O. Distribution.
A.D.V.S.
Officer Interpreter.
R.C.H.A. Brigade Ammunition Column.

S E C R E T.　　　　　　　　　　　　　　　　　　　　　　　No.G.17.

Headquarters, 5th Cavalry Division,
9th November, 1917.

To/
    O.O. Distribution.

Reference Divisional Operation Order No.40 dated 7th Nov.

In March Table for 10th, "Route" Column :-

    Add to Route for Ambala Cavalry Brigade and attached Troops - " CONTAY - AGNICOURT."

    Add to Route for Sec'bad Cavalry Brigade and attached Troops - "RUBEMPRE - MOLLIENS-AU-BOIS".

In March Table for 11th, "Route" Column :-

    Add to Route for Canadian Cavalry Brigade and attached Troops- "RUBEMPRE - MOLLIENS-AU-BOIS.

    Add to Route for Divisional Troops - "CONTAY - FRANVILLERS".

                                        Captain, G.S.,
                                      5th Cavalry Division.

--*-*-*
S E C R E T.
--*-*-*-*

No.G/19.

Headquarters, 5th Cavalry Division.
9th November 1917.

To/ O.O. Distribution
plus Cavalry Corps.

appx 141

March Table for 11th November, issued with Operation Order No.40, as amended by this office No.G/17 dated 9/11/17, is cancelled and the following substituted :-

March Table for November 11th.

FORMATION OR UNIT.	STARTING POINT.	TIME.	ROUTE.	DESTINATION.	REMARKS.
Canadian Cav Bde. R.C.H.A. Bde. Canadian C.F.A.	T roads just N. of H in HEM.	11 a.m.	DOULLENS - BEAUQUESNE - TOUTENCOURT - CONTAY.	CONTAY Area.	Not to enter CONTAY Area before 4.30 p.m.
Divnl.Hqrs(less motors) Signal Sqn(" ") H.Q.17th Bde R.H.A. 5th Field Sqdn. 17th Bde Ammn Col. R.C.H.A. Ammn Col. H.Q. A.H.T. Coy. Reserve Park(less Heavy Section).	X roads 1,000 yards S. of O in LONGUEVILLETTE.	10 a.m.	CANDAS - le VAL DE MAISON - ROBEMPRE - MOLIENS AU BOIS.	-- do --	-- do --

Acknowledge

N. T. Nicholson
Lieut-Colonel, G.S.,
5th Cavalry Division.

Appx 14²

SECRET. Copy No. 23

5TH CAVALRY DIVISION.
OPERATION ORDER No. 41.

Reference Map 1/100,000. Dated 10th November, 1917.

1.   March Table for completion of Move of Division is attached.

2.   Railheads :-

      OUTREBOIS Area ... ... CANDAS.
      CONTAY Area ... ... CORBIE.
      BRAY Area ... ... LA FLAQUE.
      Final Area ... ... TINCOURT.

3.   Completion of moves will be reported by wire or Special D.R. to Divisional Headquarters.

4.   Divisional Report Centre closes OCCOCHES at 12 noon on 11th inst., and opens at QUERRIEU at same hour.

5.   ACKNOWLEDGE.

W. T. Hodgson
Lt-Colonel, G.S.,
5th Cavalry Division.

Issued by D.R. at 10 am

To/
    Normal O.O. Distribution. Nos. 1 to 23.
    Cavalry Corps .... No. 24.

5TH CAVALRY DIVISION.

March Table for night 11/12th - (issued with Operation Order No.41).

FORMATION OR UNIT.	STARTING POINT.	TIME.	ROUTE.	DESTINATION.	REMARKS.
Ambala Cav Bde. "N" Battery R.H.A. Sec'had I.C.F.A.	FRANVILLERS.	4 p.m. 11th.	BUIRE SUR L'ANCRE - MORLANCOURT.	SUZANNE - BRAY SUR SOMME - LANEUVILLE - ETINEHEM - CHIPILLY.	Accommodation for 1 Btn. is reserved for Third Army at Bray
Sec'had Cav Bde. "N" Battery R.H.A. Sec'had I.C.F.A.	ROAD JUNCTION ½ MILE S. OF P. IN PONT NOYELLES	4 p.m. 11th.	LAMOTTE - VAUX SUR SOMME - SAILLY LAURETTE - MORCOURT	CAPPY - FROISSY - CHUIGNOLLES - PROYART - MERICOURT - MORCOURT.	

A.T.H.

5TH CAVALRY DIVISION.

March Table for night 12/13th - (Issued with Operation Order No.41).

FORMATION OR UNIT.	STARTING POINT.	TIME.	ROUTE.	DESTINATION.	REMARKS.
Ambala Cav Bde. Phow I.C.F.A.	T roads ½ mile S. of 1st E in ECLUSIER.	4.30 p.m. 12th inst.	HERBECOURT - BIACHES - PERONNE - QUES of BOIS DES FLACQUES.	Billets from A.A.& Q.M.G.	
Sec'bad Cav Bde. "N" Battery R.H.A. Sec'bad I.C.F.A.	X roads ¾ mile S. of P in PROYART.	4.30 p.m. 12th inst.	ESTREES - BRIE - VRAIGNES.	Billets from A.A.& Q.M.G.	
Canadian Cav Bde. R.C.H.A. Brigade. Canadian C.F.A.	FRANVILLERS.	4 p.m. 12th inst.	BUIRE SUR L'ANCRE - MORLANCOURT.	SUZANNE - BRAY SUR SOMME - LAMOTTE - ETINEHEM - CHIPILLY.	Accomodation for 1 Btn.in BRAY is reserved by Third Army.
Divnl.H.Q.(less motors) Signal Sqn.(") H.Q. 17th Bde R.H.A. 5th Field Squadron. 17th Bde R.H.A. Ammn.Col. R.C.H.A. Bde Ammn Col. H.Q. A.H.T. Coy Reserve Park(less Heavy Section).	Road junction ½ mile S. of P in PONT NOYELLES.	4 p.m. 12th inst.	LA NEUVILLE - VAUX SUR SOMME - SAILLY LAURETTE - MORCOURT.	CAPPY - FROISSY - CHUIGNOLIES - PROYART - MERICOURT - MORCOURT.	Billets to be allotted by D.A.A.& Q.M.G.

h. T. H.

5TH CAVALRY DIVISION.

March Table for night 13/14th - (issued with Operation Order No.41).

FORMATION OR UNIT.	STARTING POINT.	TIME.	ROUTE.	DESTINATION.	REMARKS.
Canadian Cav Bde. R.C.H.A. Brigade. Canadian C.F.A.	T roads ½ mile S. of 1st E in ECLUSIER.	4.30 p.m.	HERBECOURT - BIACHES - PERONNE - QUES of BOIS DES FLACQUES.	Billets from A.A. & Q.M.G.	
Divnl. H.Q. Group.	X roads ¾ mile S. of P in PROYART.	4.30 p.m.	ESTREES - BRIE - VRAIGNES.	Billets from A.A. & Q.M.G.	

h.G.H.

App. 143

SECRET.   No. G.21.

Headquarters, 5th Cavalry Division,
10th November, 1917.

To/
O.C. Distribution.

Reference March Table for night 12th/13th, issued with Operation Order No.41 dated 10th inst., the destination of Units will be as follows, and not as stated therein :-

UNIT.	DESTINATION.
Divisional Headquarters.	SUZANNE Village.
Signal Squadron.	- do -
Hdqrs: 17th Brigade, R.H.A.	- do -
5th Field Squadron A.H.T. Company Reserve Park (less Heavy Section)	CAPPY and BOIS OLIMPE. Representatives of these units will meet D.A.&Q.M.G. at CAPPY CHURCH at 12 NOON on 12TH.
17th Bde. R.H.A. Ammunition Column R.C.H.A. Ammunition Column	CHUIGNOLLES.
Supply Column	PROYART.
Canadian Cavalry Brigade R.C.H.A. & DE. CANADIAN C.F.A.	Camp 17, NEAR SUZANNE - BRAY-SUR-SOMME - LANEUVILLE - ETINEHEM - CHIPILLY - (inclusive) & MERICOURT-SUR-SOMME

ACKNOWLEDGE.

[signature]
for Lt-Colonel, G.S.,
5th Cavalry Division.

COPY

Orders for Troops. Appendix L

Map references to 1/40,000 maps.

(1) "A" Troop will march with Squadron H.Q. in Ambala Cav Bde Group.
"B" Troop will march with Canadian Cav Bde. Group.
"C" Troop will march with Secunderabad Cav Bde Group.

(2) Lieut GREATHEAD and 2/Lieut MATHEWSON will join their troops in concentration area.

(3) On arrival in concentration area a hot meal will be cooked and eaten. Horses will be watered and fed. Troops will water under Bde arrangements. Water points are available for Brigades from 6-20 am to 8-20 am. 8lb oats will be issued in concentration area. After feeding 4 lbs oats nosebags will be made up to 12 lbs from forage on G.S. wagons.

(4) Casualty reports to be sent daily at 6pm to Squadron H.Q. (H.Q. Ambala Bde)

(5) Iron rations will not be eaten without the order of G.O.C. Bde.

(6) No papers, orders, letters etc will be carried which could be useful to the enemy.

(7) All reports and messages must show time of despatch.

(8) While Division is in concentration area, Divnl. HQ will be at SUCRERIE, FINS. on the advance being ordered it will move to R 9 d. hent. N.E of VILLERS PLUICH. Subsequent report centres at
    (a) point midway between MARCOING and RUMILLY
    (b) LA BELLE ETOILE.
    (c) LA CROISETTE (S.W of CAUROIR)
    (d) Hill 80 (N.E. of TILLOY).

(9) Medical. Advanced dressing station, RUMILLY after commencement of cavalry operations.

(10) "B" Troop will assist Canadian Bde in cutting telegraphs and railways close to CAMBRAI on the E, N.E, & N. as the Bde moves round the town. When the Bde has taken up it's position N of CAMBRAI "B" Troop should be concentrated and rested so as to be available to rejoin Squadron HQ or undertake new work.

(11) "A" Troop will be responsible for preparing for demolition the following Bridges over the SENSEE
    (a) Road Bridge N of HEM-LENGLET
    (b) PONT-RADE (S of WASNES)
    (c) Road Bridge N of PAILLENCOURT.

(1' cont'd) "C" Troop will be responsible for preparing for demolition the following bridges over the SENSEE
    (a) Railway Bridge at AUBENCHEUL
    (b) Road Bridge at AUBENCHEUL
    (c) Road Bridge at FRESSIES.

This work is of great importance and must be completed as quickly as possible. When this is done a few men will be left at each bridge to blow if ordered and the remainder of troops should be concentrated and rested. Bridges will not be blown without the order of the G.O.C. Brigade. Completion of preparation will be reported to me without delay.

The tactical situation will decide whether "A" Troop will accompany Ambala Bde. to their bridges or whether they will be sent ahead to join the right flank of Secunderabad Bde. on the line of the SENSEE.

        (Signed) C G WOOLNER
                      Major RE
              O.C. 5° Field Coy. RE

SECRET.   appx 149   No.G.S.713/14.

                                        Headquarters, 5th Cavalry Division,
                                                  19th November, 1917.

To/   O.O. Distribution.

    The Major-General, Commanding, wishes all Officers and other ranks reminded that they must not, on any account, cross the line of our trenches with any papers, written matter or maps, that would be of value to the hostile Intelligence.

    All operation orders, instructions regarding operations, objective maps, etc., are to be destroyed before the Division crosses our trench line.

                                        W. T. Hodgson
                                                  Lt-Colonel, G.S.,
                                                  5th Cavalry Division.

Appx.15D.

S E C R E T. 　　　　　　　　　　　　　　　No.G.S.713/16.

　　　　　　　　　　　　　Headquarters, 5th Cavalry Division,

　　　　　　　　　　　　　　　　　19th November, 1917.

To/
　　O.O. Distribution.
　　Major R.H.O'D. PATERSON, 34th Horse.
　　Capt. F.H. WILKES, R.C. Dragoons.
　　Lieut. C.R.H. BENNETT, F.G. Horse.
　　Capt. A. HIATT, 7th Dragoon Guards.

　　　　ZERO hour will be 6.20 a.m. on 20th November.

　　　　ACKNOWLEDGE.

　　　　　　　　　　　　　　　　　[signature]

　　　　　　　　　　　　　　　　　LT-Colonel, G.S.,

　　　　　　　　　　　　　　　　　5th Cavalry Division.

SECRET.

No.G.S.71304.

Headquarters, 5th Cavalry Division,

16th November, 1917.

To/
O.O. Distribution.

COMMUNICATIONS.

1. **At Zero Hour.** Divisional Report Centre N.E. of FINS, near SUGAR FACTORY, will have direct telegraph and telephone communication to Cavalry Corps. Communication to Brigades will be by motor cyclist and mounted D.R.s.

2. **When the Division is ordered to advance.** The available means of communication will be :-

   From Division to Cavalry Corps :-

   (i)   Telegraph and Telephone from first forward report centre only.
   (ii) Wireless.
   (iii) Despatch Riders - motor and horse.
   (iv) Pigeons.
   (v)   Visual to Kite Balloon after dusk.

   From Division to Brigades :-

   (i)   Visual.
   (ii) Despatch Riders - Mounted at first, motor cyclist later.
   (iii) Telegraph and Telephone on existing wires when put through.

   From Regiments and Brigades to Division.

   (i)   Visual.
   (ii) Mounted Despatch Riders.
   (iii) Contact Aeroplanes.
   (iv) Pigeons.
   (v)   Telegraph and Telephone on existing wires.
   (vi) Visual to Corps Kite Balloon after dusk.

3. **First Forward Report Centre** at R.8.d.central, N.E. of VILLERS PLUICH, will be connected by telegraph and telephone to Cavalry Corps. A Visual Station will be established at about R.9b.10.7, and will be connected by wire, if possible, to Report Centre at R.8.d.central. This station should be able to communicate with the following points :-

   (i)   G.6.c.4.1. - i.e. Y road at first N in NIERGNIES.
   (ii) G.3.c.1.4. - i.e. X roads at Pt.96, 1 mile N. of RUMILLY.
   (iii) L.15.d.6.8.- X roads at B. DES NEUF, 1 mile N.W. of (MARCOING.
   (iv) L.19.central - Spur just E. of FLESQUIERES (for 1st Cav. Division).

   A relay post of D.R's will be at R.8.d.central for working back to Corps (motor cyclist) and forward to Brigades (mounted).

4. ....

S E C R E T.   No. G.S.713/4 (cont'd)
----

4. Second Forward Report Centre, at point about midway between
MARCOING and RUMILLY, will have Wireless communication to Cavalry
Corps. Telegraph and Telephone communication will be available
from MARCOING as soon as the cables laid by Corps from R.8.d.central
reach MARCOING.
    Communication forward will be by mounted D.R. only, until
motor cyclists can come up. There appears to be no opportunities
for Visual from this point.

5. Third Forward Report Centre, at LA BELLE ETOILE, will again
have Wireless communication to Cavalry Corps, and can dispose of
telegrams to Corps by Mounted D.R. to MARCOING. Forward, Visual
may be possible to ESCADOEUVRES and ground South, and to Hill ½
mile N.W. of THUN-LEVEQUE.

6. Fourth Forward Report Centre, at INN (LA CROISETTE) S.W. of
CAUROIR communication to Corps as in (5). Visual to ESCADOEUVRES
and possibly to Hill 80 N.E. of TILLOY.

7. Fifth Forward Report Centre, at Hill 80 N.E. of TILLOY.
Wireless to Corps. Visual to the following points :- (i) S.W. end
of Hill at T in THUN-LEVEQUE; (ii) Cross roads N.E. of EPINOY; and
possibly (iii) Mill S. of EPINOY. Lines will be laid to Brigades
as soon as possible.

8. Hostile Communications. The Brigade Signalling Officer,
Canadian Cavalry Brigade, should detach an experienced linesman
to the advanced regiment to assist in cutting telegraph and
telephone wires. These lines should not be cut indiscriminately
as they may be very useful to us afterwards. It is sufficient to
cut out one bay on each route met with.

9. Pigeons. Each Brigade will be given 16 birds before leaving
the concentration area N.E. of FINS. A reserve of 12 birds will
be kept at Divisional Headquarters. Pigeons fly to lofts near ROISEL
which are connected by telegraph and telephone to Cavalry Corps.
    Pigeons cannot be relied on to "home" if released before sunrise,
less than one hour before sunset, or in thick mist or fog.

10. Contact Aeroplanes. Regimental, Brigade and Divisional Headquarters will be able to communicate with contact aeroplanes by
lamp and panel. At each Divisional Report Centre mentioned above
a Message Dropping Centre will be established for receiving messages
from aeroplanes.

11. Visual to Kite Balloon. The Corps Kite Balloon will ascend near
TRESCAULT at dusk on "Z" day.

12. Visual cannot be relied upon in rainy or misty weather.

13. Particular attention is directed to para 3, Table F,
of Organisation Tables. (No G.S.524)

                                    W. T. Hodgson Lt-Colonel, G.S.,
                                                   5th Cavalry Division.

SECRET

Not to be taken in front of present H.Q.
Appx. 144 BOUVINCOURT area
17/11/17

PRECIS OF OPERATIONS.

1. The HOSTILE Line to be attacked is at present held as follows:-

IX Corps (with Headquarters at ESCADOEUVRES) with 54th Division holding line from LA VACQUERIE (exclusive) to HAVRINCOURT (inclusive) and 204th Division from HAVRINCOURT (exclusive) to a point 1½-miles N. of BOURSIES. That part of the line between GONNELIEU and LA VACQUERIE is held by 6th Regt. 9th Division.(Res.) Headquarters of 54th and 204th Divisions are in CAMBRAI and of 9th Res. Division at BEAUVOIS.

2. Information goes to show that the hostile reserves in the district are few and probably as follows :-

(Apart from resting Battalions of neighbouring Divisions in line)
 (a) The area N. of CAMBRAI,) distances of 3 and 22 miles
 (b) The LILLE-DOUAI area.) respectively from CAMBRAI.
It is possible but unlikely that there is a Division at (a) and probable that there is a Division at (b).

3. On Z day, a surprise attack is to be made on a front of 12,000 yards from 1,000-yards E. of GONNELIEU to 1,000-yards E. of HERMIES by 5 Divisions out of the line and part of 2 holding the line, assisted by 360 tanks.
 The features of the attack are :-
 (a) There is nothing at present to show that the enemy is in
   any way suspicious of attack.
 (b) There will be no preliminary bombardment.
 (c) Wire cutting is to be done by tanks.

4. The object of the operation is - to break the enemy's defensive system by a coup de main - to pass the cavalry through - to seize CAMBRAI, BOURLON WOOD and the passages over the SENSEE RIVER and to cut off the troops holding the front line between HAVRINCOURT and that River.
 The following subsidiary operations are to take place on Z day :-
 (a) By VII Corps - Capture of enemy trenches between MALAKOFF
       and GILLEMONT FARMS.
 (b) By VII and IV Corps - Feint attacks with smoke and dummies.

5. The main operations, ie., the III and IV Corps operations, will be carried out in three stages :-
 (a) First Stage:-
    The Infantry attack on the German organised
  lines, including the capture of the Canal crossings at
  MASNIERES and MARCOING and of the MASNIERES - BEAUREVOIR
  line North and East of those places.

 (b) Second Stage.
    The advance of the cavalry to isolate
  CAMBRAI and to seize the crossings over the River SENSEE,
  and of the IV Corps to capture BOURLON WOOD.

 (c) Third Stage..
    The clearing of CAMBRAI and of the quadrilateral CANAL de L'ESCAUT - SENSEE RIVER - CANAL du NORD and the overthrow of the German Divisions thus cut off.

           THE TASK OF THE CAVALRY.----------

THE TASK OF THE CAVALRY.

At Zero, 5th Cavalry Division will be just N.E. of FINS - 1st Cav Division just N.W. of FINS (under orders of IV Corps) - 2nd Cavalry Div about VILLERS FAUCON ready to follow 5th Cavalry Division.

3rd and 4th Cavalry Divisions ready to move to areas N.W. and N.E. of FINS respectively, vacated by 1st and 5th Cavalry Divisions.

Action of 5th Cavalry Division.

On order for forward movement being received, 5th Cavalry Division pushes forward its advance guard and when Cavalry Liaison Officer with Infantry reports that they have gained objectives of 1st Stage, the Division will push on its objectives with speed and vigour.:-

(a) To isolate CAMBRAI from the E. and N.E. by seizing the high ground NIERGNIES to CAUROIR and the high ground TILLOY - CUVILLERS - THUN LEVEQUE, commanding the crossings over the CANAL l'ESCAUT at ESWARS and MORENCHIES.

(b) To seize the crossings over the SENSEE River between PAILLENCOURT and AUBENCHEUL AU BAC both inclusive.

During these operations all enemy telegraph and telephone lines and following railways will be cut :-
CAMBRAI - BUSIGNY.
CAMBRAI - LE CATEAU.
CAMBRAI - SOLESMES.
CAMBRAI - LOURCHES.
SOLESMES - HASPES - VALENCIENNES

Action of 1st Cavalry Division.

The probable action of the 1st Cav. Divn. will comprise isolation of CAMBRAI from the West and the gaining of touch with 5th Cavalry Division to the North of CAMBRAI.

Action of 2nd Cavalry Division.

The 2nd Cavalry Division will follow 5th Cavalry Division and will take over objectives held by that Division as far as crossing at ESWARS - MORENCHIES, commencing by relieving troops on high ground NIERGIES - AWOINGT. The infantry will extend their defensive flank to LA BELLE ETOILE, taking over that part from 2nd Cavalry Division which will continue operating N.E. extending its left to IWUY and LIEU ST AMAND and blocking crossing over Canal l'ESCAUT at BOUCHAIN.

SECRET.   Copy No. 23

appx 147

5TH CAVALRY DIVISION.

OPERATION ORDER NO.43.

Reference Map
1/100,000 and
1/40,000.
                                              Dated.- 18th November, 1917.

1. On "Z" day a surprise attack is to be made on a front of 12,000 yards, from a point 1,000 yards E. of GONNELIEU to a point 1,000 yards E. of HERMIES.

The attack will be made by five Divisions out of the line and by part of two Divisions holding the line, assisted by 360 Tanks.

Map "A" is attached shewing :- (+ List attached)

    (a) Frontages of Corps and Divisions.
    (b) Objectives.
    (c) Headquarters of Divisions.

The following subsidiary operations will be carried out with a view to assisting the main operation :-

    (a) By the VII Corps. The capture of the enemy trenches between MALAKOFF and GILLEMONT Farms.

    (b) By the VII and IV Corps. Feint attack with smoke and dummies.

2. The object of the operation is to break the enemy's defensive system by a coup de main - to pass the cavalry through the break - to seize CAMBRAI and BOURLON WOOD and the passages over the SENSEE River and to cut off the troops holding the front line between HAVRINCOURT and that River.

3. As soon as the infantry has secured MARCOING and MASNIERES and the BEAUREVOIR - MASNIERES line, the cavalry will push forward to surround and isolate CAMBRAI by :-

    (a) Seizing points of tactical importance and blocking all exits from the Town.

    (b) By cutting the railway communication running into CAMBRAI.

4. The objectives of the Cavalry Divisions will be :-

    5TH CAVALRY DIVISION.

    (a) To isolate CAMBRAI from the E., N.E., and N. by :-

        (i) Seizing the high ground NIERGNIES to CAUROIR and the high ground TILLOY - CUVILLERS - THUN LEVEQUE commanding the crossings over the CANAL L'ESCAUT at ESWARS and MORENCHIES.

        (ii) By blocking all exits from the Town.

        (iii) By destroying the following Railways :-

            1. LE CATEAU - CAMBRAI.
            2. SOLESMES - CAMBRAI.
            3. SOLESMES - HASPRES - VALENCIENNES - DOUAI - CAMBRAI.
            4. LOURCHES - CAMBRAI,

        (b) ....

S E C R E T.   O.O. No.43 (cont'd).

    (b) Seize the crossings over the SENSEE River between PAILLENCOURT and AUBENCHEUL AU BAC (both inclusive) and, as soon as the situation admits, the crossing over the SENSEE at PALLUEL.

5. The 1ST CAVALRY DIVISION will move via METZ EN COUTURE - TRESCAULT - RIBECOURT and debouch between MARCOING and RIBECOURT, with the object of isolating CAMBRAI from W. and N.W. by occupying positions to the West and Northwest of CAMBRAI as far as railway in square S.20.d., West of TILLOY.

6. The 2ND CAVALRY DIVISION will follow the 5th Cavalry Division, two Brigades moving via LA VACQUERIE and MASNIERES and the remainder of the Division via VILLERS PLUICH and MARCOING.
    The objectives of the 2nd Cavalry Division will be :-

    (a) To take over the positions held by the 5th Cavalry Division as far as, and inclusive of, the crossings over the Canal L'ESCAUT at ESWARS and MORENCHIES, commencing by relieving the troops holding the high ground at NIERGNIES and AWOINGT.

    (b) To push patrols E. and N.E. in the area ESNES, WAMBAIX, ESTOURNEL, CARNIERES, AVESNES, IWUY and cut the BUSIGNY - CAMBRAI Railway at a point as far East as possible.

    (c) When relieved by the infantry of the IIIrd Corps, to push forward N.E., extending its left to IWUY and LIEU ST AMAND, and blocking the crossing over the Canal L'ESCAUT at BOUCHAIN.

    (d) The destruction of the Railway Bridge over the canal at NEUVILLE SUR L'ESCAUT.

7. When the Cavalry is ordered to advance, the Division will move forward as under :-

    (a) ADVANCED GUARD. CANADIAN CAVALRY BRIGADE, strength as in margin.

O.C.- Br.Gen.J.E.B.SEELY.)
Canadian Cavalry Brigade.) ROUTE.-
"B" Battery, R.C.H.A.   )   GOUZEAUCOURT - LA VACQUERIE -
No.4 M.M.G. Battery.   )   MASNIERES (via KAVANAGH ROAD from
1 Fd.Troop,5th Field Sqn.)   Q.30.b.5.3.)
Pack Sect.Can.Cav.Fd.Amb.)
Light Section, Amm. Col.) OBJECTIVES.

    (i) To seize the high ground NIERGNIES to CAUROIR and the high ground TILLOY - CUVILLERS - THUN LEVEQUE commanding the crossings over the Canal L'ESCAUT at ESWARS and MORENCHIES.

    (ii) To block all exits from CAMBRAI.

    (iii) To destroy the following railways :-

        1. LE CATEAU - CAMBRAI.
        2. SOLESMES - CAMBRAI.
        3. SOLESMES - HASPRES - VALENCIENNES - DOUAI - CAMBRAI.
        4. LOURCHES - CAMBRAI.

S E C R E T.   O.O. No.43(cont'd).

The Canadian Cavalry Brigade and Sec'bad Cavalry Brigade will each detail one squadron for a special mission. The Commanders of these squadrons will report at Divisional Headquarters at noon on "Y" day for instructions.

In the advance to its objective the Canadian Cavalry Brigade will be responsible for the protection of both flanks.

The Right Flank Guard of the Canadian Cavalry Brigade will be taken over by troops of the 5th Cavalry Brigade (2nd Cavalry Division) as soon as these troops can get up.

The Left Flank Guard will remain in position and cover the exits from CAMBRAI and the left flank of the Division until relieved by the 4th Cavalry Brigade (2nd Cavalry Division).

In the advance from MASNIERES all telegraph and telephone lines will be cut.

On gaining the crossing over the L'ESCAUT Canal at MORENCHIES, touch will be obtained with 1st Cavalry Division in the neighbourhood of TILLOY.

(b) MAIN BODY. Order of march as in margin, will advance at the same time.

Sec'bad Cav. Bde. Group.)
Divisional H.Q. Group.   ) ROUTE.-
Ambala Cav. Bde. Group.)   Track from Q.32.d.3.3. - QUEENS
No.1 "A" Echelon Group.)   CROSS - Q.23.central - VILLERS
                              PLOUICH - MARCOING Railway Bridge.

(c) The Sec'bad Cavalry Brigade after crossing the Canal at MARCOING will march on NIERGNIES and, when the Canadian Cavalry Brigade has gained the crossings at MORENCHIES and ESWARS, the Sec'bad Cavalry Brigade will cross at ESWARS and advance with following objective :-

Objective.-
Seize the crossing over the River SENSEE between PAILLENCOURT and AUBENCHEUL AU BAC (both inclusive) and, as soon as the situation admits, the crossing over the SENSEE at PALLUEL.

8. No.2 "A" Echelon will follow the same route as the Main Body of the Division but will not move until after the fighting troops of the 2nd Cavalry Division. An officer detailed by Cavalry Corps will give the order for the advance of No.2 "A" Echelon.

9. MEDICAL. The Light Sections of the Cavalry Field Ambulances will march at the head of and with No.2 "A" Echelon.
Further Medical Instructions are attached.

10. The following units will remain at FINS under the orders of Cavalry Corps :-
    (a) Heavy Sections, Field Ambulances.
    (b) 17th Bde., R.H.A. Ammunition Col.(less Light Sects.)
    (c) R.C.H.A. Bde. Ammunition Column (less Light Sects.).
    (d) Light Sections, Reserve Park.
                                                    11 ....

SECRET.   O.O. No.43 (cont'd).

./1. Prisoners of War will be sent to Divisional Report Centre where the A.P.M. will form a Collecting Station.

./2. Instructions regarding Communications have been issued separately under G.S.713/4 dated 16th November, 1917.

./3 As soon as the Division leaves FINS the Divisional Report Centre will move to R.9.b.8.8., N.E. of VILLERS PLOUICH.

./4 ACKNOWLEDGE.

                                 Lt-Colonel, G.S.,

                               5th Cavalry Division.

Issued by D.R. at 9-30am

To/
    O.O. Distribution Nos 1 to 23.
    Cavalry Corps .... No.24.
    1st Cavalry Division .. " 25.
    2nd Cavalry Division .. " 26.
    3rd Cavalry Division .. " 27.
    4th Cavalry Division .. " 28.
    Lieut.BENNETT,F.G.Horse." 29.
    Capt. A.HIATT, 7th D.G's" 30.

SECRET.   MEDICAL INSTRUCTIONS.

(Issued with Operation Order No.43.)

Pack Mounted Sections, which alone for the present represent their respective C.F.A's, move with Brigades, and under Brigade orders. Cavalry Field Ambulances, less Pack Mounted Section, march together as Divisional Troops, to the position of concentration at FINS.

Heavy Sections of Cavalry Field Ambulances remain at FINS. Light Sections will move forward with No.2 "A" Echelons of Brigades.

Bearer parties from each C.F.A., consisting of 1 Medical Officer and 24 other ranks with 12 stretchers and all available wheeled carriers will proceed on foot to RUMILLY as soon as the Cavalry advance begins, on which point all wounded able to walk or ride will be directed in the first stage of operations. This post will form the nucleus of an Advanced Dressing Station and from it Bearer parties will be available for the collection of wounded under the orders of their respective Commanding Officers as circumstances dictate. Ambulance transport moving with No.2 "A" Echelons will rendezvous here as soon as conditions permit, and evacuate wounded in accordance with instructions which will issue from A.D.M.S.

Advanced Dressing Stations and Regimental Aid Posts in the Infantry Area are as under :-

Reference Map 1/40,000, Sheet 57.C.

20th Division.

Regimental Aid Posts .... R.20.a.2.9. (XVI Ravine)
                              R.25.d.4.9.

Relay Posts .... R.25.a.8.4. (Hotel Cecil)
                              R.19.d.3.7. (near XV Ravine)

Advanced Dressing Station..... GOUZEAUCOURT. Q.36.d.6.9.

After Zero hour others will be established at R.20.a.5.9. and at R.26.c.4.9.

Walking Wounded Station ...... GOUZEAUCOURT. Q.36.b.1.4.

At Zero hour Advanced Regimental Aid Posts will be opened at R.20.d.7.4. and R.14.a.8.9.

12th Division.

                                                    (Cheshire Quarry.)
Regimental Aid Posts .... R.26.d.7.1., R.33.b.8.5., R.34.c.3.9.

Advanced Dressing Station .... VILLERS-GUISLAINS. X.9.a.3.4.

6th Division.

Regimental Aid Posts .... BEAUCAMP.   ) Map reference not
                              VILLERS-PLUICH) available.

Advanced Dressing Station .... Q.30.b.2.8.

IIIrd Corps Main Dressing Station and Collecting Post for Walking Wounded is at V.18.c.0.7. on FINS - NURLU Road.

Appx N 8

S E C R E T.   No.G.S.713/11.

Headquarters, 5th Cavalry Division.

18th November 1917.

To/
O.O. Distribution.

1. Reference O.C. No.42, para 1. Herewith March Table.

2. Divisional Report Centre will close at BOUVINCOURT at Zero - 5 hrs 30 mns and open at Sugar Factory, FINS, at same hour.

3. Maps (3 per Brigade) showing routes of advance beyond FINS are attached. (only)

H. T. Hodgson
Lieut-Colonel, G.S.,
5th Cavalry Division.

Major R.H.O'D. PATERSON. 30th Horse. - 24.
Capt F.H. WILKES. RCD's --- 25.
Lieut BENNETT. F.G.H. ---- 26.
Capt HIATT. ykD.G's ----- 24.

5TH CAVALRY DIVISION.

March Table - (Issued with G.S. No.713/11, dated 18/11/17).

FORMATION OR UNIT.	STARTING POINT.	TIME.	ROUTE.	DESTINATION.	REMARKS.
Canadian Cav Bde Group.	Junction of Roads ½ mile N. of TINCOURT.	Zero - 5 hrs 50 mns.	LONGAVESNES - LIERAMONT - NURLU - EQUANCOURT - Northern end of FINS.	Forward Concentration area, N.E. of FINS.	
Sec'ded Cav Bde Group.	--- do ---	Zero - 4 hrs 40 mns.	--- do ---	--- do ---	
Divnl. H.Q. Group.	--- do ---	Zero - 4 hrs 5 mns.	--- do ---	--- do ---	
Ambala Cav Bde Group.	--- do ---	Zero - 4 hrs	--- do ---	--- do ---	To move to starting point via BRUSLE and BOUCLY.
No.1 "A" Echelon.	--- do ---	Zero - 3hrs 20 mns.	--- do ---	--- do ---	
No.2 "A" Echelon.	--- do ---	Zero - 3 hrs 10 mns.	--- do ---	--- do ---	
Cav Field Ambulance Group.	--- do ---	ZERO - 2 hrs 35 mns.	--- do ---	--- do ---	
17th Bde RHA Amn Col (less Light Sections). R.C.H.A. Bde Amn Col (less Light Sections).	--- do ---	Zero - 2 hrs 25 mns.	--- do ---	--- do ---	
Reserve Park (less Light Sections).	--- do ---	Zero - 2 hrs 20 mns.	--- do ---	--- do ---	

TO BE DESTROYED ON LEAVING THIS AREA

SECRET

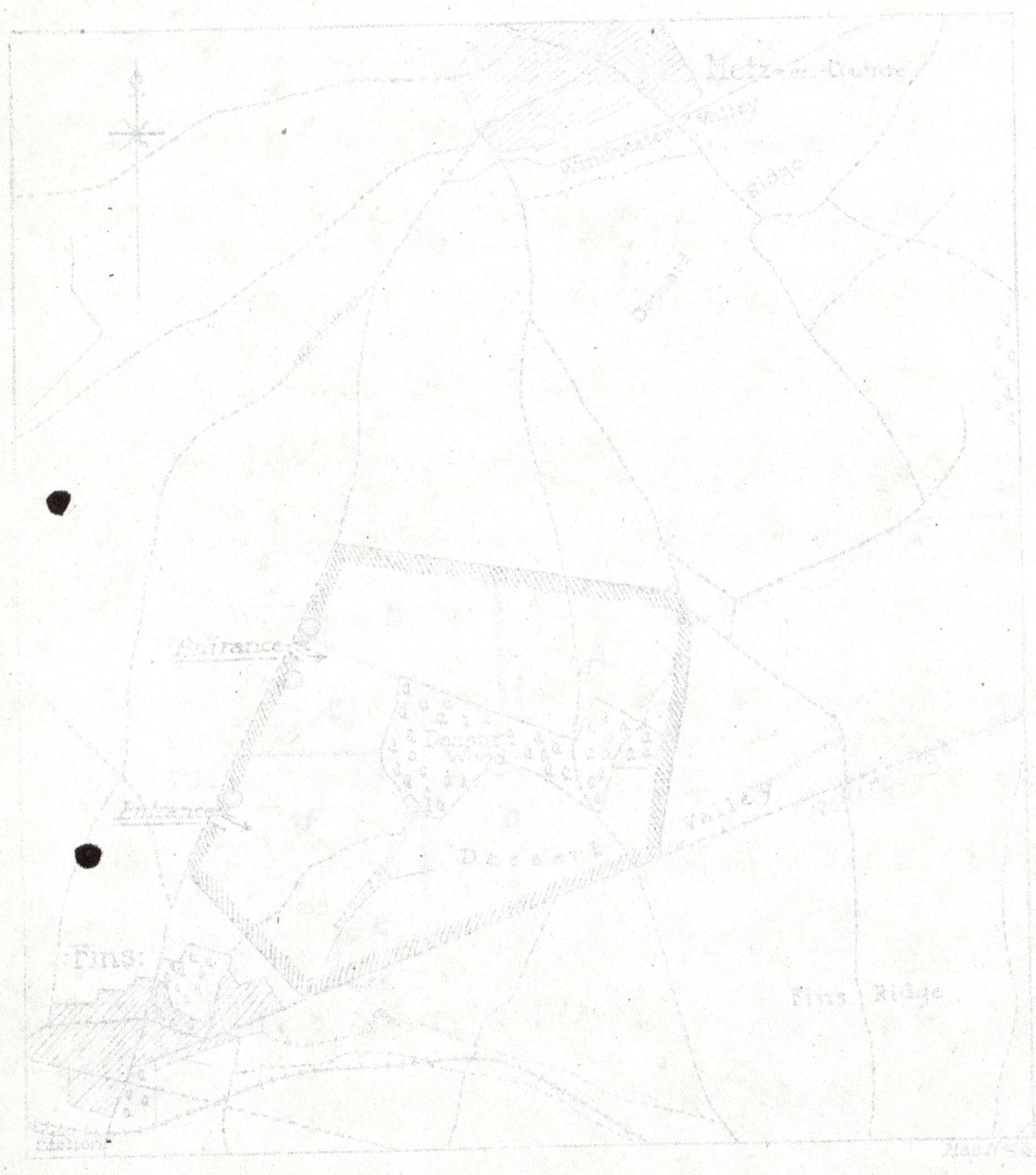

TO BE DESTROYED BEFORE LEAVING AREA SHEWN ON ATTACHED MAP.

S E C R E T.   GROUPING FOR MOVE FORWARD.

CANADIAN CAVALRY BRIGADE GROUP.

AREA
"D".
- Canadian Cavalry Brigade.
- "B" Battery, R.C.H.A.
- 1 Field Troop, R.E.
- No.4 M.M.G. Battery.
- 1 Light Section, Ammunition Column.
- Pack Section, Canadian Cavalry Field Ambulance.

SEC'BAD CAVALRY BRIGADE GROUP.

AREA
"A".
- Sec'bad Cavalry Brigade.
- "N" Battery, R.H.A.
- 1 Light Section, Ammunition Column.
- 1 Field Troop, R.E.
- Pack Section, Sec'bad Cav. Field Ambulance.

DIVISIONAL HEADQUARTERS GROUP.

AREA
"E".
- Groups I, II and III.
- 5th Signal Squadron.
- Hdqrs., 17th Brigade, R.H.A. and R.C.H.A. Brigade.
- 2 Troops, Yorkshire Dragoons.

AMBALA CAVALRY BRIGADE GROUP.

AREA.
"B".
- Ambala Cavalry Brigade.
- "A" Battery, R.C.H.A.
- 5th Field Squadron, less 2 troops.
- 1 Light Section, Ammunition Column.
- Pack Section, Lhow Cav. Field Ambulance.

No.1 "A" ECHELON GROUP.

O.C. - Lieut. BENNETT, Fort Garry Horse.

AREA
"C".
- No.1 "A" Echelon Canadian Cavalry Brigade Group.
- "   "   "   Sec'bad Cavalry Brigade Group.
- "   "   "   Divisional Headquarters Group.
- "   "   "   Ambala Cavalry Brigade Group.

No.2 "B" ECHELON GROUP.

O.C. - Capt. A. HIATT, 7th Dragoon Guards.

AREA
"F".
- No.2 "B" Echelon Canadian Cavalry Brigade Group.
- "   "   "   Sec'bad Cavalry Brigade Group.
- "   "   "   Divisional Headquarters Group.
- "   "   "   Ambala Cavalry Brigade Group.

CAVALRY FIELD AMBULANCE GROUP.

AREA
"F".
- Canadian Cavalry Field Ambulance (less Pack Section).
- Sec'bad Cavalry Field Ambulance (less Pack Section).
- Lhow Cavalry Field Ambulance (less Pack Section).

AREA "F". 17th Brigade R.H.A. Ammn. Column (less Light Sects.)

AREA "F". R.C.H.A. Brigade Ammn. Column (less Light Sections).

AREA "F". Reserve Park (less *HEAVY* Light Sections).

appx 15

5TH CAVALRY DIVISION.

Summary of Operations.

November 20th to 22nd.

Date.

20th. 8.50 a.m. The Division saddled up ready to move from Forward Concentration Area N.E. of FINS.

" 11.50 a.m. Telephone message from Cavalry Corps received ordering the Division to move forward pushing patrols up to the advancing Infantry. (Cav. Corps G.214)

" 11.55 a.m. Orders were issued by Gallopers for Division to move forward (5th Cav. Divn. G.A.508)

" 12.5 p.m. Canadian Cavalry Brigade advanced via GOUZEAUCOURT - KAVANAGH Road on MASNIERES.
Sec'bad Cavalry Brigade followed by Divisional Headquarters, Ambala Cavalry Brigade and No.1 "A" Echelon advanced by track to VILLERS PLOUICH on MARCOING.

" 1.39 p.m. Advanced Guard Canadian Cavalry Brigade reached Southern outskirts of MASNIERES and G.O.C. Canadian Cavalry Brigade got into touch with the G.O.C. of the 88th Infantry Brigade.
Situation at MASNIERES at that time was as follows :-
Troops of the 88th Infantry Brigade and one Tank had gained a footing in the village under a certain amount of hostile artillery and M.G. fire.

" 1.45 p.m. The Sec'bad Brigade Advanced Guard reached Southern outskirts of MARCOING with advanced patrols in touch with troops of the 87th Infantry Brigade.
The situation in MARCOING at that time was as follows :- The village was clear of the enemy but Railway Bridge in L.23.a. was held by hostile by rifle and M.G. fire.

" 2.0 p.m. Advanced Guard Squadron Sec'bad Cavalry Brigade (7th Dragoon Guards) crossed the L'ESCAUT River and Canal by bridge in L.23.d. gaining touch with the Infantry who were at the time held up at the Railway cutting in L.23b.
This Squadron finding that the MASNIERES - BEAUREVOIR line was still held by the enemy dismounted to prolong the right flank of the Infantry and so fill a gap which had been caused by the failure of one Company to get up.
The remainder of the Sec'bad Brigade was mounted and ready to move in L.28.c.& d.

" 2.15 p.m. MASNIERES River Bridge reported intact and clear of enemy. G.O.C. Canadian Cavalry Brigade ordered Advanced Guard Regiment, Fort Garry Horse, to cross. For action of this Squadron see Appendix "A".

5th Cavalry Division.   Summary of Operations (cont'd).

Date.	Time.	
20th.	2.15 p.m.	Finding advance East of MARCOING impracticable for the Brigade owing to the presence of enemy in MASNIERES - BEAUREVOIR line, G.O.C., Sec'bad Cavalry Brigade decided to try and cross at NOYELLES sur L'ESCAUT, and sent one Squadron, 7th Dragoon Guards under Captain Lane, to reconnoitre and make good the village and crossings at NOYELLES. The report of the action of this squadron is attached as Appendix "B".
"	3.0 p.m.	The G.O.C., 5th Cavalry Division, deciding that it was now too late for the Division to fulfil the role allotted to it for that day, asked the Cavalry Corps for instructions and received the reply given in G.228. Orders were consequently issued to Brigades to the effect that the Canadian Cavalry Brigade, if able to cross, would make RUMILLY and the high ground in G.22. and 23 its objective, but that this advance was only to be made provided that Sec'bad Cavalry were in a position to support it. (G.A.604).
"	3.0 p.m.	NOYELLES occupied by Captain LANE'S Squadron, 7th Dragoon Guards, vide Appendix "B".
"	3.30 p.m.	"B" Squadron, Fort Garry Horse crossed the canal at MASNIERES - see Appendix "A".
"	4.0 p.m.	Message received from Sec'bad Cavalry Brigade (B.M.6) asking whether the Brigade was to cross at NOYELLES.
"	4.10 p.m.	Sec'bad Cavalry Brigade instructed to cross at NOYELLES provided our infantry hold the MASNIERES - BEAUREVOIR line (G.A.600).
"	4.45 p.m.	Situation about MARCOING. Infantry held up in front of MASNIERES - BEAUREVOIR line and digging in at L.24.c. - L.23.d. - just East of Railway Station - L.18.c.
"	5.0 p.m.	Infantry in front of and to the East of MARCOING ask for dismounted help from Sec'bad Cavalry Brigade otherwise they may lose their positions during the night.
"	5.25 p.m.	Sec'bad Cavalry Brigade ordered to give every assistance the Infantry to enable them to hold their line (G.A.605).
"	6.20 p.m.	Sec'bad Brigade reports situation about MARCOING as follows :- "Infantry held up L.24.c. - L.23.d. - MARCOING Station - L.18.c. Trenches in G.13.b. and 14.c. are heavily wired. Do not consider the Brigade can support the proposed advance of the Canadians" vide (G.A.604).
"	6.50 p.m.	Sec'bad Cavalry Brigade withdrew from MARCOING to R.3.a. where they bivouacked for the night.
	7.45 p.m.	....

5th Cavalry Division.   Summary of Operations (cont'd).

Date.	Time.	
20th.	7.45 p.m.	Verbal message received from the Corps on the telephone for the Division to withdraw during the night to the FINS area.
"	8.0 p.m.	Orders for the withdrawal of Division issued under G.A.605.
"	9.30 p.m.	Phone message from Cavalry Corps received (G.236) cancelling the withdrawal of the Division and giving instructions for the Division to remain in its present position and be prepared to carry out its original role after an attack on the MASNIERES - BEAUREVOIR line by the IIIrd Corps on the following morning.
"	9.30 p.m.	Orders issued (G.A.608) in compliance with G.236 above.
"	11.30 p.m.	The Canadian Cavalry Brigade, which had marched before receipt of counter order regarding the withdrawal of the Division was stopped on KAVANAGH Road and returned to L.35.b. where it bivouacked for the night.
21st	6.0 a.m.	Sec'bad Cavalry Brigade moved to R.2.d. to a less exposed position.
"	7.0 a.m.	Squadron of 7th Dragoon Guards in NOYELLES relieved by Squadron 18th Hussars and rejoined their Regiment.
"	8.45 a.m.	From Liaison Officers with Infantry Brigades, it was ascertained that the attack referred to in Cav. Corps G.236 was to take place at 11 a.m.
"	10.45 a.m.	Division saddled up and ready to move.
"	11.0 a.m.	Infantry attack launched by 88th and 87th Brigades against MASNIERES - BEAUREVOIR line and at the same time a hostile counter-attack developed from N.E. against right of the 88th Brigade.
"	11.30 a.m.	G.O.C., 88th Brigade called on Canadian Cavalry Bde. for assistance in repelling hostile counter-attack - four M.G's were placed at the disposal of the G.O.C. 88th Brigade.
"	12.45 p.m.	Report received that the attack of the 87th Brigade was only partially successful and that by their counter-attack on the right of the 88th Brigade the Germans had succeeded in gaining some ground on the RUES DES VIGNES spur and at MON PLAISIR Farm.
"	2.30 p.m.	Instructions received from Cavalry Corps on phone that the Ambala Cavalry Brigade was to pass to the 1st Cavalry Division the G.O.C. of that Brigade being ordered to report to 1st Cavalry Division at L.21. central as soon as possible. (Cav. Corps G.257).

Orders issued ....

5th Cavalry Division. Summary of Operations (cont'd).

Date. Time.

21st. 2.30 p.m. Orders issued for the move of Ambala Cavalry Brigade
(cont'd)   to 1st Cavalry Division. (G.A.618).
              Canadian Cavalry Brigade and Sec'bad Cavalry Brigade
              ordered to be ready to withdraw.

"   5.0 p.m. Instructions received on phone from Cavalry Corps that
              the Division less Ambala Cavalry Brigade was to remain
              as situated for the night and act as reserve to the
              Infantry.

Midnight 21st/22nd. G.263 from Cavalry Corps received ordering the
              Division to remain in the vicinity of MASNIERES and
              MARCOING in order to take advantage of any opport-
              unity which might occur from the capture of RUMILLY
              by the IIIrd Corps on the following day and also
              giving instructions as regards the relief of the
              Division by the 4th Cavalry Division.

22nd 12.30 a.m. The above message - G.263 - cancelled by verbal
              message on telephone and the Division ordered to
              withdraw to area N.W. of FINS, move to be completed
              by 12 noon. (G.A.246) Orders issued accordingly.

"   5.45 a.m. Division commenced withdrawal to area N.W. of FINS.
              Ambala Cavalry Brigade rejoined Division in the area
              N.W. of FINS on the morning of the 22nd.

Appendix "A".

Report on action of "B" Squadron, Fort Garry Horse

on November 20th., 1917.

At 2.15 p.m. on November 20th., 1917, a report having been received that the bridge over the River L'ESCAUT at MASNIERES was intact the G.O.C. Canadian Cavalry Brigade ordered the Fort Garry Horse which was the Advanced Guard Regiment of the Brigade to cross. The leading Squadron of this Regiment crossed the River by the Bridge on the GOUZEAUCOURT - CAMBRAI Road at 2.30 p.m. but on arriving at the bridge over the L'ESCAUT Canal on the same road further progress was found impossible. The bridge over the Canal at this point had given way or had been blown up as a tank was crossing it.
A reconnaissance was then made and another bridge in G.27. was found which with some improvement was made passable for Cavalry. The repair of this bridge was carried out by civilian labour and men of the Canadian M.G. Squadron, the work being initiated and directed by Major Walker of the Canadian M.G. Squadron. Shortly after 3 p.m. the bridge was completed and at 3.30 p.m. the O.C. Fort Garry Horse ordered the Advanced Guard Squadron of his Regiment to cross. Throughout the repair of this bridge and the crossing of the Canal by this Squadron the hostile rifle and M.G. fire was heavy.
At the time that this Squadron was crossing General Greenly (Cmdg. 2nd Cavalry Division) had an interview with General Seely and gave instructions that no advance was to be made that evening as there was not sufficient daylight left to enable cavalry to operate.
In accordance with these instructions General Seely sent an order to the O.C., Fort Garry Horse not to cross the canal and to withdraw any of his troops that had already crossed.
This order did not reach Colonel Paterson, the O.C., Fort Garry Horse, until after "B" Squadron of his Regiment had crossed. Colonel Paterson halted the remaining two Squadrons and rode forward to recall the leading Squadron. "B" Squadron had however by this time crossed and Colonel Paterson having lamed his horse by jumping into a sunken road was unable to catch them up. Lieut. H. Strachan's account of the action of "B" Squadron is as follows :-

"   On the 20th November at 3.30 p.m. I accompanied "B" Squadron Fort Garry Horse, with Captain Campbell in Command (on a special mission).
"   The Squadron left MASNIERES by the Exit at 3.30 p.m. and crossed the Canal by a temporary bridge, after crossing some marsh ground under machine gun fire. We moved North from the Canal and entered the enemy's line by a gap cut in the wire by our own troops. At this point Capt. Campbell and one or two other ranks were hit, also by M.G. fire. We moved North and encountered the camouflaged road Southeast of RUMILLY. This we cut under M.G. fire and the Squadron went through in Sections. On crossing the road the Squadron formed line of troop columns and immediately encountered a battery of field guns. Two guns were unmanned, the crew destroyed another and the other fired one round point blank which missed. The Squadron charged the battery and those of the crew who were not killed, surrendered. The prisoners were left to be dealt with by our supports, and the Squadron then took on the enemy's infantry, who were retreating disorganised. These either took refuge in shell holes or
"   surrendered or were killed.
"   This operation ahd been carried out at the gallop and on nearing RUMILLY, the Squadron which had had about 40 casualties from M.G. fire from flanking block houses was brought down to a walk, and as we then seemed to be isolated, I took up a position in a sunken road 1 kilometre East of RUMILLY and held out till dark.

While waiting ....

Appendix "A" (cont'd).

"   While waiting for dark three telephone lines leading East were
cut. A message was sent from here in duplicate to O.C., Fort Garry
Horse and both bearers got in. After dark I decided to abandon
horses and fight our way out, all horses except five being wounded.
The horses were stampeded in order to attract the attention of the
machine guns, and the Squadron moved off in the direction of
MASNIERES. Four parties of the enemy were encountered on the
journey and retired leaving casualties. These were mostly working
parties. On reaching the wire through which   we advanced,
the Squadron had seven prisoners and two more were taken at the wire.
At this point the party became separated and Lieut. Cowen who had
previously been hit reached home with nineteen other ranks and nine
prisoners. I with one Officer and eleven other ranks entered
MASNIERES at the Eastern entrance and moved down the main street
and crossed the canal on the broken bridge where a sniper was
encountered and hit, but not captured. There were no further
casualties.

"   I would give as a conservative estimate the enemy's casualties
as 40 going out and 60 on the return trip."

Appendix "B".

Report by Captain Lane, 7th Dragoon Guards,
on Capture of NOYELLES by one Squadron 7th
Dragoon Guards.

At about 2.15 p.m. on the 20th November I was ordered to take my Squadron and make good the village and crossings at NOYELLES sur L'ESCAUT.

Lieut. Dawkins and one troop was detailed as Advance Guard. They advanced rapidly to point L.11.d. where they came under rifle and M.G. fire.

I decided to gallop the village with troops at 40 yards distance.

The M.G. fire was high and did no damage.

The advance was successful and the village was captured at 3.0 p.m. Total captures - 25 prisoners. 10 of whom were found hiding in the village.

Prisoners were handed over to a party of about 50 Infantry who came into NOYELLES shortly after the Squadron entered.

Telegraph lines were cut leading to CAMBRAI, CANTAING and CANTIGNEUL. The main bridge over the L'ESCAUT River had been blown up but I discovered three small wooden bridges (trestle) still standing over the River just S. of the Chateau in L.11.b. and held them against possible enemy enterprise.

At 4.30 p.m. a bridge was found standing over the Canal de L'ESCAUT. This bridge could have been crossed by the Brigade but it was under fire from the trench line in G.1.d. and L.6.c. which was I saw occupied by the enemy; my patrols were heavily fired on and made to retire.

The party of 50 Infantry referred to above assisted me to clear up the village and at 5 p.m. after gaining touch with the 4th Dragoon Guards just E. of BOIS DE NEUF I left the village to return to my Regiment.

On my return I received instructions to return to NOYELLES dismounted and was placed at the disposal of the O.C., 2nd Royal Fusiliers for outpost duty during the night.

I was relieved by a squadron of 18th Hussars at 5 a.m. on November 21st.

The night of the 20th/21st was uneventful except for spasmodic bombing along the canal.

5TH CAVALRY DIVISION.

MARCH TABLE — (ISSUED WITH OPERATION ORDER No 44)

FORMATION OR UNIT.	STARTING POINT.	TIME	ROUTE.	DESTINATION	REMARKS.
AMBALA CAV. BDE. MHOW CAV. FD. AMB. LCE.	EASTERN EXIT OF ETRICOURT ON ETRICOURT - EQUANCOURT ROAD	7 A.M.	ETRICOURT - MANANCOURT - MOISLAINS - BOUCHAVESNES - CLERY - MARICOURT.	BILLETS TO BE ALLOTTED BY D.A.A.&Q.M.G.	
CANADIAN CAV. BDE. R.C.H.A. BDE (AND LIGHT SECTION AMMN. COLUMN). CANADIAN CAV. FD. AM. LCE.	— DITTO —	7.50 A.M.	— ditto —	— DITTO —	
DIVISIONAL HDQRS. H.Q. 17TH BDE. R.H.A. 5TH SIGNAL SQDN. 5TH FIELD SQDN.	— DITTO —	9 A.M.	— DITTO —	— DITTO —	
SEC'BAD CAV. BDE. 'N' BTY. R.H.A. (AND LIGHT SECT. AMMN. COL). SEC'BAD CAV. FD. AM. BCE.	— DITTO —	9.10 A.M.	— DITTO —	— DITTO —	
17TH BDE. R.H.A. AMMN. COL. (LESS LIGHT SECTS) R.C.H.A. AMMN. COL. (LESS LIGHT SECTS.)	— DITTO —	10.10 A.M.	— DITTO —	— DITTO —	
RESERVE PARK (LESS HEAVY SECTION)	— DITTO —	10.25 A.M.	— DITTO —	— DITTO —	TAIL TO BE CLEAR OF ETRICOURT BY 11 A.M.

App. 153

SECRET.   Copy No. 21

5TH CAVALRY DIVISION

OPERATION ORDER No. 45.

Ref. Map 1/100,000   Dated 26th November 1917.

1. The Division will move to the "D" Area (MONCHY LAGACHE) to-morrow, the 27th inst., in accordance with the attached March Table.

2. Divisional Hdqrs Group will march under orders of C.R.H.A.

3. "B" Echelon will march with Brigades and units of Divisional Troops.

4. Light Sections, Ammunition Column will march with Brigades and, on arriving at ESTREES-EN-CHAUSSEE, they will march direct to the Ammunition Column Area at MONCHY LAGACHE.

5. Motor Ambulances and Sanitary Section will move under orders to be issued by A.D.M.S.

6. Reserve Park Heavy Section and Dismounted Reinforcements will join the Division on the 27TH under orders to be issued by Cavalry Corps. On arrival in MONCHY LAGACHE Area Dismounted Reinforcements will rejoin their units.

7. A distance of 200 yards will be maintained between Regiments and Batteries and similar units.

8. The Divisional Report Centre will close at SUZANNE at 11. a.m. on 27th and open at MONCHY LAGACHE at the same hour.

9. ACKNOWLEDGE

N. T. Hodgson
Lt. Colonel
G.S.
5th Cavalry Division

Issued by D.R. at 8.30 pm.

20/1   O.O. Distribution 1-23.   Nos.

5TH CAVALRY DIVISION.

MARCH TABLE Issued with O.O. No 46.

FORMATION OR UNIT.	STARTING POINT	TIME.	ROUTE.	DESTINATION.	REMARKS.
17th Bde. Amm. Col. (Searchlight Sections) R.H.A. Bde Amm. Col. (two Light Sections).	East E. of BOIS OLIMPE	8 A.M.	VILLERS CARBONNEL – BRIE – ESTRÉES-EN-CHAUSSEE.	MONCHY LAGACHE	To be clear of ESTREES DENIECOURT by 10 A.M.
Divisional H.Q. H.Q. 17th Bde. R.H.Q. 5th Signal Sqdn. 5th Field Sqdn. H.Q. A.H.T. Coy.	Fork roads ½ mile SOUTH of MARICOURT.	9 A.M.	CLERY – ST. DENIS – DOINGT – road junction ½ mile E. of ESTREES -EN-CHAUSSEE.	MONCHY LAGACHE (AREA).	Head to reach road junction ½ mile E. of ESTREES-EN-CHAUSSEE at 2.30 p.m.
Canadian Cav. Bde. R.C.H.A. Bde. and Light Section Ammt. Column. Can. Cav. Field Ambulance.	Fork roads ½ mile SOUTH of MARICOURT.	9.30 A.M.	CLERY – ST. DENIS – DOINGT – Road junction ½ mile E. of ESTREES-EN-CHAUSSEE	MERANCOURT (AREA)	

5TH. CAVALRY DIVISION.

MARCH TABLE ISSUED WITH O.O. No. 45 (CONT'D)

FORMATION OR UNIT.	STARTING POINT.	TIME.	ROUTE.	DESTINATION	REMARKS.
Sec. Cav. Bde. "N" Battery, R.H.A. and Light Sect. Amm. Column. Sec. Cav. 3d. Ambulance.	Cross roads just N. of R in ESTREES (DENIECOURT)	10 A.M.	VILLERS-CARBONNEL-BRIE-ESTREES-EN-CHAUSSEE.	TREFCON (AREA)	To be clear of road junction ½ mile E. of ESTREES-EN-CHAUSSEE by 1.30 p.m.
Ambulance Cav. Bde. Show Cav. 3d. Ambulance.	—do.—	11 am.	—do.—	TERTRY (Area)	To be clear of road junction just E. of ESTREES-EN-CHAUSSEE by 2.30 p.m.

Fighting troops and A. Echelon may pass B. Echelons provided this can be done without blocking the traffic.

T.H.

SECRET.   Urgent appx 154

No.G.S.722.

Headquarters, 5th Cavalry Division,
23th November, 1917.

To/
O.O. Distribution.

1. The Division has been warned to be prepared to take over a sector of the line at short notice.

It is probable that the Divisional Sector will be the same as held by the Division in the Summer, 1917.

2. The Dismounted Establishments of units of the Division will be the same as those approved by G.S.570/4 dated 10th May, 1917, and subsequent amendments.

Sec'bad and Ambala Brigades will forward as soon as possible any alteration that they consider necessary in the Establishment of the British Regiments of their Brigades owing to the reduction in strength of the Dismounted Reinforcements.

W. T. Wilson
Lt-Colonel, G.S.,
5th Cavalry Division.

```
S E C R E T.                                          Copy No. 43
```

appx 155

5TH CAVALRY DIVISION.

OPERATION ORDER NO. 46.

Ref. Map 1/20,000.   Dated.- 29th November, 1917.

1. The Division will take over the front now occupied by the 17th Infantry Brigade - Right Brigade of the 24th Division - in accordance with attached Table of Relief.
    The 4th Cavalry Division will relieve the Centre Brigade of the 24th Division on 30th.Nov./1st.Dec. on the front G.13.d. to G.2.a.
    The Sector S. of the OMIGNON River is held by the 5th French Division, III Corps.

2. Brigadiers will make all arrangements with regard to the details of relief direct with the G.O.C., 17th Infantry Brigade and the Battalion Commanders concerned.

3. The Artillery relief will be carried out on December 2nd and 3rd under orders to be issued by the C.R.H.A.

4. The relief of the Machine Guns of the 17th Infantry Brigade will be carried out on the night 2nd/3rd December under orders to be issued by Major Walker, Canadian M.G. Squadron who will act as Divisional Machine Gun Officer.

5. Brigades, C.R.H.A. and Divn'l M.G. Officer will report the completion of reliefs to Divisional Headquarters by the code word LEOPARD.

6. The Canadian Cavalry Brigade will remain in its present area as a Mounted Reserve to the Divisional Sector.

7. Orders with regard to moves of Field Ambulances and relief of Medical units will be issued by the A.D.M.S.

8. The Command of the Sector will pass from the 17th Infantry Brigade to 5th Cavalry Division at 10 am on December 2nd.

9. Divisional Headquarters and Report Centre will be at MONCHY LAGACHE.

10. ACKNOWLEDGE.

                              [signed] Lt-Colonel, G.S.,
                                         5th Cavalry Division.

Issued by D.R. at 8-15 pm

To/
        O.O. Distribution Nos. 1 to 23.
        24th Division.   ... No. 24.
        17th Infantry Brigade. No. 25.
        Cavalry Corps   ... No. 26.

Relief Table for December 1st/2nd. (Issued with O.O.46.)

Relieving Force.	Formation to be relieved.	Frontage.	Date.	Remarks.
Brig.Gen.C.RANKIN,C.M.G., D.S.O. Ambala Cavalry Brigade. 1 Field Troop.R.E.	Right Battalion, 17th Inf.Bde.	Sub-Sector A.1. M.8.c. to G.31.a.	1st/2nd December.	Bde.H.Qrs.at VADENCOURT.- will get into touch with the French Inf.H.Qrs.at about R.35.c.
Brig.Gen.C.L.GREGORY. Sec'bad Cav.Bde. 1 Field Troop R.E.	Left Battalion, 17th Inf.Bde.	Sub-Sector A.2. G.31.a. to L.24.a.5.8.	1st/2nd December	Bde H.Qrs at R.8.b.2.2.
Headquarters, 5th Cavalry Division.	H.Q.17th Inf.Bde.	Sector A. M.8.c. to L.24.a.5.8.	10 a.m., December 2nd.	5th Cavalry Div.H.Qrs,remaind at MORCHY LeGACHE.

appx 156

SECRET.   Copy No. 23

5TH CAVALRY DIVISION.

OPERATION ORDER NO. 47.

Ref. Map 1/100,000.   Dated 30th November, 1917.

1. The Division will rendezvous at once as under :-

    Ambala Cavalry Brigade Head at road junction ½ mile E. of ESTREES-EN-CHAUSSEE tail towards CAULINCOURT.

    Sec'bad Cavalry Brigade in billets ready to follow Ambala Cavalry Brigade.

    Canadian Cavalry Brigade Head at road junction ½ mile East of ESTREES-EN-CHAUSSEE tail towards MERANCOURT.

    5th Field Squadron will follow Sec'bad Cavalry Brigade.

    Divisional Headquarters, 5th Signal Squadron and Hdqrs, 17th Brigade, R.H.A. will follow Canadian Cavalry Brigade.

2. Batteries and Cavalry Field Ambulances will march with Brigades.

3. "A" Echelon will march in rear of Brigades and Divisional Troops.

4. The following will remain in billets ready to move.

    "B" Echelon.
    Ammunition Column. *(less light Sect which follows Canadian)*
    Reserve Park Heavy Section.
    Hdqrs., Aux. H.T. Coy.

5. Brigadiers, C.R.H.A. and O.C., 5th Field Squadron will meet the Divisional Commander at Road junction ½ mile East of ESTREES-EN-CHAUSSEE at once.

6. Divisional Report Centre in rear of Canadian Cavalry Brigade.

7. ACKNOWLEDGE.

                                            J. O'Rorke Capt fr
                                            Lt-Colonel, G.S.,
                                            5th Cavalry Division.

Issued by D.R. at 10 am.

To/
        O.O. Distribution Nos. 1 to 23.
        Cavalry Corps   No. 24.

SECRET.

Appendix A

Copy No. 8

5TH CAVALRY DIVISION.

OPERATION ORDER NO. 40.

Reference Map 1/100,000.   Dated 7th November, 1917.

1. The Division will move SOUTH on November 9th, 10th and 11th in accordance with attached March Table.

   Orders for the March of the Division on the 12th inst. will be issued later.

2. "B" Echelons will march with Brigades and Divisional Troops.

3. Divisional Troops will march on the 10th and following days under orders to be issued by C.R.H.A. through Divn'l Signals.

4. Motor Ambulances and Sanitary Section will march under orders to be issued by A.D.M.S.

5. Divisional Headquarters will close at FRESSIN at 11 a.m. on the 10th inst. and open at OCCOCHES at the same hour.

6. ACKNOWLEDGE.

W. T. Hodgson
Lt-Colonel, G.S.,
5th Cavalry Division.

Issued by D.R. at 9 p.m.

To/
     Normal O.O. Distribution Nos. 1 to 23.
     Cavalry Corps .... No. 24.

5TH CAVALRY DIVISION.

March Table for Nov. 9 - (issued with Operation Order No.40).

FORMATION OR UNIT.	STARTING POINT.	TIME.	ROUTE.	DESTINATION.	REMARKS.
Ambala Cav Bde. Mhow I.C.F.A.	PLUMOISON Church.	9 a.m.	CONCHY SUR CANCHE – BONNIERES.	OUTRE BOIS Area. Billets to be allotted by D.A.A.& Q.M.G.	To be East of ABBEVILLE-HESDIN road by 10.30 am
Sec'bd Cav Bde. "N" Battery R.H.A. Sec'bd I.C.F.A.	HESDIN Railway Station.	10.30 a.m.	LABROYE – AUXI LE CHATEAU.	---- do ----	In moving to starting point, troops of Sec'bd Bde will not use HESDIN-MARESQUEL road.
Canadian Cav Bde. R.C.H.A. Bde. Canadian C.F.A.	Brigade arrangements.	10 a.m.	No restrictions.	BOUIN-AUBIN ST.VAAST- CONTES-ECQUEMICOURT- MARESQUEL-BEAURAINVILLE -LOISON.	Canadian M.G. Sqdn. will remain night of 8/9th at LESPINOY.
17th Bde R.H.A. Ammn. Column. R.C.H.A. Ammn. Column.	V.ROCHOCQ.		FRUGES – RUISSEAU- VILLE – LA LOGE.	CAVRON ST.MARTIN- WAMBERCOURT.	
Reserve Park(less Heavy Section). Hqrs.A.H.T.Coy.	HERLY.	10.30 a.m.	HENOVILLE – EMBRY.	OFFIN-HESMOND- BOUBERS.	
5th Field Squadron.	REMTY.	10 a.m.	COUPELLE VIEILLE – CREQUY.	LEBIEZ.	

5TH CAVALRY DIVISION.

March Table for No. 10th - (issued with Operation Order No.40).

FORMATION OR UNIT.	STARTING POINT.	TIME.	ROUTE.	DESTINATION.	REMARKS.
Canadian Cav Bde. R.C.H.A. Bde. Canadian C.F.A.	PLUMOISON Church.	9 a.m.	LABROYE - AUXI LE CHATEAU.	OUTREBOIS Area. Billets to be allotted by D.A.A.& Q.M.G.	
Divnl.H.Q.(less motors) Signal Sqn.(" ") Hqrs 17td 3de R.H.A. 5th Field Squadron R.E. 17th Bde R.H.A. Ammn.Col. R.C.H.A. Bde Ammn Col. Reserve Park(less Heavy Section). Hqrs A.H.T. Coy.	X Roads at W of Pt. WAAIH.	9 a.m.	HESDIN-2nd N in MARCONNE-ST.GEORGES-CANCHY SUR CANCHE-BONNIERES.	---- do ----	
Ambala Cav Bde. Ihow.I.C.F.A.	T roads just N. of H in HEM.	9.30 a.m.	-BEAUQUESNE - TOUTENCOURT.	DOULLENS CONTAY Area. Billets to be allotted by D.A.A.& Q.M.G.	
Sec'bed Cav Bde.N.Bty.RHA Sec'bed I.C.F.A.	FIENVILLERS.	9.30 a.m.	CANDAS - le VAL DE MAISON.	---- do ----	

--*-*-*
S E C R E T.
--*-*-*

No.G/19.

Headquarters, 5th Cavalry Division.
9th November 1917.

To/ O.O. Distribution
plus Cavalry Corps.

March Table for 11th November, issued with Operation Order No.40, as amended by this office No.G/17 dated 9/11/17, is cancelled and the following substituted :-

March Table for November 11th.

FORMATION OR UNIT.	STARTING POINT.	TIME.	ROUTE.	DESTINATION.	REMARKS.
Canadian Cav Bde. R.C.H.A. Bde. Canadian C.F.A.	T roads just N. of H in HEM.	11 a.m.	DOULLENS - BEAUQUESNE - TOUTENCOURT - CONTAY.	CONTAY Area.	Not to enter CONTAY Area before 4.30 p.m.
Divnl.Hqrs(less motors) Signal Sqn(" ") H.Q.17th Bde R.H.A. 5th Field Sqdn. 17th Bde Ammn Col. R.C.H.A. Ammn Col. H.Q. A.H.T. Coy. Reserve Park(less Heavy Section).	X roads 1,000 yards S. of O in LONGUEVILLETTE.	10 a.m.	CARDAS - le VAL DE MAISON - ROBEMPRE - MOLLIENS AU BOIS.	-- do --	-- do --

Acknowledge

[signature]
Lieut-Colonel, G.S.,
5th Cavalry Division.

Appendix B.

SECRET.

No. G.14.

Headquarters, 5th Cavalry Division,
7th November, 1917.

To/
   Normal C.O. Distribution
   plus D.A.D.O.S. and Supply Column.
----

1.   Dismounted Reinforcements, less the R.H.A. reinforcements now with 5th Field Squadron, will assemble to-morrow at WAHIN proceeding there in the empty supply lorries.

2.   The R.H.A. Reinforcements with 5th Field Squadron and the P.B. men with Divisional Headquarters will assemble at WAHIN on the 9th inst under orders to be issued later.

3.   Major R.H.O'D. PATERSON, 34th Horse, will command the Dismounted Reinforcements of the Division.

4.   Brigades and Divisional Troops will render to this office, by 9th inst., a nominal roll, in duplicate, showing all officers and O.R's. who have joined the Dismounted Reinforcements at WAHIN.

                                            Lt-Colonel, G.S.,
                                            5th Cavalry Division.

Copy to :-
   Major R.H.O'D. PATERSON, 34th Horse.

SECRET.   H.Q., 17th Brigade R.H.A.

Appendix C

OPERATION ORDER No. 25.   Copy No...7.

Reference Map
LENS 11, 1/100,000.   5th November 1917.

1. Divisional Troops will move south on the 10th inst. to the OUTREBOIS area under the orders of the C.R.H.A., in accordance with the attached March Table.

2. Billets will be allotted by D.A.A.G. &.M.G.
Advance parties should proceed well ahead of units to obtain allocation of billets.

3. Rations for 11th consumption will be delivered to units in the new area by supply lorry.

4. Both the 17th Brigade R.H.A. Ammunition Column and the R.C.H.A. Ammunition Column will march under the orders of Captain H.J. CAFFES, R.H.A., who will make his own arrangements as to the order in which the Columns march.

5. ACK OF RECPT.

T.A.M. Bond
  Captain
for C.R.H.A. 5th Cavalry Division.

Copy No. 1. Div'l H.Q.
         2. Signal Squadron.
         3. 17th Bde R.H.A. Am. Col.
         4. R.C.H.A. Bde A.M. Col.
         5. H.Q., A.M.T. Coy.
         6. Reserve Park.
         7. File. 9th Field Squadron
         8. file.

March Table (to accompany O.O. No.25).

Unit.	Starting Point.	Time.	Route.	Destination.	Remarks.
Divisional H.Q.	X roads at N of Et. WAMIN.	9.a.m.	HESDIN - 2nd N in MARCONNE - ST.GEORGES - CANCHY sur CANCHE - BONNIERES.	OCCOCHES - OUTREBOIS.	500 yards to be maintained between units.
Signal Squadron.	do.	9.10 a.m.	do.	do.	
H.Q., 17th Bde R.H.A.	do.	9.20 a.m.	do.	MEZEROLLES.	
5th Field Squadron.	do.	9.30 a.m.	do.	REMAISNIL.	
17th Bde R.H.A.) Amm.Cols. R.C.H.A.	do.	9.40 a.m.	do.	MON PLAISIR FARM MAGTER FARM HARDINVAL.	
H.Q.,A.H.T.Coy.	do.	10 a.m.	do.	BARLY.	
Reserve Park (less Heavy Sectn)	do.	10.15 a.m.	do.	BARLY.	

SECRET.

Appendix D

H.Q. 17th Brigade R.H.A.
10th November 1917.

March Orders to Divisional Troops.

Reference Maps:
LENS 11 , 1/100,000.
AMIENS 17, 1/100,000.

1. The time table and route for the march of Divisional Troops on the 11th inst. is altered in accordance with the attached March Table.

2. The CONTAY area must not be entered before 4.30 p.m.

3. 200 yards interval will be maintained between units and a halt of 10 minutes will be made every hour at the hour.

4. The march will be continued on the 12th and 13th inst. for which days March orders will be issued later.

5. Railhead for the CONTAY area will be CORBIE,

6. ACKNOWLEDGE.

J.A.M. Burns
Captain R.F.A.
for C.R.H.A. 5th Cavalry Division.

Copy No. 1. Div'l H.Q.
2. Camp Commandant.
3. Signal Squadron.
4. 17th Bde R.H.A. A.C.
5. R.C.H.A. Bde A.C.
6. H.Q.,A.H.T.Coy.
7. Reserve Park.
8. 5th Field Squadron.

March Table.

Unit.	Starting Point.	Time.	Route.	Destination.
Div'l H.Q.	X roads 1000 yds South of O in LONGUEVILLETTE,	10 a.m.	CANDAS - le VAL de MAISON - RUBEMPRE - MOLLIENS au BOIS.	QUERRIEU.
Signal Squadron.	do.	10.10 a.m.	do.	do.
H.Q., 17th Bde R.H.A.	do.	10.20 a.m.	do.	do.
5th Field Squadron.	do.	10.30 a.m.	do.	LA HUSSOYE.
17th Bde R.H.A. Amm. Col.) R.G.H.A Amm. Col.)	do.	10.40 a.m.	do.	PONT NOYELLES.
H.Q., A.H.T.Coy.	do.	10.50 a.m.	do.	FRECHENCOURT.
Reserve Park (less Heavy Sectn)	do.	11 a.m.	do.	FRECHENCOURT.

Wheels of Awid troops will march by CANDAS - TALMAS - VILLERS BOCAGE - MOLLIENS AU BOIS going to ticle of road. Route to training ground to be carefully reconnitred ....

C.R.E., Cavalry Corps. R.E.

O.C., 2nd. Field Squadron. R.E.
O.C., 3rd. Field Squadron. R.E.

Appendix E

The detachments of the 1st. Field Squadron now with the 2nd. Field Squadron. R.E. and of the 5th. now with the 3rd. will change places as soon as possible. The change should be completed by evening 11th. at latest. The 5th. and 1st. Field Squadron officers should make themselves conversant with what are known as the East and West COLOGNE areas respectively.

                      (sgd)   W.H.EVANS.

                              Lieut. Colonel R.E.

10/11/17.
                            C.R.E., Cavalry Corps.

Copy to:-

Major Thackwell.
1st. Field Squadron. R.E.
5th. Field Squadron. R.E.

                              Lieut. Colonel R.E.

Appendix F

SECRET.   Copy No. 7

5TH CAVALRY DIVISION.
OPERATION ORDER No. 41.

Reference Map 1/100,000.   Dated 10th November, 1917.

1. March Table for completion of Move of Division is attached.

2. Railheads :-

OUTREBOIS Area	CANDAS. Exchange
CONTAY Area	CORBIE.
BRAY Area	LA FLAQUE.
Final Area	TINCOURT.

3. Completion of moves will be reported by wire or Special D.R. to Divisional Headquarters.

4. Divisional Report Centre closes OCCOCHES at 12 noon on 11th inst., and opens at QUERRIEU at same hour.

5. ACKNOWLEDGE.

W. T. Hodgson
Lt-Colonel, G.S.,
5th Cavalry Division.

Issued by D.R. at 10 am

To/
Normal O.O. Distribution. Nos. 1 to 23.
Cavalry Corps .... No.24.

5TH CAVALRY DIVISION.

March Table for night 12/13th - (issued with Operation Order No.41).

FORMATION OR UNIT.	STARTING POINT.	TIME.	ROUTE.	DESTINATION.	REMARKS.
Ambala Cav Bde. Thow I.C.F.A.	T roads ¼ mile S. of 1st E in ECLUSIER.	4.30 p.m. 12th inst.	HERBECOURT - BIACHES - PERONNE - QUES of BOIS DES FLACQUES.	Billets from A.A.& Q.M.G.	
Sec'bed Cav Bde. "N" Battery R.H.A. Sec'bed I.C.F.A.	X roads ¾ mile S. of P in PROYART.	4.30 p.m. 12th inst.	ESTREES - BRIE - VRAIGNES.	Billets from A.A.& Q.M.G.	
Canadian Cav Bde. R.C.H.A. Brigade. Canadian C.F.A.	FRANVILLERS.	4 p.m. 12th inst.	BUIRE SUR L'ANCRE - MORLANCOURT.	SUZANNE - BRAY SUR SOMME - LAMEUVILLE - ETINEHEM - CHIPILLY.	Accomodation for 1 Btn. in BRAY is reserved by Third Army.
Divnl.H.Q.(less motors) Signal Sqn.(" ") H.Q. 17th Bde R.H.A. 5th Field Squadron. 17th Bde R.H.A. Ammn.Col. R.C.H.A. Bde Ammn Col. H.Q. A.H.T. Coy. Reserve Park(less Heavy Section).	Road junction ½ mile S. of P in PONT NOYELLES.	4 p.m. 12th inst.	LA NEUVILLE - VAUX SUR SOMME - SAILLY LAURETTE - MORCOURT.	CAPPY - FROISSY - CHUIGNOLLES - PROYART - MERICOURT - MORCOURT.	Billets to be allotted by D.A.A.& Q.M.G.

H.T.H.

5TH CAVALRY DIVISION.

March Table for night 13/14th - (issued with Operation Order No.41).

FORMATION OR UNIT.	STARTING POINT.	TIME.	ROUTE.	DESTINATION.	REMARKS.
Canadian Cav Bde. R.C.H.A. Brigade. Canadian C.F.A.	T roads ½ mile S. of 1st E in ECLUSIER.	4.30 p.m.	HERBECOURT - BIACHES - PERONNE - QUES of BOIS DES FLACQUES.	Billets from A.A.& Q.M.G.	
Divnl. H.Q. Group.	X roads ⅔ mile S. of P in PROYART.	4.30 p.m.	ESTREES - BRIE - VRAIGNES.	Billets from A.A.& Q.M.G.	

h.G.H.

SECRET.   H.Q., 17th Brigade R.H.A.

Appendix G

OPERATION ORDER No. 27.

Reference Map
AMIENS 17, 1/100,000.   11th November 1917.

1.   The march will be continued on the night of the 12/13th inst. in accordance with the attached March Table.

2.   Railhead for the BRAY area will be LA FLAQUE.

3.   Representatives of Div'l H.Q., H.Q., 17th Bde R.H.A. 5th Signal Squadron, 5th Field Squadron, A.H.T.Coy, and Reserve Park (less Heavy Section) will meet the D.A.A.& Q.M.G. at CAPPY Church at 12 noon on the 12th.

4.   O.C. 5th Field Squadron will detail one officer to be at the Starting Point to check the time heads of units pass.
        The Camp Commandant will detail 2 M.M.P. to be at the Starting Point at 4 p.m. to remain there until all units are clear. They will march at the rear of the last unit and report to the C.R.H.A. on completion of the march

5. ACKNOWLEDGE.

                                        Captain,
               for C.R.H.A. 5th Cavalry Division.

Addressed : Units Div'l Troops.

MARCH TABLE. for 12th Nov.

(to accompany Operation Order No.27).

Unit.	Starting Point.	Time.	Route.	Destination.	Remarks.
H.Q., 17th Brigade R.H.A.	Road junction ½ mile South of P in PONT NOYELLES.	4 p.m.	LA NEUVILLE - VAUX sur SOMME - SAILLY LAURETTE - MORCOURT.	CAPPY.	200 yds interval to be maintained between units. Halt for 10 minutes every clock hour. Reports to head of column.
Signal Squadron.	do.	4.10 p.m.	do	do.	
Div'l H.Q.	do.	4.20 p.m.	do.	do.	
17th Bde R.H.A. Amm. Col.) R.C.H.A. Bde Amm. Col.)	do.	4.30 p.m.	do.	CHUIGNOLLES.	
5th Field Squadron.	do.	4.40 p.m.	do.	ME.CAPPY and BOIS OLIMPE.	
A.H.T Coy.	do.	4.50 p.m.	do.	do.	
Reserve Park (less Heavy Section)	do.	5 p.m.	do.	do.	

SECRET.   H.Q., 17th Brigade R.H.A.

OPERATION ORDER No. 28.

Appendix H

Reference Maps:
AMIENS 17, 1/100,000.
ST.QUENTIN 18, 1/100,000.   13th November 1917.

1.   The march will be continued on the 13th inst. in accordance with the attached March Table.

2.   Railhead for the final area will be TINCOURT.

3.   All units must be clear of CAPPY by 4 p.m. on 13th.

4.   ACKNOWLEDGE.

T.A.M. Boyd Captain,
for C.R.H.A. 5th.Cav. Divn.

Copy No. 1. 5th Cav. Divn. G.
    2. Camp Commandant.
    3. Signal Squadron.
    4. 5th Field Squadron.
    5. 17th Bde R.H.A. Amm. Col.
    6. H.C.R.A. Bde Amm. Col.
    7.
    8.

MARCH TABLE for 13th.
(to accompany Operation Order No.28.)

Unit.	Starting Point.	Time.	Route.	Destination.	Remarks.
Div'l H.Q.	S.E. exit of CAPPY on the FAY road.	3.20 p.m.	ESTREES - ERIE.	As allotted by A.A.& Q.M.G.	200yds interval to be maintained between units. Reports to head of column.
Signal Squadron.	do.	3.25 p.m.	do.	do.	
H.Q., 17th Brigade R.H.A.	do.	3.30 p.m.	do.	do.	
5th Field Squadron	do.	3.35 p.m.	do.	do.	
A.H.T.Coy.	do.	3.40 p.m.	do.	do.	
Reserve Park.	do.	3.45 p.m.	do.	do.	
R.H.A.& R.C.H.A. Ammunition Columns.	X roads ¾ mile South of the P in PROYART.	4 p.m.	do.	do.	

Appendix J

C.R.E., Cavalry Corps. E.A.674

O.C., Det. 5th. Field Squadron. R.E., TREFCON.

Reference my E.A.655 of 11/11/17.

You will move tomorrow afternoon 13th. inst. to BIAS WOOD to rejoin your Squadron.

A lorry, which can do two trips will report to you at noon.

You will hand over to an officer of the 2nd. Field Squadron.

(sgd) W.H.EVANS.

Lieut. Colonel R.E.

12/11/17.　　　　　　　　C.R.E., Cavalry Corps.

Copy to:-
O.C., 2nd. Field Squadron. R.E.
O.C., 5th. Field Squadron. R.E.
Major Thackwell.
4th. Cavalry Division.

Lieut. Colonel R.E.

SECRET

C.R.E., Cavalry Corps. E.A. ~~1710~~
****
1710.

O.C., 1st. Field Squadron. R.E.
O.C., 2nd. Field Squadron. R.E.
O.C., 3rd. Field Squadron. R.E.
O.C., 4th. Field Squadron. R.E.
O.C., 5th. Field Squadron. R.E.

Appendix K

****

Will you please satisfy yourself regarding the water supply for your division in the forward concentration area. You should arrange with the Officer in charge to take it over before the arrival of your division.

The positions of the troughs and the general arrangements have been communicated to you verbally.

Troughs must be used from both sides and good policing arrangements are essential.

Lieut. Colonel R.E.
C.R.E., Cavalry Corps.
****

15/11/17.
******

Appendix M

Orders for A Echelon.

Map reference to 1:40000 map.

(1) A Echelon consists of :- 2 x Ray M, SSM, CQMS and OR ws Saddlers, 4 doubles toolcarts, cds (cooks cart) water cart, maltese cart, LGS (Res Parks)

(2) Echelon will march in rear of A. ich. A Bn Hos, RHQ (Australian Cav Bde Group).

(3) Echelon will parade in marching order at 1.45 am 20th inst & march to conc. station area via ME of FINS via CARTIGNY, BRUSLE BOUCLY X roads (½ mile N. of TINCOURT, LONGAVESNES LIERAMONT, NURLU EQUANCOURT MOISLAINS and N of FINS Crossroads BOUCLY to be passed at 3.0 am A Echelon hereon. Division ahead at the Checking Point (X roads ¼ N. of TINCOURT)

(4) Echelon Sub-section will be commanded by Capt Hirst 7 D.G.

(5) LGS wagon (Res Parks) will report in concentration area.

(6) On arrival in concentration area a hot meal will be cooked & eaten. Horses will be watered and fed. Sub tion water point (V6 d 6.7) will be available from 8.30 - 9.30 am. Pltn nets will be issued in conc. area. After feeding 4 hrs oats ration will be made up to 12 hrs from forage.

on Echelon wagons.

(7) Echelon will advance with fighting troops and A. Echelon of 2nd Cav. Divn.

(8) Casualty reports to be sent daily at 6 p.m. to Squadron H.Q. (c/o Ambala Bde)

(9) Iron rations will not be eaten without the order of Capt. Hiatt.

(10) No papers, orders, letters, etc. will be carried which could be useful to the enemy.

(11) All reports & messages must show time of despatch.

                                              Wooten

19/10/17
                                              Major R.E.
                         O.C. 5th Fld Sqdn R.E.

Appendix N

Orders for B Echelon and Dismounted Reinforcements

(1) B Echelon consists of :- G.S. wagon (Technical)
Trestle wagon, Maxo Cart, Bicycles,
S/Sgt Winton, Cpl Austry and O.R. as
detailed.

(2) Dismounted Reinforcements consist of :-
Sgt Whamond and O.R. as detailed,
including detachment under Sgt Brackland.

(3) During morning of 20th inst. Dis. Rein. will
move all Rugs, 2nd Blankets, latrine buckets,
Tarred covers and other Ordnance stores to
dumps at Xroads 800y North of camp.
Sgt Nixon will be left in charge of this dump.
DADOS will arrange for him to join Dis Rein.
at BOUCLY when these stores are collected by
DADOS.
Dis Rein. will also clean up Camp, leaving
it Spotlessly tidy.

(4) Cpl Hodgkins will report to Capt Wilken RCD
at Xroads BOUCLY at 2 pm on 20th
for attachment to Pickets. He will know
numbers of men, horses, wagons in
B Echelon & Dis. Rein. He will meet
the column when it arrives in BOUCLY.

(5) B Echelon & Dis Rein. will move (?) at
2.15 pm forward to BOUCLY via
CARTIGNY and BRUSLE.

Dismounted men will march in rear of squadron.

(6) Dis Rein. at present with Lt Greathead will join at BOUCLY.

(7) Iron rations will not be eaten without the order of a Brigadier.

(8) No papers, letters etc will be carried which could be of use to the enemy.

19/11/17   A. Woolven
             Major RE
             OC. 5th Field Squadron RE

Appendix "O"

SECRET.   COPY No 7

5TH. CAVALRY DIVISION

OPERATION ORDER No. 44.

REF. MAP 1/100,000.   DATED 22ND NOVEMBER, 1917.

1. The Division will move to the BRAY area on the 23rd instant in accordance with the attached March Table. 17 miles

2. The rate of march will be 4½ - miles per hour - 200 - yards distance will be maintained between Regiments, Batteries and Transport Echelons.

3. Route for Cyclists - NURLU - PERONNE - BIACHES - HERBECOURT.

4. Motor Ambulances will move under orders of the A.D.M.S.

5. Divisional Report Centre will close at EQUANCOURT at 11 a.m. and open at SUZANNE at the same hour.

6. Staff Captains & Representatives of Divnl. Troops will meet D.A.A. & Q.M.G at 11-0 Am at SUZANNE Chateau
   8.0 Start.

Copies.
Normal O.O. Dist: 1-23
    Cav. Corps. 24.

                          N.T. Hodgson Lieut Col.
                          G.S, 5th Cav: Divn.

Issued by D.R at 10 pm

5TH CAVALRY DIVISION.

MARCH TABLE - (ISSUED WITH OPERATION ORDER No 44)

FORMATION OR UNIT.	STARTING POINT.	TIME	ROUTE.	DESTINATION	REMARKS.
AMBALA CAV. BDE. MHOW CAV. FD. AMB. LCE.	EASTERN EXIT OF ETRICOURT ON ETRICOURT-EQUANCOURT ROAD	7 A.M.	ETRICOURT - MANANCOURT - MOISLAINS - BOUCHAVESNES - CLERY - MARICOURT.	BILLETS TO BE ALLOTTED BY D.A.A.& Q.M.G.	
CANADIAN CAV. BDE. R.C.H.A. BDE (AND LIGHT SECTION, AMMN. COLUMN). CANADIAN CAV. FD. AMLCE.	- DITTO -	7.50 A.M.	- ditto -	- DITTO -	
DIVISIONAL HDQRS. H.Q. 17TH BDE. R.H.A. 5TH SIGNAL SQDN. 5TH FIELD SQDN.	- DITTO - Start 8.30 am	9 A.M.	- DITTO -	- DITTO -	
SEC'BAD CAV. BDE. 'N' BTY. R.H.A. (AND LIGHT SECT. AMMN.COL). SEC'BAD CAV. FD. AMBCE.	- DITTO -	9.10 A.M.	- DITTO -	- DITTO -	
17TH BDE. R.H.A. AMMN. COL (LESS LIGHT SECTS) R.C.H.A. AMMN. COL. (LESS LIGHT SECTS)	- DITTO -	10.10 A.M.	- DITTO -	- DITTO -	
RESERVE PARK (LESS HEAVY SECTION)	- DITTO -	10.25 A.M.	- DITTO -	- DITTO -	TAIL TO BE CLEAR OF ETRICOURT BY 11 A.M.

Appendix P

SECRET   No. GA 635.   HQrs 5th Cavdn
                        23-11-17.

Warning Order

Operation Order Distribution

1. The Division will be prepared, from 8 A.M. 24th November, to move from their present billets in one hour after receipt of orders at Divisional Headquarters. (Approximately 40 minutes after receipt of orders by Brigades and Div Troop Units)

2. ACKNOWLEDGE.

                    A. T. A[...]
                        Lieut Col
                        G 5th Cavdn.

Appendix Q.

<u>SECRET</u> GA 640

HQ 5th Cav Bn
24-11-14
25

To O.O. Distribution –

This Office No GA 635 df 23-11-14 – placing the Division at "1 hours" notice to move – is hereby cancelled.

2. Acknowledge

J O'Brien Capt
for 5th Cavalry Bn

SECRET.   Appendix R
Copy No. 2

5TH CAVALRY DIVISION

OPERATION ORDER No. 45.

Ref. Map 1/100,000   Dated 26th November 1917.

1. The Division will move to the "D" Area (MONCHY LAGACHE) to-morrow, the 27th inst., in accordance with the attached March Table.

2. Divisional Hdqrs Group will march under orders of C.R.H.A.

3. "B" Echelon will march with Brigades and units of Divisional Troops.

4. Light Sections, Ammunition Column will march with Brigades and, on arriving at ESTREES-EN-CHAUSSEE, they will march direct to the Ammunition Column Area at MONCHY LAGACHE.

5. Motor Ambulances and Sanitary Section will move under orders to be issued by A.D.M.S.

6. Reserve Park Heavy Section and Dismounted Reinforcements will join the Division on the 27th under orders to be issued by Cavalry Corps. On arrival in MONCHY LAGACHE Area Dismounted Reinforcements will rejoin their units.

7. A distance of 200 yards will be maintained between Regiments and Batteries and similar units.

8. The Divisional Report Centre will close at SUZANNE at 11. a.m. on 27th and open at MONCHY LAGACHE at the same hour.

9. ACKNOWLEDGE

N. T. Hodgson
Lt.-Colonel,
G.S.
5th Cavalry Division

Issued by D.R. at 8.30 pm.

20/   Nos.
O.O. Distribution 1-23.

5TH CAVALRY DIVISION.

MARCH TABLE ISSUED WITH O.O. No 45.

FORMATION OR UNIT.	STARTING POINT.	TIME.	ROUTE.	DESTINATION.	REMARKS.
17th Bde. Amm. Col. (Searchlight Sections) R.H.A. Bde. Amm. Col. (two Light Sections).	East E. of BOIS OLIMPE	8 A.M.	VILLERS CARBONNEL - BRIE - ESTREES-EN-CHAUSSEE.	MONCHY LAGACHE	To be clear of ESTREES DENIECOURT by 10 A.M.
Divisional H.Q. H.Q. 17th Bde. R.H.A. 5th Signal Sqdn. 5th Field Sqdn. H.Q. A.H.D. Coy.	Fork roads ½ mile SOUTH of MARICOURT.	9 A.M.	CLERY - ST. DENIS - DOINGT - road junction ½ mile E. of ESTREES - EN - CHAUSSEE.	MONCHY LAGACHE (AREA)	Head to reach road junction ½ mile E. of ESTREES-EN-CHAUSSEE at 2.30 p.m.
Canadian Cav. Bde. R.C.H.A. Bde. and light section Amm. Column. Can. Cav. Field Ambulance.	Fork roads ½ mile SOUTH of MARICOURT.	9.30 A.M.	CLERY - ST. DENIS - DOINGT - Road junction ½ mile E. of ESTREES-EN-CHAUSSEE	MERANCOURT (AREA)	

5TH CAVALRY DIVISION.

MARCH TABLE ISSUED WITH O.O. No. 45 (CONT'D)

FORMATION OR UNIT.	STARTING POINT.	TIME.	ROUTE.	DESTINATION	REMARKS.
2c'tac Cav. Bde. "N" Battery, R.H.A. and light-dect. Amm. Column. 2c'tac Tan. 3d. Ambulance.	Cross roads just N. of R in ESTREES (DENIECOURT)	10.A.M.	VILLERS-CARBONNEL -BRIE-ESTREES-EN-CHAUSSEE.	TREFCON (AREA)	To be clear of road junction ½ mile E. of ESTREES-EN-CHAUSSEE by 1.30 p.m.
Ambala Cav. Bde. Mhow Cav. Bde. 3d. Ambulance.	—do.—	11 a.m.	—do.—	TERTRY (Area)	To be clear of road junction just E. of ESTREES-EN-CHAUSSEE by 2.30 p.m.

Fighting Troops and A. Echelon may pass B. Echelons provided this can be done without blocking the traffic.

M.J.H.

SECRET.

H.Q. 17th Brigade R.H.A.
26th November 1917.

Appendix S

March Orders to Divisional Troops.

Reference Maps
AMIENS 17, 1/100,000.
ST.QUENTIN, 1/100,000.

1. Divisional Troops will march to the "D" Area (MONCHY LAGACHE) tomorrow the 27th inst. in accordance with the attached March Table.

2. "B" Echelons will march with units of Divisional Troops.

3. A distance of 200 yards will be maintained between units.
Halt for 10 minutes every clock hour.
A halt will be made at DOINGT to water and feed.

4. Head of column to reach road junction ½ mile E. of ESTREES - en - CHAUSSEE at 2.30 p.m.

5. Cyclists must move in a formed body.

6. ACKNOWLEDGE.

J.A.M. Bond
Captain,
for C.R.H.A. 5th Cavalry Division.

Copy No.1 H.Q.,5th Cav. Divn.G.
2. Camp Commandant.
3. 5th Signal Squadron.
4. 5th Field Squadron. ✓
5. H.Q.,A.H.T.Coy.
6. File.

March Table for Divisional Troops.

Unit.	Starting Point.	Time.	Route.	Destination.	Remarks.
H.Q. 17th Bde R.H.A.	Fork roads ½ mile South of MARICOURT.	9 a.m.	CLERY - ST.DENIS - POIGNY - road junction ½ mile E. of ESTREES-en- CHAUSEE.	MONCHY LAGACHE (area)	Reports to head of column.
Div'l H.Q.	do.	9.5 a.m.	do.	do.	
5th Signal Squadron.	do.	9.10 a.m.	do.	do.	
5th Field Squadron.	do.	9.15 a.m.	do.	do.	
H.Q.,A.H.T.Coy.	do.	9.20 a.m.	do.	do.	

SECRET

URGENT.

C.R.E., Cavalry Corps. E.A. 786

Appendix T

O.C., 5th. Field Squadron. R.E.

1. Your Division is going to take over the 17th. Brigade Sector of the 24th. Division line on the night of December 1st. - 2nd.

2. Will you please arrange to take over all R.E. work in the sector from No. 104 Field Company R.E., who are located at Q.1.a.8.8. MILIEU COPSE.

3. Weekly reports of work with a tracing showing progress will be required by 6 p.m. every Saturday.

4. A further communication regarding the supply of stores will be sent you.

Lieut. Colonel R.E.

28/11/17.

C.R.E., Cavalry Corps.

SECRET. Urgent   No.G.S.722.

Appendix U

Headquarters, 5th Cavalry Division,
29th November, 1917.

To/
O.O. Distribution.

1. The Division has been warned to be prepared to take over a sector of the line at short notice.

It is probable that the Divisional Sector will be the same as held by the Division in the Summer, 1917.

2. The Dismounted Establishments of units of the Division will be the same as those approved by G.S.570/4 dated 10th May, 1917, and subsequent amendments.

Sec'bad and Ambala Brigades will forward as soon as possible any alteration that they consider necessary in the Establishment of the British Regiments of their Brigades owing to the reduction in strength of the Dismounted Reinforcements.

W. T. Hodgson
Lt-Colonel, G.S.,
5th Cavalry Division.

SECRET.

SECRET.   Copy No. 2

Appendix V.

5TH CAVALRY DIVISION.

OPERATION ORDER NO. 46.

Ref. Map 1/20,000.   Dated.- 29th November, 1917.

1.   The Division will take over the front now occupied by the 17th Infantry Brigade - Right Brigade of the 24th Division - in accordance with attached Table of Relief.
   The 4th Cavalry Division will relieve the Centre Brigade of the 24th Division on 30th.Nov./1st.Dec. on the front G.13.d. to G.2.a.
   The Sector S. of the OMIGNON River is held by the 5th French Division, III Corps.

2.   Brigadiers will make all arrangements with regard to the details of relief direct with the G.O.C., 17th Infantry Brigade and the Battalion Commanders concerned.

3.   The Artillery relief will be carried out on December 2nd and 3rd under orders to be issued by the C.R.H.A.

4.   The relief of the Machine Guns of the 17th Infantry Brigade will be carried out on the night 2nd/3rd December under orders to be issued by Major Walker, Canadian M.G. Squadron who will act as Divisional Machine Gun Officer.

5.   Brigades, C.R.H.A. and Divn'l M.G. Officer will report the completion of reliefs to Divisional Headquarters by the code word LEOPARD.

6.   The Canadian Cavalry Brigade will remain in its present area as a Mounted Reserve to the Divisional Sector.

7.   Orders with regard to moves of Field Ambulances and relief of Medical units will be issued by the A.D.M.S.

8.   The Command of the Sector will pass from the 17th Infantry Brigade to 5th Cavalry Division at 10 a.m. on December 2nd.

9.   Divisional Headquarters and Report Centre will be at MONCHY LAGACHE.

10. ACKNOWLEDGE.

                             N. T. Hodgson, Lt-Colonel, G.S.,
                                         5th Cavalry Division.

Issued by D.R. at 8-15 p.m.

To/
      O.O. Distribution Nos. 1 to 23.
      24th Division.   ...   No. 24.
      17th Infantry Brigade.   No. 25.
      Cavalry Corps   ...   No. 26.

Relief Table for December 1st/2nd.(Issued with C.O.46.)

Relieving Force.	Formation to be relieved.	Frontage.	Date.	Remarks.
Brig.Gen.C.RANKIN,C.M.G., D.S.O. Ambala Cavalry Brigade. 1 Field Troop,R.E.	Right Battalion, 17th Inf.Bde.	Sub-Sector A.1. K.8.c. to G.31.a.	1st/2nd December.	Bde.H.Qrs.at VADENCOURT.- will get into touch with the French Inf.H.Qrs.at about R.35.c.
Brig.Gen.C.L.GREGORY. Sec'bad Cav.Bde. 1 Field Troop R.E.	Left Battalion, 17th Inf.Bde.	Sub-Sector A.2. G.31.a. to L.24.a.5.8.	1st/2nd December	Bde H.Qrs at R.8.b.2.2.
Headquarters, 5th Cavalry Division.	H.Q.17th Inf.Bde.	Sector.A. M.8.c. to L.24.a.5.8.	10 a.m., December 2nd.	5th Cavalry Div.H.Qrs,remaind at MONCHY LAGACHE.

SECRET.   Copy No. 4

Appendix W

5TH CAVALRY DIVISION.

OPERATION ORDER NO. 47.

Ref. Map 1/100,000.   Dated 30th November, 1917.

1.   The Division will rendezvous at once as under :-

       Ambala Cavalry Brigade Head at road junction ¾ mile E. of ESTREES-EN-CHAUSSEE tail towards CAULINCOURT.

       Sec'bad Cavalry Brigade in billets ready to follow Ambala Cavalry Brigade.

       Canadian Cavalry Brigade Head at road junction ½ mile East of ESTREES-EN-CHAUSSEE tail towards MERANCOURT.

       5th Field Squadron will follow Sec'bad Cavalry Brigade.

       Divisional Headquarters, 5th Signal Squadron and Hdqrs, 17th Brigade, R.H.A. will follow Canadian Cavalry Brigade.

2.   Batteries and Cavalry Field Ambulances will march with Brigades.

3.   "A" Echelon will march in rear of Brigades and Divisional Troops.

4.   The following will remain in billets ready to move.

       "B" Echelon.
       Ammunition Column. (less Light Sect which follows Canada)
       Reserve Park Heavy Section.
       Hdqrs., Aux. H.T. Coy.

5.   Brigadiers, C.R.H.A. and O.C., 5th Field Squadron will meet the Divisional Commander at Road junction ½ mile East of ESTREES-EN-CHAUSSEE at once.

6.   Divisional Report Centre in rear of Canadian Cavalry Brigade.

7.   ACKNOWLEDGE.

                                            J. O'Rorke Capt. for
                                               Lt-Colonel, G.S.,
                                               5th Cavalry Division.

Issued by D.R. at 10 am.

To/
       O.O. Distribution Nos. 1 to 23.
       Cavalry Corps   No. 24.

appx 116

S E C R E T.   Copy No. 23

5TH CAVALRY DIVISION.

OPERATION ORDER NO.42.

Reference Map
1/100,000.   Dated 19th November, 1917.

1.   The Division (less "B" Echelon, Sanitary Section, A.H.T.Coy, Heavy Section Reserve Park and Dismounted Reinforcements) will march to a forward Concentration Area, N.E. of FINS on Y/Z night in accordance with a March Table which will be issued later.

        The Grouping for this move and the subsequent forward moves of the Division is shown in Appendix "A", attached.

2.   In moving to the forward Concentration area, wherever possible, squadrons will move off the roads. All wheels will move by the roads only. Squadrons and wheels will move closed up.

3.   On arrival in the forward Concentration Area there will be a halt of two and a half hours during which horses will be watered and fed.
        After feeding, nosebags will be refilled from forage dumps which have been prepared in this area.
        Arrangements will be made by Brigades and O's.C. Divisional Troops for a hot meal to be ready for the men in this area.

4.   The Division will be ready to move forward from the FINS area at ZERO plus 2½ hours.

5.   Brigades and O's.C. Divisional Troops will arrange for guides to meet units at NURLU and direct them to their places in the FINS area.

6.   "A" Echelon will be sub-divided into No.1 "A" Echelon and No.2 "A" Echelon as under :-

                No.1 "A" Echelon.   No.2 "A" Echelon.

        Mobile Veterinary Sections will march with and form part of No.2 "A" Echelon.

                                                proportion with Squadrons)

        Three S.A.A. limbers will accompany the fighting troops of the Machine Gun Squadrons.

7.   The following moves will be completed by 12 noon on Y day under orders to be issued by C.R.H.A. and O.C., 5th Field Squadron, respectively :-
        (a) Light Sections Ammunition Column to Batteries.
        (b) One Field Troop, R.E. to Canadian Cavalry Brigade.
        (c) One Field Troop, R.E. to Sec'bad Cavalry Brigade.

8.   The Dismounted Reinforcements of all units and "B" Echelons, Divisionalised, will be assembled at BOUCLY by 4 p.m., on Z day.

                                Owing to ....

S E C R E T.   Copy No. 23

5TH CAVALRY DIVISION.

OPERATION ORDER NO.42.

Reference Map
1/100,000.   Dated 19th November, 1917.

1. The Division (less "B" Echelon, Sanitary Section, A.H.T.Coy, Heavy Section Reserve Park and Dismounted Reinforcements) will march to a forward Concentration Area, N.E. of FINS on Y/Z night in accordance with a March Table which will be issued later.

The Grouping for this move and the subsequent forward moves of the Division is shown in Appendix "A", attached.

2. In moving to the forward Concentration Area, wherever possible, squadrons will move off the roads. All wheels will move by the roads only. Squadrons and wheels will move closed up.

3. On arrival in the forward Concentration Area there will be a halt of two and a half hours during which horses will be watered and fed.

After feeding, nosebags will be refilled from forage dumps which have been prepared in this area.

Arrangements will be made by Brigades and O's.C. Divisional Troops for a hot meal to be ready for the men in this area.

4. The Division will be ready to move forward from the FINS area at ZERO plus 2½ hours.

5. Brigades and O's.C. Divisional Troops will arrange for guides to meet units at NURLU and direct them to their places in the FINS area.

6. "A" Echelon will be sub-divided into No.1 "A" Echelon and No.2 "A" Echelon as under :-

No.1 "A" Echelon.	No.2 "A" Echelon.
Signal Troop Limber.	Supply Limbers.
Brigade Tool Limber.	Mess Carts. (4 per Bde. only)
Regt'l and Sqdn. S.A.A.	Water Carts, Cook Carts.
and Explosive Limbers	Technical Carts.
M.G., S.A.A. Limbers.	Officers' Pack Horses (less proportion with Squadrons)

Three S.A.A. limbers will accompany the fighting troops of the Machine Gun Squadrons.

7. The following moves will be completed by 12 noon on Y day under orders to be issued by C.R.H.A. and O.C., 5th Field Squadron, respectively :-
(a) Light Sections Ammunition Column to Batteries.
(b) One Field Troop, R.E. to Canadian Cavalry Brigade.
(c) One Field Troop, R.E. to Sec'bad Cavalry Brigade.

8. The Dismounted Reinforcements of all units and "B" Echelons, Divisionalised, will be assembled at BOUCLY by 4 p.m., on Z day.

Owing to ....

S E C R E T.   O.O. No.42 (cont'd).

      Owing to the return of the 5th Cavalry Battalion the full complement of officers as laid down in Organization Tables will be required to accompany the Dismounted Reinforcements.

      Duplicate nominal rolls of officers and men will be rendered to this office by 1 p.m., Y day.

      Major R.H.O'D. PATERSON, 34th Horse will command the Dismounted Reinforcements of the Division. Captain F.H. WILKES, Royal Canadian Dragoons will command "B" Echelon Divisionalised.

9.   Officers detailed in 5th Cavalry Division No.A/5544 dated 3rd November, 1917, and in G.A.578 of 16th November, 1917, for duty as Liaison Officers and Gallopers with Divisional Headquarters will report to the General Staff Office at 2 p.m., on Y day. Attention is drawn to Organization Tables, Table "F", para.1.

11.   ACKNOWLEDGE.

                            W.T. Hodgson
                                      Lt-Colonel, G.S.,

                                       5th Cavalry Division.

Issued by D.R. at 8·30 p.m.

To/
      O.O. Distribution. Nos. 1 to 23 (as in G.S.525/4.)
      M.M.G. Battery No.24
      Major R.H.O'D. PATERSON,
           34th Horse .... " 25
      Captain F.H. WILKES, R.C.D." 26
      Lieut. G.R.H. BENNETT,
           Fort Garry Horse.." 27.
      Capt.& Sr. A. HIATT,
           7th Dragoon Guards. " 28.

S E C R E T.　　　　　　　APPENDIX "A".

(Issued with Operation Order No.42.)

GROUPING FOR FORWARD MOVE.

CANADIAN CAVALRY BRIGADE GROUP.

Canadian Cavalry Brigade.
"B" Battery, R.C.H.A.
1 Field Troop, R.E.
M.M.G. Battery.
1 Light Section Ammunition Column.
Pack Section, Canadian Cav. Field Ambulance.

SEC'BAD CAVALRY BRIGADE GROUP.

Sec'bad Cavalry Brigade.
"N" Battery, R.H.A.
1 Light Section, Ammunition Column.
1 Field Troop, R.E.
Pack Section, Sec'bad Cav. Field Ambulance.

DIVISIONAL HEADQUARTERS GROUP.

Groups I, II and III.
5th Signal Squadron.
Hdqrs., 17th Brigade, R.H.A. and R.C.H.A. Brigade.
2 Troops, Yorkshire Dragoons.

AMBALA CAVALRY BRIGADE GROUP.

Ambala Cavalry Brigade.
"A" Battery, R.C.H.A.
5th Field Squadron less 2 troops.
1 Light Section, Ammunition Column.
Pack Section, Mhow Cav. Field Ambulance.

No.1 "A" ECHELON GROUP.

O.C. - Lieut. G.R.H. BENNETT, Fort Garry Horse.

No.1 "A" Echelon　Canadian Cavalry Brigade Group.
　"　　"　　"　　Sec'bad Cavalry Brigade Group.
　"　　"　　"　　Divisional Headquarters Group.
　"　　"　　"　　Ambala Cavalry Brigade Group.

No.2 "A" ECHELON GROUP.

O.C. - Captain and Qr.Mr. A. HIATT, 7th Dragoon Guards.

No.2 "A" Echelon　Canadian Cavalry Brigade Group.
　"　　"　　"　　Sec'bad Cavalry Brigade Group.
　"　　"　　"　　Divisional Headquarters Group.
　"　　"　　"　　Ambala Cavalry Brigade Group.

CAVALRY FIELD AMBULANCE GROUP.

Canadian Cavalry Field Ambulance (less Pack Section).
Sec'bad Cavalry Field Ambulance (less Pack Section).
Mhow Cavalry Field Ambulance (less Pack Section).

17th Brigade R.H.A. Ammunition Column (less Light Sections).

R.C.H.A. Brigade Ammunition Column (less Light Sections).

Reserve Park (less ~~Light~~ HEAVY Sections).

appx 152

SECRET.　　　　　　　　　　COPY No. 23

5TH. CAVALRY DIVISION

OPERATION ORDER No. 44.

REF. MAP 1/100,000.　　　　DATED 22ND NOVEMBER, 1917.

1. The Division will move to the BRAY area on the 23rd instant in accordance with the attached March Table.

2. The rate of march will be 4½ miles per hour - 200 yards distance will be maintained between Regiments, Batteries and Transport Echelons.

3. Route for Cyclists - NURLU - PERONNE - BIACHES - HERBECOURT.

4. Motor Ambulances will move under orders of the A.D.M.S.

5. Divisional Report Centre will close at EQUANCOURT at 11 a.m. and open at SUZANNE at the same hour.

6. Staff Captains & Representatives of Divnl. Troops will meet D.A.A. & Q.M.G at 11-0 Am at SUZANNE Chateau

Copies.
Normal O.O. Dist: 1-23
　Cav. Corps. 24.

N. T. Hodgson Lieut Col.
G.S, 5th Cav: Divn.

Issued by D.R at 10pm

War Diary.
5th Cavalry Division.
G.S.
December 1917.

WAR DIARY
or
INTELLIGENCE SUMMARY
(Erase heading not required.)

S-E-C-R-E-T

Instructions regarding War Diaries and Intelligence Summaries are contained in F.S. Regs., Part II. and the Staff Manual respectively. Title pages will be prepared in manuscript.

GENERAL STAFF, 5TH CAVALRY DIVISION.

Army Form C. 2118.

244

Place	Date	Hour	Summary of Events and Information	Remarks and references to Appendices
	DECEMBER, 1917.			
E.5.a.	1st }		An account of the operations 30th November to 2nd December is attached as an Appendix.	Appx. 157.
E.5.c.	2nd }			
HEUDECOURT.	3rd		Orders issued that Ambala Cavalry Brigade on withdrawal to E.23. will be ready to move up in support of Cavalry Corps Sector (X.13.c.8.5. - GAUCHE WOOD). The Divisional Report Centre closed at HEUDECOURT and opened at LONGAVESNES at 12 noon. The Division, less Artillery and 5th Field Squadron, on withdrawal from the line moved - Canadian Brigade to S.E. of ROISEL - Sec'bad Brigade to E.14. - Ambala Brigade to E.29. Orders issued to Dismounted Men working in BROWN LINE W.18.d.8.7. - W.5.a.1.9. as to their action in case of attack.	Appx. 158
do. LONGAVESNES.	4th		Ambala Cavalry Brigade, strength 650 rifles, ordered to occupy the BROWN LINE as above on the night of the 4th/5th. 13th Machine Gun Squadron ordered to occupy the BROWN LINE on the night 4th/5th under arrangements with Cavalry Corps Machine Gun Officer.	
do.	5th		Ambala Dismounted Brigade and 13th M.G. Squadron in occupation of the BROWN LINE under the orders of G.O.C., Cavalry Corps Sector. Sec'bad and Canadian Brigades ready to move up to the BROWN LINE in the event of an attack on the Cavalry Corps Sector. Situation on this front reported normal. On the night of the 5th/6th Ambala Dismounted Rifles and 13th M.G. Squadron withdrawn from the BROWN LINE and rejoined their Brigades at VILLERS FAUCON and E.14. respectively.	
do.	6th		Field Squadron left forward position about JACQUENNE COPSE, E.5.central and arrived at VILLERS FAUCON. Dismounted Men of the Division (200) who were working on the BROWN LINE under C.R.E. Cavalry Corps returned to ATHIES. G.A.882 issued for movement of Batteries to rejoin Brigades on relief.	Appx. 159
do.	7th		Operation Order No.48 issued.	Appx. 160
do.	8th		Movements took place in accordance with O.O.48 (amended). Divisional Headquarters opens at MONCHY LAGACHE at 2 p.m. 9th.	

SECRET.   5TH CAVALRY DIVISION.

Army Form C. 2118.

WAR DIARY
or
INTELLIGENCE SUMMARY
(Erase heading not required.)

DECEMBER, 1917.

Instructions regarding War Diaries and Intelligence Summaries are contained in F. S. Regs., Part II. and the Staff Manual respectively. Title pages will be prepared in manuscript.

Place	Date	Hour	Summary of Events and Information	Remarks and references to Appendices
	DECEMBER, 1918.			
MONCHY LAGACHE.	9th.		Location of the Division as follows :- Divisional Headquarters MONCHY LAGACHE - Ambala Cavalry Brigade CARTIGNY and BRUSLE - SEC'BAD CAVALRY BRIGADE H.Q. Road in V.4.d., 2 regiments V.3.central, 1 regiment BUIRE, 13th M.G. Squadron BRUSLE - Canadian Cavalry Brigade ROISEL - R.H.A. in line covering Southern Sector of Cavalry Corps front i.e. N. of River OMIGNON.	
do.	10th.		Orders issued for the movement of officer students to Cavalry Corps Equitation School on December 11th to report CAYEUX-sur-MER on evening of 11th. G.S.722/4 and 722/5 issued regarding action of the Division when called upon to act as Reserve to 24th Infantry Division in Cavalry Corps Sector.	Appx.161 & 162
do.	11th.		Warning order received from Cavalry Corps for 13th, 14th and Canadian Machine Gun Squadrons to move to GOMIECOURT reporting there on 12th. These Squadrons to form a mounted reserve for the VI Corps. Warning order sent to Brigades by wire and orders issued at 8.25 a.m. for M.G. Squadrons to rendezvous at DOINGT and march under Major WALKER, Canadian M.G. Squadron, on the 11th to BEAULENCOURT and on 12th to GOMIECOURT. G.57 issued ordering Dismounted Reinforcements of Ambala and Sec'bad Brigades to move to PONUILLY to work under C.R.E., Cavalry Corps. Weather dull, frost at night.	Appx.163
do.	12th.		Orders issued for Canadian Cavalry Brigade to find a working party of 300 to report at road junction S.E. of HESBECOURT (L.13.c.8.2.) at 3.30 p.m. This party is for work under 24th Division. Message received from Cavalry Corps stating that information obtained from prisoners of a German offensive in the morning which might extend South into Cavalry Corps Sector. Ambala Cavalry Brigade is ordered to be saddled up and ready to move from 7 a.m. on 13th. Weather fine but dull.	
do.	13th.		Gun fire to the North throughout the night 12th/13th becoming intensive from 5.30 to 6.30 a.m. At 8.30 a.m. Ambala Cavalry Brigade ordered to off-saddle but to be ready to move at one hour's notice.	
do.	15th.		15th	....

SECRET.

Army Form C. 2118.

DECEMBER, 1918.   5TH CAVALRY DIVISION.

WAR DIARY
INTELLIGENCE/SUMMARY.

(Erase heading not required.)

Instructions regarding War Diaries and Intelligence Summaries are contained in F. S. Regs, Part II. and the Staff Manual respectively. Title pages will be prepared in manuscript.

Place	Date 1918.	Hour	Summary of Events and Information	Remarks and references to Appendices
ONCHY LAGACHE.	15th.		Orders issued for Ambala Cavalry Brigade to take over the working party supplied by Canadian Cavalry Brigade on night 16th/17th. Sec'bad Cavalry Brigade come on one hour's notice to move at 8 a.m. on 16th at which time Ambala Cavalry Brigade ceases to be at short notice.	
do.	16th.		Operation Order No.49 issued for the movement of Canadian Cavalry Brigade, Sec'bad Cavalry Brigade and Divisional Troops into MONCHY LAGACHE area.	Appx.164
do.	17th.		Heavy snow fell during the night 16th/17th. Movements ordered in O.O.49 completed by 2 p.m.	
do.	19th.		G.S.722/5/1 issued. Working parties are supplied by Brigades to clear snow and ice from the roads to permit passage of motor transport. Weather very cold and still.	Appx.165
do.	20th.		Orders issued for Sec'bad Cavalry Brigade to take over on the night 20th/21st the working party supplied by Canadian Cavalry Brigade for work in 24th Division area. Machine Gun Squadrons of the three Brigades rejoined the Division and are billeted in Brigade areas. Canadian Cavalry Brigade comes under one hour's notice relieving Sec'bad Cavalry Brigade. Weather cold and still.	
do.	21st.		9th Hodson's Horse and 14th M.G. Squadron billeted in TERTRY Area. 18th Lancers and Mhow Cavalry Field Ambulance ordered to move into TERTRY Area on 22nd. Ambala Brigade H.Q. and 8th Hussars remain at CARTIGNY until TERTRY Area cleared of the French.	
do.	22nd.		Orders received for Division to find a working party of 600 O.R's for work on the night of the 24th/25th. Orders issued accordingly, G.57/5.	Appx.166
do.	23rd.		Ambala Brigade Headquarters opened at TERTRY and Ambala Brigade (less 8th Hussars at CARTIGNY) is billeted in TERTRY area. Permanent and Training Staff for Divisional School move to BUSSY-LES-DAOURS where School is to be located.	
do.	24th.		600 men of Sec'bad Brigade complete wiring task on the night 24th/25th and return to billets. 26th.	

SECRET.

Army Form C. 2118.

Instructions regarding War Diaries and Intelligence
Summaries are contained in F. S. Regs., Part II.
and the Staff Manual respectively. Title pages
will be prepared in manuscript.

WAR DIARY 5TH CAVALRY DIVISION.
or
INTELLIGENCE SUMMARY.

(Erase heading not required.)

DECEMBER, 1917.

Place	Date	Hour	Summary of Events and Information	Remarks and references to Appendices
MONCHY LAGACHE.	DECEMBER, 1917. 26th.		G.S.722/11 issued regarding the use of Reserves in the Cavalry Corps Sector. Work in progress on Divisional Gas School.	Appx.167
do.	27th.		Reference G.S.722/11 the line from BIHECOURT - R.2.b.0.7. is reconnoitred by the Staff of the Division and the Staff of the three Brigades. Brigades submit their plans in the event of their being ordered up to hold the above line.	
do.	28th.		Division informed by Cavalry Corps that BUSSY-LES-DAOURS is definitely given to 5th Cavalry Division for Divisional School. 2nd Cavalry Divisional School ordered to leave.	
do.	29th.		G.S.722/14 issued shewing roles of Brigades up to January 25th. Amendment to G.S.722/14 issued.	Appx.168 Appx.169.
do.	30th.		Orders received that wiring party of 300 which had been working under C.R.E. 24th Division is no longer required. Orders issued accordingly.	
do.	31st.		Orders issued for attendance of students at Divisional Gas School commencing January 4th. Frost and snow alternately with slight thaws since December 12th.	

H.S.Hopper

Lt-Colonel, G.S.,
5th Cavalry Division.

App 157

5TH CAVALRY DIVISION.

Summary of Operations – 30th November to 2nd December, 1917.

30th November.

Time.

8.50 am. Telephone message received from Cavalry Corps for the Division (which was billeted in the MONCHY LAGACHE Area) to be prepared to move at short notice. All units were informed.

9.20 am. G.C.113 received ordering Division to move to VILLERS FAUCON at once and to send a Staff Officer to H.Q., 55th Infantry Division at E.22.b.5.0. Units were informed immediately by telephone and wire and given the Starting Point of Road junction ½ mile East of ESTREES EN CHAUSSEE. Orders for the march were issued. Reserve Park, A.H.T. Coy., "B" Echelon, Heavy Section Ammunition Column and Dismounted Men remained in billets.

10.30 am. Staff Officer returning from 55th Infantry Division met G.O.C. Division and Brigadiers at Starting Point and gave the situation on VII Corps front. The Division was to move to the valley East of VILLERS FAUCON.

12.15 pm. The leading Brigade – Ambala Cavalry Brigade – arrived East of VILLERS FAUCON at 12.15 pm. followed by Sec'bad and Canadian Cavalry Brigades.

1.20 pm. Operation Orders (under G.A.81) were issued for the advance of the Division after a Conference between the Divisional and Cavalry Corps Commanders at H.Qs. of the 55th Infantry Division.

1.45 pm. Orders were received from Cavalry Corps (G.2) for the 5th Cavalry Division to move at once with the objective – the enemy's flank between VILLERS GUISLAIN and GOUZEAUCOURT. The 4th Cavalry Division had orders to support the 5th Cav. Division as their attack developed.
This was in confirmation of the Conference mentioned above. Cavalry Corps Advanced Headquarters at E.22.b.5.0.
The Ambala Cav. Bde. moved forward as Advanced Guard to the Division with orders to attack the enemy's flank with vigour at BOIS GAUCHE and to the North of that place. (G.A.82 from the Division timed 2.25 pm.)

2.0 pm. Rear Report Centre of the Division at E.23.c.9.0. and Adv. Report Centre at E.5.b.2.4., where Supply Section "A" Echelon, Light Section Ammunition Column and Field Ambulances halted on arrival.

2.25 pm. The Sec'bad Cav. Bde. moved from VILLERS FAUCON with orders to move on the left flank of Ambala Cav. Bde. with GONNELIEU as its objective.
The Canadian Cav. Bde. moved to Divisional Reserve following Sec'bad Cav. Bde. as far as W.29.central. Fighting Section "A" Echelon followed Canadian Cav. Bde. to about E.5.b. and Field Squadron halted at JACQVENNE COPSE.

2.30 pm. Ambala Cav. Bde. got into touch with West Surrey Regiment at W.18.b. and finding our Infantry holding VAUCELLETTE FARM pushed on towards BOIS GAUCHE (Ambala B.M.40).

3.0 pm. ....

30th November (cont'd).

Time.

3.0 pm. Ambala Cav. Bde. Advanced Guard - 8th Hussars - held up by M.G. fire ½ mile South of GOUZEAUCOURT and enemy reported in X.1.& 7. 8th Hussars ordered to attack GAUCHE WOOD and 9th Horse sent up in support. Remainder of the Brigade about CLENIN WELL COPSE. A wired line existed between W.18.a. and X.1.a.
Sec'bad Cav. Bde. directed its Advanced Guard on GOUZEAUCOURT, the main body being at the time about W.5.central.

3.30 pm. The Advanced Guard Sec'bad Cav. Bde. arrived at GOUZEAUCOURT which had just been occupied by the Guards.
The 5th Cavalry Brigade - 2nd Cavalry Division - was held up at Southern edge of GOUZEAUCOURT by M.G. fire from the direction of GONNELIEU. As the left flank of the Guards at GOUZEAUCOURT Station was in the air one squadron, 7th Dragoon Guards, was pushed forward to connect up that point with the nearest troops on the left. Right flank of the 20th Division was found to rest at R.25.b. Patrols were pushed forward towards GONNELIEU with a view to mounted attack but that place was found to be defended by wire and M.G's.

3.50 pm. The Ambala Cav. Bde. (8th Hussars and 9th Horse) occupied the sunken road in W.6.c.& d. and the enemy in W.6.d. were driven back.

4.0 pm. The advance of the Ambala Cav. Bde. (8th Hussars) from the sunken road W.6.c.& d. was stopped by a counter-attack from the ridge running just East of BOIS GAUCHE. The counter-attack was repulsed.
The Canadian Cav. Bde. was pushed forward to co-operate on the right of Ambala Cav. Bde. with VILLERS GUISLAIN as their objective. The Divisional Commander considering this to be the best method of assisting Ambala Cav. Bde. to gain GAUCHE WOOD.

4.30 pm. In accordance with the orders of Cavalry Corps Commander, who had been with the Divisional Headquarters at E.5.b. since 3.30 p.m., the Lucknow Cav. Bde. came under the orders of the 5th Cavalry Division.
At this time H.Q. of the 4th Cavalry Division and Lucknow Cavalry Brigade were with H.Q., 5th Cavalry Division in E.5.b.
Lucknow Cavalry Brigade became Divisional Reserve to 5th Cavalry Division in E.5.central.

4;55 pm. The Lucknow Cav, Bde, was ordered to get into touch with the Infantry Commander in the front PEZIERE - VAUCELLETTE FARM and to send one regiment to W.24.b.& c. to act as support to the above line as it was reported that the enemy was massing for an attack on this front.

5.0 pm. Canadian Cav. Bde. after getting into touch with the Infantry about VAUCELLETTE FARM established a line just East of VAUCELLETTE FARM - X.13.a.3.0. - W.18.central. Brigade H.Q. W.18.d.7.4. Patrols were pushed out along the front and touch was gained with Ambala Cav. Bde. on the left. One prisoner was captured near BEET FACTORY. BEET FACTORY, CHAPEL CROSSING and ground in X.8.c. was held by enemy and M.G's. Ambala Cav. Bde. held sunken road in W.6.b.& d. and touch was gained with 20th Hussars towards their left rear. The enemy was holding the railway line in X.1. and X.7. H.Q., Ambala Cav. Bde. W.17.central.

5.30 p.m. . . . .

30th November (cont'd).

5.30 pm. The Sec'bad Cav. Bde. was about W.5.central with one squadron covering the left of the Guards Brigade.

6.35 pm. The Squadron covering the left of the Guards Brigade about GOUZEAUCOURT Station was withdrawn as touch was gained between the Guards and the 20th Division..

8.30 pm. Warning Order was received from the Cavalry Corps that the Cavalry Corps, les 1st and 3rd Cavalry Divisions, would co-operate with the IIIrd Corps on December 1st.

10.0 pm. G.A.659 issued ordering Sec'bad Cav. Bde. to withdraw into Divisional Reserve to E.5.a.
At this time the R.H.A. batteries of the Division which had been allotted to Brigades when moving forward ("A" Battery, R.C.H.A. to Ambala Cav. Bde.) were in action as follows :-

"B" Battery, R.C.H.A. ... W.18.c. covering Canadian front.

"A" Battery, R.C.H.A. ... W.17.d. covering Ambala front.

"N" Battery. R.H.A. ... W.18.a.

C.R.H.A. was at Divisional H.Q., E.5.b., throughout the operations.

11.30 pm. G.A.662. Orders were issued for the Division to attack VILLERS GUISLAIN - GAUCHE WOOD in conjunction with tanks. <u>Lucknow Cav. Bde.</u> on the Right to attack VILLERS GUISLAIN. <u>Ambala Cav. Bde.</u> on the Left to attack GAUCHE WOOD.

December, 1st.

12.30 am. G.20 was received from the Cavalry Corps giving orders for the attack of the Division and Lucknow Cav. Bde. on VILLERS GUISLAIN - GAUCHE WOOD. 8 Tanks crossing a N. and S. line through W.12.central were to co-operate with the attack on GAUCHE WOOD and 6 tanks crossing the line VAUCELLETTE FARM - CHAPEL HILL were to cooperate with the attack on VILLERS GUISLAIN. Tanks to cross the above mentioned line at 6.30 a.m.
Simultaneous with the attack of 5th Cavalry Division the 4th Cavalry Division was to attack the ridge in X.10. and X.16. and the Guards Division was to seize the QUENTIN MILL ridge.
2nd Cavalry Division to be concentrated West of GOUZEAUCOURT

1.15 am. The Adjutant of the Tanks which were to co-operate in the attack arrived at Divisional H.Q. and a Conference was held at which representatives of Canadian, Ambala and Lucknow Brigades (General GAGE), & C.R.H.A. attended. The action of the Cavalry in conjunction with the Tanks was decided on and the Artillery was brigaded under C.R.H.A. to co-operate with the attack.

3.30 a.m. B.M.50 received from Lucknow Cav. Bde. - O.O. for the attack on VILLERS GUISLAIN.

5.15. am. A message was received from the tanks that on account of delay in coming up all tanks would start from GUENIN WELL COPSE and not as previously arranged. This message had also been sent direct from the Adjutant of the Tanks to the Brigades concerned.

7.15 a.m. ....

1st December. (cont'd). 4.

Time.

7.15 am. The tanks crossed the railway at X.1.c. moving East. (Ambala Cav. Bde.B.M.56). 18th Lancers followed the tanks supported by the 9th Horse, 8th Hussars being in Brigade Reserve.

7.20 am. Lucknow Cav. Bde. B.M.52 received saying the Brigade would co-operate with tanks from VAUCELLETTE FARM when they were seen moving on VILLERS GUISLAIN as they had no time to alter their dispositions and conform with the new starting point of the tanks.

7.27 am. G.A.664 sent to Lucknow Cav. Bde. ordering the Brigade to do everything possible to support the tanks and carry the objective VILLERS GUISLAIN.

7.45 am. Indian Cavalry seen entering GAUCHE WOOD.

8.30 am. 18th Lancers and Guards consolidating the Eastern and Southern edges of GAUCHE WOOD which was entirely in our hands. 4 M.G's sent up to the Wood by Ambala Cav. Bde. One officer, 5 N.C.O's and 37 O.R's were taken prisoner during the attack on BOIS GAUCHE. In addition one M.G. was captured and 10 more wounded prisoners were sent back to the rear without coming to Divisional Headquarters.

8.55 am. Guards on the left of Ambala Cav. Bde. held up about R.31. central. G.A.666 issued ordering Sec'bad Cav. Bde. to re-inforce Ambala Cav. Bde. with one regiment and ordering Ambala Cav. Bde. to attack Northwards after occupying GAUCHE WOOD to assist the Guards.

9.0 am. Lord Strathcona's Horse, Canadian Cav. Bde., taking advantage of the advance of the Ambala Cav. Bde. pushed forward and captured ten prisoners and one M.G. near CHAPEL CROSSING.

9.45 am. 7th Dragoon Guards ordered by Ambala Cav. Bde. to attack North from GAUCHE WOOD. 7th Dragoon Guards supported by the 9th Horse pushed forward and filled the gap between N.E. corner of GAUCHE WOOD and R.32.c. gaining touch with Guards at this point.

10.0 am. B.M.53 received from Lucknow Cav. Bde. stating that patrols had been forward since 8 a.m.

11.15 am. B.M.54 timed 10.30 a.m. received from Lucknow Cav. Bde. stating that two attempts had been made to push forward from VAUCELLETTE FARM on VILLERS GUISLAIN but that these were held up by M.G. fire from X.14.a. and X.13.d.3.1. Two squadrons had also been pushed forward towards GAUCHE WOOD with a view to attacking VILLERS GUISLAIN from the West but were held up by M.G. fire.
6 tanks had been seen returning West but none were seen going near VILLERS GUISLAIN.

12 noon. Situation on Ambala Cav. Bde. front as follows :-
One Squadron. 9th Horse between CHAPEL CROSSING and X.7. central. - Grenadiers from X.7.central to S.W. corner of GAUCHE WOOD - S.& E. from GAUCHE WOOD held by Grenadiers and 18th Lancers - 7th Dragoon Guards from N.E. corner of GAUCHE WOOD to R.32.central.

12.40 p.m. ....

1st December (cont'd).

Time.

12.40 pm. G.A.674 issued.- under orders from Cavalry Corps Lucknow Cav. Bde. passes to the 4th Cavalry Division.

1.15 pm. Orders issued for the attack of the Canadian Cav. Bde on the objective - Outskirts of VILLERS GUISLAIN - Eastern edge of GAUCHE WOOD, at 3 p.m. The 4th Cavalry Division with Lucknow Cav. Bde. on its left were attacking VILLERS GUISLAIN and the high ground S.E. of the valley in X.10., at the same time. The dividing line between Lucknow Cav. Bde. and Canadian Cav. Bde. was VAUCELLETTE FARM - X.13. central - X.8.central - X.2.d.9.0.

3.0 pm. Lord Strathcona's Horse moved forward to attack.

3.20 pm. CHAPEL CROSSING and one M.G. captured.

4.0 pm. One Squadron Lord Strathcona's Horse reached S.E. corner of GAUCHE WOOD, moving on objective. This squadron was followed closely by another squadron of Lord Strathcona's Horse. An enemy trench running East and West in X.7.c. reported strongly held by enemy and M.G's. Lucknow Cav. Bde attack did not appear to be progressing on the right flank.

4.5 pm. Enemy retiring towards VILLERS GUISLAIN from X.7.d. Four prisoners and one M.G. were taken.

4.20 pm. Strong enemy counter-attack from direction of BEET FACTORY.

4.50 pm. Owing to Lucknow Cav. Bde. attack having made no progress on the right and the enemy having counter-attacked from that direction advance by Canadian Cavalry Brigade on final objective was impossible.

5.40 pm. G.A.679 issued in accordance with Cav. Corps G.20 ordering Sec'bad Cav. Bde. to relieve Ambala Cav. Bde. and hold the front from road in X.7.c. to BOIS GAUCHE, inclusive, which was allotted to 5th Cavalry Division - 4th Cavalry Division holding VAUCELLETTE FARM, exclusive, to road in X.7.c., inclusive.- 7th Dragoon Guards to come under orders of Sec'bad Cav. Bde. when relief commenced - C.R.H.A. to arrange to barrage the front in conjunction with 4th Cav. Division on the right and Guards Division on the left.

6.25 pm. Lord Strathcona's Horse ordered by Canadian Cav. Bde. not to attempt to gain their final objective but to co-operate with the troops holding GAUCHE WOOD.

7.14 pm. G.A.680 issued in accordance with instructions received from Cavalry Corps ordering a strong M.G. barrage to be arranged from GAUCHE WOOD up valley X.2.b. - R.33.b.

8.0 pm. Barrages arranged as above by 13th M.G. Squadron assisted by 6 M.G's from 14th M.G. Squadron.

2nd December.

12.10 am. G.A.684 issued on receipt of G.43 from Cav. Corps stating that a strong hostile attack was to be expected this morning. The Division to hold the line it now occupied at all costs. Orders for the action of the Division in the event of the hostile attack taking place issued.

1.30 a.m. ....

2nd December (cont'd).

Time.		
1.30	am.	Relief of Canadian Cav. Bde. by 4th Cavalry Division completed. Brigade, less Brigade H.Q., one regiment and one section of M.G's, moved to E.5.central - 1 regiment and one section M.G's remained at W.24.a. during the night as hostile attack was expected.
5.0	am.	Ambala Cav. Bde. relieved in the line by Sec'bad Cav. Bde. 8th Hussars and 14th M.G. Squadron remained up as Reserve to Sec'bad Cav. Bde. Ambala Cav. Bde., less 8th Hussars and 14th M.G. Squadron, moved to W.29.
7.0	am.	8th Hussars and 6 M.G's, 14th M.G. Squadron, moved up into Brigade Reserve to Sec'bad Cav. Bde. to W.10.d.
8.40	am.	G.A.686 issued ordering G.O.C., Sec'bad Cav. Bde. to report as early as possible his method of holding the line and plan of defence in case of attack.
10.10	am.	B.M.12 received from Sec'bad Cav. Bde. stating line held as follows :- X.7.a.1.2. held by two troops of Deccan Horse - X.7.a.central held by two troops of Deccan Horse - 2 Squadrons, Deccan Horse in trench line X.7.b.0.7. - X.8.a.2.9. Support Squadron of Deccan Horse and Regt'l H.Q. at X.1.c.17. Eastern edge of GAUCHE WOOD held by 3 squadrons Poona Horse, and Regt'l H.Q. and supporting squadron in GAUCHE WOOD. 7th Dragoon Guards in sunken road W.6.c.& b. in support to front line. Brigade H.Q. and 8th Hussars in Brigade Reserve in W.10.d.
11.15	am.	G.X.51 issued reporting large bodies of the enemy seen South of VILLERS GUISLAIN.
12 noon.		Personal interview between G.O.C. Sec'bad Cav. Bde. and G.O.C. 35th Infantry Brigade when arrangements were made for action in case of attack.
12.40	pm.	G.A.688 issued ordering Canadian Cav. Bde. to stand to ready to move.
1.25	pm.	G.53 received from Cav. Corps placing 5th Field Squadron under C.R.E. Cavalry Corps for work on strong points in 2nd line. O.C., 5th Field Squadron informed.
2.15	pm.	G.A.689 issued - 1st Cavalry Division would relieve 5th Cavalry Division in the line on the night 2nd/3rd.
2.30	pm.	G.A.690 issued to Sec'bad Cav. Bde. reporting continuous movement of hostile troops in X.4. and X.5. (as was stated in Cav. Corps I.G.45).
3.0	pm.	G.A.691 issued ordering each Brigade to find a Working Party of 3 officers and 65 O.R's. for work in the 2nd line under C.R.E. Cavalry Corps in accordance with Cavalry Corps G.53.
4.0	pm.	Divisional Report Centre closed at E.5.a. and opened at HEUDECOURT.

5.0 p.m. ....

2nd December (cont'd).

Time.

- 5.0 pm. A body of the enemy moved against S.E. corner of GAUCHE WOOD. 10 succeeded in entering the Wood of whom 8 were killed. The enemy were driven off.

- 6.20 pm. GAUCHE WOOD was heavily shelled.

- 6.45 pm. G.60 received from Cavalry Corps ordering the Division to move to area about LONGAVESNES.

- 8.0 pm. Relief of the sector held by 5th Cavalry Division commenced. Command passed at midnight 2nd/3rd. and the Sec'bad Cav. Bde. moved to W.22., 8th Hussars and 14th M.G. Squadron rejoining Ambala Cav. Bde.

- 10.0 pm. 400 Dismounted Men from 4th and 5th Cavalry Division arrived at HEUDECOURT and moved up under arrangements made by the 5th Cavalry Division to work in the 2nd line of Cavalry Corps sector under the C.R.E. Cavalry Corps.

- 11.0 pm. G.A.697 issued ordering the Division, less Artillery, to move to LONGAVESNES, Area S.E. of ROISEL in E.23. and Area in E.14. Field Squadron remained in forward area under the orders of C.R.E. Cavalry Corps.

3rd December.

- 10.0 am. The Dismounted Men of 4th and 5th Cavalry Divisions billeted North of road in W.16.c. reported to all concerned.

    Withdrawal of the Division to areas round LONGAVESNES complete by 1.15 p.m. Divisional H.Q. at LONGAVESNES.

The total number of prisoners captured by the Division during the operations was :-

By Ambala Cav. Bde. ...... 55 and 1 M.G.
(Of these 43 passed through Divisional H.Q. Remainder went direct to Ambualnces.)

By Canadian Cav. Bde. ... 15 and 4 M.G's.

1 M.G. passed through Divisional H.Q., 1 passed to D.A.D.O.S. and 2 were left in the line in action.

&&&&&&&&&&&&&&&&&&&&&&&&&&

5th Cavalry Division,
6th December, 1917.

Intelligence Summary – 30th Nov. to 2nd Dec.

The most valuable identification obtained was that given by the first prisoner captured (by F.S.H. on the evening of 30.11.17). He belonged to the 25 I.R., 208th Division.

A map captured at GOUZEAUCOURT earlier in the day shewed the 25th I.R. as attached to the 34th Division, which was known, before the 5th Cavalry Division took part in the operations, to be already in the line. But there was no indication whatever that the whole of the 208th Division was present on this front until the capture of this prisoner. The Division was only relieved 3 days before in the ST. MINIEL salient. The prisoner gave the information that there were two regiments of his Division in immediate reserve, of which, without him, we should have known nothing. One of these Regt. was identified by prisoners on the evening of the next day, 1st December, being the 185th I.R., of whom 4 prisoners were taken by the L.S.H. Their battalion had come into line the same morning (1st Dec.), as stated by the prisoner of the 25th I.R.. This identification was valuable as giving an indication of the extent to which the enemy was using up the reserves immediately available.

The other prisoners captured were of the 145. I.R. of the 34th Divn., (43 by G.H. and 9 with 2 M.G. by L.S.H.). Among these were a few of the 30. I.R. (34th Divn.) who had lost their way after carrying back wounded.

These men ----

These men of the 145.I.R. were captured at different points between CHAPEL CROSSING and GAUCHE WOOD, and therefore gave an indication of the extent of front occupied by that Regt., and as belonging to different companies and battalions, of the extent to which that Regt. had been used up in the fighting.

Among the papers sent to Divisional H.Q. perhaps the most valuable was a set containing a map issued by the German Staff before operations, shewing the various barrages, the direction of the various units advance, and its limits; this was accompanied by a Divisional Order, shewing the tactics employed in the attack by all arms, even down to transport arrangements.

SECRET AND URGENT. No. G.A. 795.

Headquarters, 5th Cavalry Divn.
4th December, 1917.

To/ Canadian Cavalry Brigade.
   Sec'bad Cavalry Brigade.
   Ambala Cavalry Bde.
   C.R.H.A.
   5th Field Squadron.
   5th Signal Squadron.
   A.D.M.S.
   A.P.M.
   A.A. & Q.M.G.
   2nd Cavalry Divn.
   Cavalry Corps.

1. The 2nd Cavalry Division will relieve the 1st Cavalry Division in the line tonight 4th/5th December.

2. The Ambala Cavalry Brigade (less 14th M.G. Sqdn.), strength 650 rifles, will be in support to the 2nd Cavalry Divn. and will move dismounted into the BROWN LINE this afternoon. Move to be completed by 4 p.m. at which time the Ambala Cav. Bde. will come under orders of the 2nd Cavalry Divn.

3. The 14th M.G. Sqdn. and horses of the Ambala Bde. will remain at VILLERS FAUCON.

4. The 13th M.G. Sqdn. was placed under the orders of the G.O.C. Cavalry Corps Sector at 9 a.m. this morning and now occupies positions in the BROWN LINE.

5. The Canadian and Sec'bad Brigades will act as Reserve to the Cavalry Corps Sector.

(a) The Sec'bad Bde (less M.G. Sqdn) strength 650 rifles, will be ready to move at ½ hour's notice by day and 1 hour's notice by night to a position of readiness at W.1.a.9.1.

The Brigade will move dismounted and the horses of the Brigade will remain in the present area.

The above state of readiness will come into force from 2 p.m. to-day.

On orders being received for the Brigade to move a Staff Officer will immediately report to G.O.C. Cavalry Corps Sector at W.1.d.3.0. for orders.

(b)..................

No. G.A. 795 (cont'd.)

(b) The Canadian Bde. will remain in its present area, and, in the event of the Sec'bad Bde. being ordered forward, will receive orders to saddle-up and stand-to ready to move, to the position of readiness at W.16.d.9.1.

A Staff Officer will at the same time be sent to W.16.d.3.0. for orders.

6. Orders for the moves of Cavalry Field Ambulances will be issued by A.D.M.S.

7. Divisional Report Centre remains at LONGAVESNES, E.25.d.5.9.

8. Canadian, Sec'bad and Ambala Brigades to ACKNOWLEDGE.

J. D. Rorke Capt
for
Lt Col.
G.S., 5th Cavalry Div.

Issued at 4.30 pm.

SECRET.
No. G.A. 882.
Headquarters, 5th Cavalry Divn.
6th December, 1917.

App. 159

To/
    Canadian Cavalry Brigade.   5th Field Sqdn.
    Sec'bad Cavalry Brigade   5th Signal Sqdn.
    Ambala Cavalry Brigade   A.D.M.S.
    17th Brigade, R.H.A.   O.C. A.S.C.
    R.C.H.A. Brigade.   A.P.&.M.S.
    17th Bde. R.H.A. Ammn. Col.

1. The Cavalry Corps, less Artillery, was relieved in the line last night.

2. The State of Readiness ordered in this office No. G.A. 795 dated 4th inst., ceases, but Sec'bad Cavalry Brigade will until further orders be ready to move out at short notice, i.e. exercise parties must not go far from camp.

3. The 17th Brigade, R.H.A. and R.C.H.A. Brigade will be relieved to-night and on relief will move as under :-

    H.Q. 17th Bde. R.H.A. .... LONGAVESNES.
        (Bivouacs from Camp Comdt.)

    R.C.H.A. Bde. .... ROISEL area
        (Route - SAULCOURT - VILLERS FAUCON)
        (Bivouacs from Staff Captain,)
        (Canadian Cav. Bde.)

    "N" Battery, R.H.A. .... to E.14.b.
        (bivouacs from Staff Captain Sec'bad Cav. Bde.)

Light Sections, Ammunition Column will move with Batteries.

4. When the movements in para. 3 have been completed the Division will remain in its present area.

5. ACKNOWLEDGE.

J. P. Burke
Captain, G.S.
5th Cavalry Division

Appx. 100

```
-----------
S E C R E T.                                    Copy No. 23
-----------
```

5TH CAVALRY DIVISION.

Operation Order No.48.

Ref. 1/40,000 Map.   Dated 7th December, 1917.

1. The Sec'bad Cavalry Brigade, Ambala Cavalry Brigade and Reserve Park will move to-morrow in accordance with attached March Table.

2. The remainder of the Division, including 5th Field Squadron, will remain as at present located.
   The Canadian Cavalry Brigade will be ready to move at one hour's notice.

3. "B" Echelons of Ambala and Sec'bad Cavalry Brigades will accompany Brigades.

4. Staff Captains of Ambala and Sec'bad Cavalry Brigades and a Representative of Reserve Park will meet A.A.& Q.M.G. at fork roads J.32.d.9.9. at 11 a.m. to-morrow for allotment of areas.

5. Distance of 200 yards to be maintained between regiments and Transport Echelons.

6. Divisional Report Centre remains at LONGAVESNES.

7. ACKNOWLEDGE.

                                   W. T. Hodgson Lt-Colonel, G.S.
                                                 5th Cavalry Division.

Issued by D.R. at 10 30 pm

To/
        O.O. Distribution Nos 1 to 23.

SECRET

5TH CAVALRY DIVISION.

MARCH TABLE (ISSUED WITH OPERATION ORDER NO. 48)

FORMATION OR UNIT	STARTING POINT	TIME	ROUTE	DESTINATION	REMARKS.
Ambala Cav. Bde. Mhow Cav. Fd. Amb.	Brigade arrangements	—	ROISEL – S. of River COLOGNE.	CARTIGNY – BRUSLE	Head not to enter BRUSLE before 2 p.m.
Sec'd Cav. Bde. Sec'd Cav. Fd. Amb.	Brigade arrangements	—	LONGAVESNES – TINCOURT.	BUIRE – COURCELLES.	Head not to enter BUIRE before 2 p.m.
Reserve Park (less Heavy Section)	To follow	Decided leav. Bde.		CARTIGNY.	—

App. 161

```
*-*-*-*-*-*-*                           No. G.S. 722/4.
S E C R E T.
*-*-*-*-*-*-*            Headquarters, 5th Cavalry Division.
                                   10th December 1917.
```

To/
    O.O. Distribution.

Reference Map
1/40,000.
----

1.   In the event of the 5th Cavalry Division being ordered to reinforce the Infantry holding the line, the following movements will take place at once:-

       CANADIAN CAVALRY BRIGADE.- will concentrate in K.18.b.

       AMBALA CAVALRY BRIGADE.- will move by the most direct route as far as K.24.d.

       SEC'BAD CAVALRY BRIGADE.- will concentrate in K.29.a. Units of the Brigade billetted in the CARTIGNY Area will follow Ambala Brigade as far as K.29.a., remainder of the Brigade will move via VRAIGNES - HANCOURT.

2.   "A.1" Echelon will accompany Brigades.

3.   Reserve Park, A.H.T. Coy, Ammunition Column (less S.A.A. limbers), "A.2" Echelon, "B" Echelon and Dismounted Men will remain as at present located.
      Brigades will concentrate "A.2" Echelons, "B" Echelons and Dismounted Men in their present areas and report location to Advanced Divisional Report Centre.

4.   S.A.A. limbers with 17th Bde R.H.A. and R.C.H.A. Ammunition Columns will concentrate on road N.W. of HERVILLY, K.23.c., where they will receive orders to join "A.1" Echelons of Brigades.

5.   Liaison Officers and Gallopers will report to Advanced Divisional Headquarters.

6.   Advanced Divisional Headquarters will open at cross roads, HERVILLY, K.23.d.5.3.

7.   ACKNOWLEDGE.

                                             Lieut-Colonel, G.S.,
                                             5th Cavalry Division.

SECRET.   No.G.S.722/5.

Appx. 162

Headquarters, 5th Cavalry Division,

10th December, 1917.

To/
    O.O. Distribution.

1. Until further orders the Division is to be ready to turn out at short notice and from 6.30 a.m. to 8 a.m. units will stand to ready to saddle up.

2. Exercise will not take place until after 10 a.m. and no horses are to be taken far from the squadron lines.

3. The Canadian Cavalry Brigade will contiue to be held in readiness to move at one hour's notice.

4. From reports received there are still indications that the enemy may continue his attacks.

5. In the case of a serious attack the 4th Cavalry Division will move to a position of readiness in the valley S. of SMALLFOOT WOOD in Squares R.8., R.14., R.15., R.20. and from this position will be ready to :-

    (a) Hold the second line from BIHUCOURT inclusive to strong point in L.31.d. inclusive.

    (b) Reinforce any part of the intermediate line from the soutern boundary to FERVAQUE FARM inclusive.

    (c) Deliver an attack in that area.

    (d) Move North to a second position of readiness about JEANCOURT, squares L.26.b., L.20.d. and L.21.c. should a strong attack take place in the 24th Division sector.

6. Similarly the 5th Cavalry Division will move to a position of readiness near HERVILLY to be ready to :-

    (a) Hold the second line from strong point in L.31.d., exclusive, to the northern boundary of the Corps area.

    (b) Reinforce any part of the intermediate line from FERVAQUE FARM to the northern boundary.

    (c) Man the Corps switch running from FERVAQUE FARM through squares L.9.b. and d., L.8.b. and d. to the second line in square L.7.d.3.1.

    (d) Move South to a second position of readiness between JEANCOURT and MONTIGNY FARM in case of a successful attack on the right sector of the line. (enemy)

7. In the case of (a). The Division will hold the second line as under :-

                                                        (i) ....

No.G.S.722/5 (cont'd).

7.(cont'd).

    (i) Ambala Cavalry Brigade. From strong point in L.31.d., exclusive, to road L.13.d.2.1., inclusive.

    (ii) Canadian Cavalry Brigade. From L.13.d.2.1., exclusive, to COLOGNE River S. of GEORGES COPSE, L.1.c.

    (iii) Sec'bad Cavalry Brigade. Will be in reserve West of HERVILLY about K.29.a.

In case (b).

Ambala Cavalry Brigade will reinforce from FERVAQUE FARM, exclusive, and TEMPLEUX - HARGICOURT Road, L.4.c.8.5., inclusive.

Canadian Cavalry Brigade, will reinforce from the TEMPLEUX - HARGICOURT Road L.4.c.8.5., exclusive, to cutting F.22.central., inclusive.

In case (c). The Ambala Cavalry Brigade will occupy the Corps switch L.16.a.4.3. - L.15.b.1.9. - L.9.c.2.2. - L.8.d.5.3. - L.8.c.5.7. - L.7.d.5.2.

In case (d). The Division will move South with a view to mounted action.
    The Sec'bad Cavalry Brigade will be the Advanced Guard of the Division.

Reconnaissances of the lines to be occupied, lines of approach and lines to be reinforced will be carried out by Brigades at once.

8. Report Centres are as under :-

    Right Brigade, 24th Division.- HERVILLY, K.24.c.4.3.

    Left Brigade, 24th Division.- HAUT WOODS, L.7.c.4.4.

    24th Division.- NOBESCOURT FARM, K.32.b.9.9.

    3rd Dismounted Bde - R.8.6.1.2.

The Advanced Report Centre of the 5th Cavalry Division will be at HERVILLY, K.23.d.5.3.

9. ACKNOWLEDGE.

                                     Lt-Colonel, G.S.,
                                       5th Cavalry Division.

War Diary
App 163

No. G.57.

Headquarters, 5th Cavalry Division,

11th December, 1917.

To/
O.C., Dismounted Reinforcements,
5th Cavalry Division.

1. The following party to be detailed by O.C., Dismounted Reinforcements will march to-morrow at 11 a.m. from FOURQUES to POEUILLY for work under the C.R.E. Cavalry Corps :-

O.C.- .... Major RISLEY, 18th Lancers.
Actg. Adjutant and Q.Mr. To be detailed by O.C. Dismounted
(Reinforcements.

From Indian Dismounted Reinforcements, Ambala Cavalry Brigade.

1 British Officer, 2 Indian Officers, 75 Other Ranks.

From Indian Dismounted Reinforcements, Sec'bad Cavalry Brigade.

1 British Officer, 2 Indian Officers, 75 Other Ranks.

2. The O.C., Dismounted Reinforcements will detail the necessary cooks, batmen, etc., in addition to the above numbers.

3. The A.A.& Q.M.G. will detail 3 L.G.S. Wagons from the Reserve Park and 1 water wagon to accompany the party.

4. The necessary Medical personnel will be detailed by the A.D.M.S.

5. Accommodation at POEUILLY will be allotted by Cavalry Corps "Q".

6. The O.C., L.S.C. will detail one lorry to be at Hdqrs., Dismounted Reinforcements FOURQUES at 10.30 a.m. to-morrow to convey the kits of the party to POEUILLY.

7. The O.C., Dismounted Reinforcements will render to this office a statement shewing the names of the officers accompanying the party and the number of O.R's by units.

8. ACKNOWLEDGE. (O.C. Dismounted Reinforcements only).

R. T. Hodgson
Lt-Colonel, G.S.,
5th Cavalry Division.

Copies to :- C.R.E. Cavalry Corps.
Canadian Cav. Bde.
Sec'bad Cav. Bde.
Ambala Cav. Bde.
Q.
O.C. ASC
ADMS. / for information & necessary action

SECRET.   Copy No. 23

5TH CAVALRY DIVISION.
OPERATION ORDER NO.49.

Ref. Map 1/40,000.   Dated 16th December, 1917.

1.   Movements will take place on the 17th inst., in accordance with the attached March Table.

2.   Dismounted Reinforcements will move under orders to be issued by A.A.& Q.M.G.

3.   Orders have been issued direct to 7th Dragoon Guards, Sec'bad Cavalry Field Ambulance and Light Section Reserve Park.

4.   ACKNOWLEDGE.

                                            Captain, G.S.,
                                            5th Cavalry Division.

Issued by D.R. at 5 p.m.

To/
    O.O. Distribution Nos 1 to 23
    7th Dragoon Guards.... No. 24
    Sec'bad Cav. Fd. Amblce " 25
    Light Section Reserve Pk." 26
    Cavalry Corps   27

5TH CAVALRY DIVISION.

MARCH TABLE - (Issued with Operation Order No.49)

FORMATION OR UNIT.	STARTING POINT	TIME	ROUTE	DESTINATION.	REMARKS.
Canadian Cavalry Brigade (less R.C.H.A. Brigade) Can. M.G. Squadron) Canadian Cav. Fd. Amb.	Cross roads in K.33.a.	10.30 a.m.	HANCOURT - VRAIGNES.	MERAUCOURT AREA.	
17th Bde. R.H.A. Ammn. Column. R.C.H.A. Bde. Ammn. Col.	Church at DEVISE	3.0 a.m.	DEVISE - MERAUCOURT	MONCHY LAGACHE	
Reserve Park (less Light Section).	- do -	9.15 a.m.	- do -	- do -	
Sec'bad Cavalry Brigade (less "N" Battery R.H.A., 7th Dragoon Guards, 15th M.G. Squadron and Sec'bad Cav. Fd. Ambulance.)	MONTECOURT	11.0 a.m.	MERAUCOURT - TERTRY.	TREFCON AREA.	
7th Dragoon Guards, Sec'bad Cav. Fd. Amb. Light Sect. Res.Park.	Cross roads BIAS P.9.c.	10.0 a.m.	Direct Route.	TREFCON AREA.	Will march under orders of 7th Dragoon Guards, Light Section, Reserve Park move to MONCHY LAGACHE from road junction in . P.30.d.

Appx 16

S E C R E T.   No. G.S.722/5/1.

                                    Headquarters, 5th Cavalry Division,
                                            19th December, 1917.

To/
    O.C. Distribution.

        Reference G.S.722/5 of 10th December.

        Paras. 1 and 2 relating to the Division standing to from 6.30 a.m. to 8 a.m. and to the hour of "Exercise" are cancelled.

        The Sec'bad Cavalry Brigade will continue to be ready to move at one hour's notice.

                        [signature]   Lt-Colonel, G.S.,
                                        5th Cavalry Division.

URGENT.

No G.57/5.

Headquarters, 5th Cavalry Division.

22nd December 1917.

To

Ambala Cavalry Brigade.
Sec'bad Cavalry Brigade.
A.A and Q.M.G.
O.C., A.S.C.
Camp Commandant.

---

1. The working party of 300 men at present found by the Sec'bad Cavalry Brigade for work under the G.R.E.24th Division will, on the 24th instant, be found by the Ambala Cavalry Brigade.

2. The O.C., A.S.C. will detail 15 lorries to report at Ambala Cavalry Brigade Headquarters at 1-45 p.m., on the 24th and on the following days to convey the party to TEMPLEUX LE GUERARD.
   The lorries will bring the party back to TERTRY on completion of the night's work.

3. The Sec'bad Cavalry Brigade will find 600 men, with proportion of Officers and N.C.O's, on the night of the 24th instant for wiring under the 129th Company R.E., 24th Division.
   The 600 men will be organised in four parties, each of 150, and the work is to be completed in one night.

4. The four officers detailed to command these four parties will meet the O.C. 129th Field Company R.E., at his Headquarters, at ROISEL, tomorrow, 23rd inst, at 9-45 a.m., and proceed with him to reconnoitre the work and arrange tasks, etc.
   A Divisional car will report at the Headquarters Sec'bad Cavalry Brigade at 8-30 a.m., tomorrow for the use of these officers.

5. Orders regarding rendezvous of Sec'bad Party and conveyance to and from rendezvous, will be issued later.

ACKNOWLEDGE.

(sd) W.T.HODGSON.Lieut Colonel.

G.S., 5th Cavalry Division.

Appx 16?

SECRET.
No. G.S.722/11.

Headquarters, 5th Cavalry Division,

26th December, 1917.

To/
C.O. Distribution.

Ref. Map 1/40,000.

1. The following instructions regarding the use of the Reserves in the Cavalry Corps Sector will come into force at 7 a.m. on December 27th and the orders issued under G.S.722/5 and para.4 of G.S.57/4 will at that hour be cancelled.

2. The troops available for the defence of the Corps Sector are 5th Cavalry Divisions and the 24th Division.
   These Divisions are situated as follows :-

   "C" Cavalry Division (3rd Cav. Div.) holding the Right Sector with horses N.W. of AMIENS.

   "B" Cavalry Division (2nd Cav. Div.) holding the Centre Sector with horses S.W. of AMIENS.

   24th Division holding the Left Sector.

   "A" Cavalry Division (1st Cav. Div.) in the DOINGT area)
   "D" Cavalry Division (4th Cav. Div.) in the ATHIES area) Mobile
   "E" Cavalry Division (5th Cavalry Div.) in the   ) reserve.
                                            CAULAINCOURT area)

3. In the case of an attack on a large scale and the Reserve being ordered to move forward the Divisions in Mobile Reserve will act as under :-

   (a) "E" Cavalry Division (5th Cav.Div.)

       One Brigade will man the defences of the 2nd Line from the River MIGNON - grid line in R.2.b.0.7., inclusive.
       The remainder of the Division will move to a position of readiness about Squares R.14., 15. and 20.

   (b) "A" Cavalry Division (1st Cav.Div.)

       One Brigade will man the defences of the 2nd Line from grid line in R.2.b.0.7., exclusive to the work in L.19.d.7.5., exclusive.
       The remainder of the Division will move to a position of readiness in K 28 and 29 with Divisional Headqrs at HERVILLY.

   (c) "D" Cavalry Division (4th Cav.Div.)

       Will move to position of readiness between HANCOURT and BEAUMETZ with Divisional Headquarters at BOUVINCOURT.

   The 2nd Line from the work in L.19.d.7.5. to the Northern boundary of the Corps will be held by the 24th Division.

4. In the event of the Division being called on to carry out the role allotted in para.3 (a) above

(i) ....

No.G.S.722/11 (cont'd)

(i) The Sec'bad Cavalry Brigade, which after 7 a.m. on 27th inst. will be at one hour's notice, will move at once to occupy the 2nd Line from the River OMIGNON to R.2.b.0.7. inclusive.
Route - CAULAINCOURT - VERMAND.

The necessary reconnaissances will be carried out at once and a report under the following headings will be submitted to Divisional Headquarters by 6 p.m. on 27th inst.

(a) Method and plan for holding the line, giving dispositions.
(b) Plan of the M.G. defence, giving positions of guns.
(c) Position of led horses.
(d) Position of No.1 "A" Echelon.
(e) Position of Brigade Report Centre.

(ii) The remainder of the Division, less R.H.A., Ammunition Column, 5th Field Squadron, Reserve Park, Aux. H.T. Coy., "B" Echelon and Dismounted Reinforcements, will concentrate about R.14., 15., and 20, units moving as under :-

	Route.
Divisional Hdqrs. and Signal Sqdn.	- CAULAINCOURT - VERMAND.
Canadian Cavalry Brigade	- Road junction East of ESTREES-EN-CHAUSSEE - POEUILLY - SOYECOURT.
Ambala Cavalry Brigade	- CAULAINCOURT - VERMAND.

Exact points of concentration for the Canadian and Ambala Cavalry Brigades will be notified later.

(iii) No.1 "A" Echelon and Cavalry Field Ambulances will accompany Brigades.

(iv) The following units will hook in and remain in their present areas ready to move :-
"B" Echelon.
Reserve Park.
Aux.H.T. Company.
Ammunition Column.
A representative of each reporting to A.A.& Q.M.G. at Divn'l Hdqrs., MONCHY LAGACHE, for orders.

5. Reference para.4 (i) the role allotted to the Sec'bad Cavalry Brigade will be taken by each Brigade in turn for a period of 6 days as under :-
Sec'bad Cav. Bde. from 7 a.m. 27th Dec.'17 to 4 pm. 1st Jan.'18.
Ambala Cav. Bde. from 4 p.m. 1st Jan.'18 to 4 p.m. 7th Jan.'18.
Canadian Cav. Bde. from 4 pm. 7th Jan.'18 to 4 p.m. 13th Jan.'18.

Ambala and Canadian Cavalry Brigades will in consequence carry out the reconnaissances ordered in para.4 (i) above and send in their reports to this office by December 31st and January 6th, respectively.

6. Movement will where possible be across country and by the shortest route.

7. Dismounted Reinforcements will stand to in Brigades' Areas.

8. In the event of the moves ordered above being carried out the Divisional Report Centre will open at CHURCH, VENDELLES.

9. ACKNOWLEDGE.

J. O'Rorke
Captain, G.S.,
5th Cavalry Division.

Copy to Cav Corps

```
S E C R E T.
```
Appx 168 War Diary

No. G.S. 722/14.

Headquarters, 5th Cavalry Division,
29th December, 1917.

To/
O.O. Distribution.

Reference this office No.G.S.722/11 dated 26.12.17, "Instructions regarding the use of the Reserves in the Cavalry Corps Sector".

1. From Para.1 of above quoted memo. delete "and para.4 of G.S.57/4".

2. The Division, in addition to the role described in para.3 (a) of G.S.722/11, will place one Brigade at the disposal of the G.O.C., Dismounted Divisions in the line, (H.Q. BOUVINCOURT).

3. The Brigade whose role it is to occupy the line R. OMIGNON to R.2.b.0.7., will not be at one hour's notice.

4. The duties of Brigades will be as in the attached table.

5. ACKNOWLEDGE.

W.T. Hodgson Lt. Col.
G.S.,
5th Cavalry Division.

SECRET.

TABLE OF DUTIES OF BRIGADES. (issued with G.S.722/14 dated 29.12.17).

1. Brigade.	2. 27th December to 4 pm. 1st Jan.	3. 4 pm. Jan 1st to 4 pm. Jan. 7th.	4. 4 pm. Jan. 7th. to 4 pm. Jan. 13th.	5. 4 pm. Jan. 13th. to 4 pm. Jan. 19th.	6. 4 pm. Jan.19th to 4 pm. Jan.25th.
SEC'BAD CAV. BDE.	Prepared to occupy the line R.OMIGNON-R.2.b.0.7.	One hour's notice to act as mounted Reserve to Dismounted Divisions.	Working Party for 24th Division.	As in Column 2	As in Column 3 and so on.
AMB.LA CAV. BDE.	Working Party for 24th Division.	Prepared to occupy the line R.OMIGNON to R.2.b.0.7.	One hour's notice to act as mounted Reserve to Dismounted Divisions.	- do -	- do -
CANADIAN CAV.BDE.	One hour's notice to act as mounted Reserve to Dismounted Divisions.	Working Party for 24th Division.	Prepared to occupy the line R.OMIGNON to R.2.b.0.7.	- do -	- do -

W.T.H.

The Brigade under orders to occupy the line R. OMIGNON to R.2.b.0.7. will on receipt of orders to move send a Staff Officer at once to Dismounted Divisions Hdqrs., SMALLFOOT WOOD.

The Brigade under orders to act as mounted Reserve to Dismounted Divisions will on receipt of orders to move send a Staff Officer to BOUVINCOURT.

No.G.S.722/15.

Headquarters, 5th Cavalry Division,
30th December, 1917.

To/ C.O. Distribution.

     Reference Table of Duties of Brigades issued with this office No.G.S.722/14 dated 29th inst., for " 4 p.m." read "12 noon" throughout the Table.

A. T. Hodgson.
Lt-Colonel, G.S.,
5th Cavalry Division.

SECRET.

Army Form C. 2118.

WAR DIARY or INTELLIGENCE SUMMARY

GENERAL STAFF, 5TH CAVALRY DIVISION.

(Erase heading not required.)

Instructions regarding War Diaries and Intelligence Summaries are contained in F.S. Regs., Part II. and the Staff Manual respectively. Title pages will be prepared in manuscript.

Place	Date	Hour	Summary of Events and Information	Remarks and references to Appendices
MONCHY LAGACHE	1st. to 5th		Division billeted as follows - Divisional Hdqrs. MONCHY LAGACHE; Ambala Cavalry Brigade TERTRY; Sec'bad Cavalry Brigade TREFCON; Canadian Cavalry Brigade MERAUCOURT (Sheet 62.C., 1/40,000). Division supplies working parties for work in Cavalry Corps Area. Frost and snow continues at intervals.	
do.	6th.		Students for the Divisional School left for BUSSY-LES-DAOURS. Party of 1 B.O., 12 B.O.R. and 24 horses left for HAUTEAVESNES as Riding Establishment to teach Equitation to Infantry Officers at XVII Corps School. G.S.722/16 issued, "Forecast of Probable Reliefs".	Appx. 170.
do.	9th.		Conference of Brigade Majors at Divn'l Headquarters reference going into the line. 'Phone message received that the Division will not go into the line as all Indian units will probably be sent overseas.	
do.	11th.		G.S.722/18 issued, cancelling G.S.722/16.	Appx. 171.
do.	12th.		Sec'bad Cavalry Brigade find a working party, 120 strong, for work under 258th Tunnelling Coy., and daily from this date.	
do.	13th.		G.S.722/19 and G.S.722/20 issued regarding "Instructions for Reserves" and Table of Duties for Brigades.	Appx. 172. Appx. 173.
do.	15th.		Thaw sets in. Heavy rain and wind.	
do.	16th.		Rain and wind.	
do.	17th.		A party, 300 strong, was found by Sec'bad Cavalry Brigade for work on BROWN Line, Cavalry Corps Southern Sector, and daily from this date. Party found from Sec'bad Cavalry Brigade for work under 258th Tunnelling Coy. was struck off work from to-day, inclusive.	
do.	18th.		A party, 700 strong, was found from Ambala Cavalry Brigade for work on buried cable, and daily from this date. 23rd.	

SECRET.

WAR DIARY GENERAL STAFF,
or 5TH CAVALRY DIVISION.
INTELLIGENCE/SUMMARY.
(Erase heading not required.)

Army Form C. 2118.

JANUARY, 1918.

Instructions regarding War Diaries and Intelligence Summaries are contained in F. S. Regs., Part II. and the Staff Manual respectively. Title pages will be prepared in manuscript.

Place	Date	Hour	Summary of Events and Information	Remarks and references to Appendices
MONCHY LAGACHE	23rd.		Orders issued for working parties, strength 300, to be found - 150 from Canadian Cavalry Brigade - 150 from Dismounted Reinforcements. Ambala and Sec'bad Cavalry Brigades, to work on the BROWN Line, commencing 10 a.m. 25th inst. All other working parties to cease from this time. Warning order issued (G.S.722/24) for Division to relieve 1st Dismounted Division in the line.	Appx.174.
do.	24th.		Operation Order No.50 issued advising ordering relief of 1st Dismounted Division.	Appx.175.
do.	25th.		Information received that 4th Cavalry Division will relieve 2nd Dismounted Division in the line on night 27th/28th. Relief referred to in Operation Order No.50 carried out.	Appx.176.
do.	26th.		Relief referred to in Operation Order No.50 carried out. Orders issued (O.O.51) for that portion of Division not in line to move to 3rd Cavalry Division area, DOMART Area.	Appx.177.
do.	27th.		Headquarters, Division took over Command of Centre and Right Sectors of Cavalry Corps front at 10 a.m.	
BOUVINCOURT	31st.		Troops of Division disposed in line as per attached statement.	

Lt-Colonel, G.S.,
5th Cavalry Division.

SECRET.

No. G.S.722/16.

Headquarters, 5th Cavalry Division,
6th January, 1918.

To/
    O.O. Distribution.

Copy of Cavalry Corps letter No.G.X.283/237
dated 5th January, 1918 to 5th Cavalry Divn.

Forecast of probable reliefs.

1.   5th Dismounted Division will relieve 3rd Dismounted Division in the line by the 15th January.
    4th Dismounted Division will relieve 2nd Dismounted Division in the line by 20th January.

2.   Major-General H.J.M. MACANDREW and Staff will relieve Major-General VAUGHAN and Staff in command of the Dismounted Divisions, as soon as the relief of the 3rd Dismounted Division is completed.

3.   On relief, the 2nd and 3rd Cavalry Divisions will each in turn supply a Labour Battalion of 600 other ranks for work in forward area, commencing with the 3rd Cavalry Division. Accommodation for this Battalion will be found by the 5th Cavalry Division in their present area.

4.   1st Cavalry Division will continue to be in Corps Reserve.

5.   A Brigade of 24th Division will be detailed as Corps Reserve from the date of the completion of the relief of 3rd Dismounted Division by 5th Dismounted Division.

For information.

Reference para.3 above, the accommodation for the 600 men will be found by the Sec'bad Cavalry Brigade.

ACKNOWLEDGE

Lt-Colonel, G.S.,
5th Cavalry Division.

Appx. 171

S E C R E T.   No.G.S.722/18.

Headquarters, 5th Cavalry Division,
11th January, 1918.

To/
    O.O. Distribution.

1.   5th Cavalry Division No.G.S.722/16 dated 6th January, 1918 is cancelled.

2.   The 1st Dismounted Division will relieve the 3rd Dismounted Division in the line by January 15th.

3.   On relief the 3rd Dismounted Division will form a Pioneer Regiment of 600 working men which will be located at TREFCON.
    The A.A.& Q.M.G. will arrange with Sec'bad Cavalry Brigade for the accommodation of this Regiment.

4.   ACKNOWLEDGE.

                                      Lt-Colonel, G.S.,
                                      5th Cavalry Division.

SECRET.

No. G.S.722/19.

Headquarters, 5th Cavalry Division,
13th January, 1918.

To/
O.O. Distribution.

The following instructions regarding the use of Reserves will come into force at midnight 13th/14th January and will be substituted for those issued under G.S.722/11 dated 26th December, 1917 :-

1. The Reserves at the disposal of the Cavalry Corps will be :-

    1 Brigade of 24th Division located at VRAIGNES and HANCOURT with Brigade Headquarters at VRAIGNES.

    The Canadian Cavalry Brigade.

2. The Canadian Cavalry Brigade will keep 1 Regiment at 1 hour's notice from midnight 13th/14th January.

3. In case of serious attack the Canadian Cavalry Brigade will

    (i) Move to a position of readiness in square R.14.
    (ii) Send a Staff Officer to the Brigade Hd. Qrs. in R.8.b. (SMALL FOOT WOOD) to learn the situation and receive orders from Cavalry Corps.
    (iii) Be prepared to man the defences of the BROWN LINE from the OMIGNON River to the grid line in R.2.b.0.7., inclusive.

The necessary reconnaissances will be carried out at once.

4. The remainder of the Division will be extensively employed during the next few weeks as working parties.
These parties will act in accordance with this office No.G.57/7 of 30th December, 1917, and, if an attack takes place during the hours that they are at work, will come under the orders of the G.O.C. of the Sector at whose Headquarters they report, vide para.2 of G.S. 57/7.

5. ACKNOWLEDGE.

Lt-Colonel, G.S.,
5th Cavalry Division.

Appx 173

SECRET. No.G.S.722/20.

Headquarters, 5th Cavalry Division,
13th January, 1918.

To/
O.O. Distribution.

The following Table of Duties of Brigades is issued in substitution of that forwarded with this office No.G.S.722/14 dated 29th December, 1917 :-

Date.	Canadian Cav. Bde.	Sec'bad Cav. Bde.	Ambala Cav. Bde.
January 14th.	CORPS RESERVE. (Prepared to man the defences of the BROWN LINE from the Corps Southern Boundary on OMIGNON River to the grid line in R.2b.0.7., inclusive).	2 Offers, 120 O.R's for work under 258th Tunnelling Coy. 50 O.R's for hutting, VERMAND.	
January 15th.	- do -	- do -	
January 16th.	- do -	As for 14th. plus 300 men for work on S. Sector, Brown Line.	
January 17th.	- do -	- do -	
January 18th.	- do -	- do -	700 men for work on buried cable.
January 19th. and onwards.	- do -	- do -	- do -

J O'Rurke
Captain, G.S.,
5th Cavalry Division.

S E C R E T.   Appx. 174   No.G.S.722/24.

Headquarters, 5th Cavalry Division,
23rd January, 1918.

To/
O.O. Distribution.

WARNING ORDER.

1. 5th Dismounted Division will relieve 1st Dismounted Division in the line on the nights 25th/26th and 26th/27th January.

2. Dismounted Brigades will take over as follows :-

     Right Sub-sector   ...   Ambala Dismounted Brigade.

     Left Sub-sector   ...   Canadian Dismounted Brigade.

     Brigade in Support   ...   Sec'bad Dismounted Brigade.

3. Sufficient men will be left with the horses to enable them to move while the Dismounted Division is in the line.

4. Major-General MACANDREW and Staff will relieve Major-General MULLINS and Staff in command of the Dismounted Divisions at 10 a.m. on 27th January.

5. ACKNOWLEDGE.

J. O'Rorke
Captain, G.S.,
5th Cavalry Division.

DISMOUNTED DIVISIONS LOCATION REPORT.

Shewing positions at 6 a.m. 17th January, 1918.

Unit.	Location of Headquarters.
DISMOUNTED DIVISIONS H.Q.	BOUVINCOURT (SANTIN FARM).

RIGHT SECTOR.

1st Dismounted Division H.Q. ...	SMALL FOOT WOOD (R.8.b.8.6.)
do. do. Wagon Lines.	R.32.a.2.8.

BRIGADES IN LINE.

1st Dis. Bde. H.Q. (Right Sub-sector)	R.11.c.8.8.
5th Dragoon Guards (in line)	R.6.a.4.3.
2nd " " (in line)	M.1.d.4.3.
11th Hussars (support)	R.5.d.1.5.
1st M.G. Squadron	L.28.a.4.2.
2nd Dis. Bde. H.Q. (Left Sub-sector)	L.28.c.2.1.
18th Hussars (in line)	L.23.d.45.70.
9th Lancers (in line)	L.29.b.8.0.
4th Dragoon Guards (support)	L.28.a.5.4.
2nd M.G. Squadron	L.34.a.3.1.

BRIGADE IN SUPPORT.

9th Dis. Brigade H.Q.	R.17.a.2.9.
15th Hussars	do.
Bedfordshire Yeomanry ...	do.
19th Hussars	L.34.a.3.8.
9th M.G. Squadron	M.7.d.5.9.

S E C R E T.
Copy No. 23

Appx. 175

5TH CAVALRY DIVISION.
OPERATION ORDER No. 50.

Reference Map 1/40,000.   Dated 24th January, 1918.

1.   The 5th Dismounted Division will relieve the 1st Dismounted Division in the line in accordance with the attached Table of Reliefs.

2.   The 5th Dismounted Division will be commanded by G.O.C., Canadian Cavalry Brigade and the following Staff :-

    Brigade Major   ... - Major BROOKE, Canadian Cavalry Brigade.
    Staff Captain   ... - Captain HALLIFAX, Sec'bad Cav. Brigade.
    Asst. Brigade Major   - To be detailed by Canadian Cav. Brigade.
    Divisional M.G. Officer   - Major WATSON, 13th M.G. Squadron.
    Intelligence Officer   - Lieut. WOELLWORTH, Ambala Cav. Brigade.
    Signalling Officer   - Canadian Cavalry Brigade Signal Officer.
    Transport Officer   ... - To be detailed by O.C., A.S.C.
    Divn'l Gas N.C.O.   ... - Canadian Cavalry Brigade.

3.   Each Dismounted Brigade will be commanded by G.O.C., Brigade and Staff, less personnel employed on 5th Dismounted Division H.Q.; any shortage being filled by Officers detailed from within the Brigade.

4.   The C.C., 5th Signal Squadron will arrange for a Signal Troop personnel being drawn from all three Brigades for duty with the 5th Dismounted Division Headquarters.

5.   All orders regarding the relief of Machine Guns will be issued by the Divn'l M.G. Officer, 5th Dismounted Division (Major WATSON, 13th M.G. Squadron).

6.   Orders regarding the relief of the 1st Field Squadron by 5th Field Squadron will be issued later.

7.   No Artillery reliefs will take place.

8.   The A.D.M.S., 5th Cavalry Division will arrange direct with A.D.M.S., Dismounted Divisions regarding the relief of Medical Units.

9.   All Trench Stores, Maps, Defence Schemes, etc., will be taken over and receipts given.

10.   Command of the Right Sector will pass to G.O.C., 5th Dismounted Division on completion of relief.

11.   O.C., A.S.C. will detail 15 Limbered G.S. Wagons from Reserve Park for the transport of rations to Regimental H.Q. The following additional transport will be detailed by Brigades to report to 5th Dismounted Division Transport Officer at VERMAND on relief :-

N.C.O.	Drivers.	Vehicles.	Riding Horses.	L.D. Horses.
1 (in charge)	6/12 2	3/6 L.G.S. wagons. 2 Water carts.	1	12/24 4

One Shoeing-smith will be detailed by Sec'bad Cavalry Brigade to accompany the Transport.

12. ....

S E C R E T.   O.O. No. 50 (cont'd).

12.   Completion of relief will be reported to the Division by the Code Word V I C T O R Y.

13.   ACKNOWLEDGE.

[signature]

Captain, G.S.,

5th Cavalry Division.

Issued by D.R. at 8am

To/
    O.O. Distribution Copies Nos. 1 to 23.
    Cavalry Corps   "   "   24
    H.Q., Dismounted Divisions "   25
    1st Dismounted Division   "   26
    2nd Dismounted Division   "   27

SECRET.

TABLE OF RELIEFS. (Issued with Operation Order No.50 dated 24th January 1918).

Serial No.	Date.	Unit to be Relieved.	To be relieved by.	Advanced Parties.	Remarks.
1	24th.	—	—	Advance Parties, 5th Dis. Division H.Q's to reconnoitre dispositions, reporting at 1st Dis. Division at 3 p.m. (H.Q.)	
2	25th.	—	—	Advance Parties of Reserve Dis. Bde. 5th Dis. Division (Sec'bad Bde.) report.- Party of one Regiment at FORT DYCE, LE VERGUIER (L.34.a.3.6.) and parties remainder of Brigade at H.Q., Reserve Dis. Bde., VADENCOURT. Both at 9 a.m.	
3	25th.	—	—	Advance Party Ambala Dis. Brigade report at H.Q., A.1. (R.11.c.8.8.) at 4 p.m. Advance Party Canadian Dis. Brigade report at H.Q., A.2. (L.28.c.2.1.) at 4 p.m.	
4	Night 25th/26th.	All M.G's 1st Dis. Div.	All M.G's 5th Dis. Divn.		Details of reliefs to be arranged direct between Divn'l M.G. Officers.
5	Night 25th/26th.	Reserve Dis. Brigade at VADENCOURT (less 1 Regt.)	Sec'bad Dis. Brigade. (less 1 Regt.)		Units of Sec'bad Dis. Brigade to arrive VADENCOURT at 4.45 p.m. 25th January.

Serial No.6 ....

S E C R E T.

23

TABLE OF RELIEFS. (Issued with O.O. No.50 cont'd).

Serial No.	Date.	Unit to be Relieved.	To be relieved by.	Advanced Parties.	Remarks.
6	Night 25th/26th.	1 Regt., Reserve Dis. Brigade at LE VERGUIER.	1 Regiment, Sec'bed. Dis. Brigade.		Regiment of Sec'bed Dis. Brigade to arrive at LE VERGUIER at 4.45 p.m.
7	Night 26th/27th.	Dis.Bde. of 1st Dis.Divn. in front line in Sub-sector A.1.	Ambala Dismounted Brigade.		Ambala Dis. Brigade to arrive at cross-roads BIHECOURT, R.21.b.9.9. at 4.30 p.m.
8	Night 26th/27th.	Dis.Bde. of 1st Dis. Division in front line in Sub-sector A.2.	Canadian Dismounted Brigade.		Canadian Dis. Brigade to arrive at Western exit, LE VERGUIER on JEANCOURT road at 4.30 p.m.
9	25th Jan.	Transport of all M.G's. and Reserve Dismounted Brigade will be relieved by transport of all M.G's., 5th Dismounted Division and Sec'bed Dismounted Brigade.			
10	26th Jan.	Transport of Dismounted Brigades in A.1. and A.2. Sub-sectors will be relieved by transport of Ambala and Canadian Dismounted Brigades respectively.			

S E C R E T.   Copy No. 23

Appx. 176

5TH CAVALRY DIVISION OPERATION ORDER NO. 51.

Reference Map 1/100,000.

Dated 26th January, 1918.

1. That portion of 5th Cavalry Division not employed in the line (vide Operation Order No.50 dated 24th January, 1918) will move to the 3rd Cavalry Division Area as shown on attached March Table.

2. 17th Brigade, R.H.A., R.C.H.A. Brigade, Field Squadron, 17th Brigade R.H.A. Ammunition Column and R.C.H.A. Brigade Ammunition Column will remain as at present located.

3. "B" Echelon will accompany Brigades and Divisional Troops.

4. The Officer Commanding, mounted Brigade and attached Troops, is responsible that the strictest march discipline be maintained during the march, and, that the column is kept well closed up and on the right of the road; no Officers or O.R's are to march level with the column.
    A distance of 200 yards will be kept between regiments and every lot of 25 wagons.

5. Led horses will move saddled up and the rider will change mounts at intervals.

6. Colonel ADAMS, 20th Deccan Horse, will command the Division in the back area.

7. Rear Report Centre will open at DOMART EN PONTHIEU at 12 noon, January 30th., under arrangements to be made by O.C., 5th Signal Squadron.

8. Motor Ambulances and Sanitary Section will move under the orders of A.D.M.S.

9. ACKNOWLEDGE.

Captain, G.S.,
5th Cavalry Division.

Issued by D.R. at 9.30 am

To/
    O.O. Distribution, Nos. 1 to 23.
    Cavalry Corps ...   No. 24.

    3rd Cavalry Division   " 25.
    Col. ADAMS, 20th Horse.   " 26.
    A.P.M., AMIENS.   " 27.
    Area Comdt. VILLERS
            BRETONNEUX.   " 28.

S E C R E T.   MARCH TABLE. (Issued with 5th Cavalry Division Operation Order No.51).

Formation or Unit.	Starting Point.	Time.	Route.	Destination.	Remarks.
Canadian Cav. Brigade. Canadian Cav. Field Ambulance.	Cross roads at PRUSLE.	10 a.m. 28th January.	BRIE - FOUCAUCOURT.	HARBONNIERES, GUILLAUCOURT, VIENCOURT, BAYONVILLERS, WARFUSEE-ABANCOURT, LAMOTTE, MARCELCAVE.	To be clear of BRIE Bridge by 11.30 a.m.
- ditto -	Road junction 400 yards N. of LL in VILLERS BRETONNEUX.	9 a.m. 29th January.	AMIENS (Southern Boulevard) - LONGPRE - ARGOEUVES (vide Brown Line on attached map issued only to Brigades, A.H.T. Company and Reserve Park).	VIGNACOURT, FLESSELLES, HAVERNAS, WARGNIES, NAOURS, BERTEAUCOURT.	
- ditto -		30th. January.		PROUVILLE AREA. Billets from A.A.& QMG.	
Ambala Cav. Brigade (less Mhow C.F.A.) Reserve Park H.Q., A.H.T. Coy.	Eastern exit of MONS-EN-CHAUSSEE	9.50 a.m. 30th January.	BRIE - FOUCAUCOURT.	HARBONNIERES, GUILLAUCOURT, VIENCOURT, BAYONVILLERS, WARFUSEE-ABANCOURT, LAMOTTE, MARCELCAVE.	To be clear of BRIE Bridge by 11.30 a.m.
- ditto -	Road junction 400 yards N. of LL in VILLERS BRETONNEUX.	9 a.m. 31st. January.	AMIENS (Southern Boulevard) - LONGPRE - ARGOEUVES (vide Brown Line on attached map issued only to Brigades, A.H.T. Coy. and Reserve Park.)	VIGNACOURT FLESSELLES HAVERNAS WARGNIES NAOURS BERTEAUCOURT	

1st February ....

SECRET.   MARCH TABLE (cont'd.) Issued with Operation Order No.51.   5TH CAVALRY DIVISION.

Formation or Unit.	Starting Point.	Time.	Route.	Destination.	Remarks.
Ambala Cav. Brigade. (less Mhow C.F.A.) Reserve Park. H.Q., A.H.T. Coy.	—	1st. February.	—	AILLY-LE-HAUT-CLOCHER AREA.	Billets from A.A.& Q.M.G.
Sec'bed Cav. Brigade.	Cross roads at PRUSLE.	10 a.m. 1st. February.	BRIE - FOUCAUCOURT.	HARBONNIERES, GUILLAUCOURT, WIENCOURT, BAYONVILLERS, WARFUSEE-ABANCOURT, LAMOTTE, MARCELCAVE.	To be clear of BRIE Bridge by 11.30 a.m.
Sec'bed Cav. Field Ambulance.	Road junction 400 yards N. of LL in VILLERS BRETONNEUX.	9 a.m. 2nd. February.	AMIENS (Southern Boulevard) - LONGPRE - ARGOEUVES. (vide Brown Line on attached map issued only to Brigades, A.H.T. Company and Reserve Park).	VIGNACOURT AREA.	Billets from A.A.& Q.M.G.
- ditto -					

ooooooooOOOOooooooooo

SECRET.

Army Form C. 2118.

Instructions regarding War Diaries and Intelligence
Summaries are contained in F. S. Regs., Part II.
and the Staff Manual respectively. Title pages
will be prepared in manuscript.

WAR DIARY
or
INTELLIGENCE/SUMMARY.
(Erase heading not required.)

5TH CAVALRY DIVISION.

FEBRUARY, 1918.

Place	Date	Hour	Summary of Events and Information	Remarks and references to Appendices
BOUVINCOURT	1st.		Moves of Brigades in accordance with O.O.No.51 dated January 25th 1918 continued.	
	2nd.		Moves of Brigades in accordance with O.O.No.51 dated January 25th 1918 completed. Location of units as per attached list of billets.	Appx.178.
	8th.		Orders received that 4th and 5th Cavalry Divisions would be broken up and portions proceed to EGYPT (G.S.790/1 dated 8.2.18)	Appx.179
	11th.		Warning order received from Cavalry Corps to the effect that 1st Cavalry Division will relieve 5th Cavalry Division in the line on the nights 15th/16th and 16th/17th. The 5th Cavalry Division, less 7th Dragoon Guards, 8th Hussars and Canadian Cavalry Brigade, will proceed to their back area. Canadian Brigade and the 2 British Regiments will remain in the forward area.	
	12th.		Orders for relief of 5th Dismounted Division received from Cavalry Corps (5th Dismounted Divn. duly received them from Dismounted Divisions) Dismounted Divisions Order No.7 attached.	Appx.180.
	15th.		Half relief ordered in Dismounted Divisions Order No.7 completed by 6 p.m.	
	16th.		For actions of 5th Dismounted Division see "5th Dismounted Division War Diary" attached.	Appx. 181.
PONT DE METZ.	17th.		Divisional Headquarters established at PONT DE METZ with Brigades as follows :- Canadian Cav. Bde. - Dismounted Brigade under Cavalry Corps in forward area, remainder in billets around BERNAVILLE. Sec'bad Cav. Bde. - H.Q., BELLOY SUR SOMME, 20th Horse, and 34th Horse and 13th M.G.Squadron billets around BELLOY SUR SOMME. Dismounted 7th Dragoon Guards under Cavalry Corps in forward area. Remainder " " " in billets around PICQUIGNY. Ambala Cav. Bde. - H.Q., LONGUET. 9th Horse, 18th Lancers and 14th M.G. Squadron in billets around LONGUET. Dismounted 8th Hussars under Cavalry Corps in forward area. Remainder " " in billets around AILLY-LE-HAUT CLOCHER. 5th Cavalry Divisn on Rear Report Centre closed at DOMART and opened at PONT DE METZ at 1 p.m. 18th	

SECRET. FEBRUARY, 1918.

Army Form C. 2118.

WAR DIARY 5TH CAVALRY DIVISION.
or
INTELLIGENCE/SUMMARY.
(Erase heading not required.)

Instructions regarding War Diaries and Intelligence Summaries are contained in F.S. Regs., Part II. and the Staff Manual respectively. Title pages will be prepared in manuscript.

Place	Date	Hour	Summary of Events and Information	Remarks and references to Appendices
PONT DE METZ.	18th 19th 20th		Division organising for pending move to EGYPT.	
	18th.		Information received that Canadian Cavalry Brigade would come under Dismounted Divisions from noon to-day and would take over a sector of the line S. of OMIGNON River with H.Q. at VERMAND.	
	19th.		Orders received for Light Section Canadian Cavalry Field Ambulance to move by 3 stages, commencing on 21st., to VERMAND.	
	21st.		Light Section Canadian Cavalry Field Ambulance marched as above. Orders issued for entraining to TARANTO and MARSEILLES to commence on 22nd inst. For details of these moves please see 5th Cavalry Division "Q" Summary.	

Captain, G.S.,
for Lt-Colonel, G.S.,
5th Cavalry Division.

S E C R E T.   DISMOUNTED DIVISIONS LOCATIONS REPORT.   Appx 77

Forecasting Positions for 6 a.m. on 3rd February.

Unit.	Location of Headquarters.
DISMOUNTED DIVISIONS H.Q.	BOUVINCOURT (SANTIN FARM)

RIGHT SECTOR.   5th Dismounted Division H.Q.   SMALL FOOT WOOD (R.8.b.8.5.)

Brigades in Line :-
Right Sub-sector.-
Ambala Dismounted Brigade H.Q.	R.11.c.6.9.
8th Hussars (in line)	M.7.b.5.6.
9th H. Horse. (in line)	R.6.b.6.5.
18th Lancers (support)	R.5.d.1.5.
14th M.G. Squadron	COOKERS QUARRY.

Left Sub-sector.-
Canadian Dismounted Brigade H.Q.	L.28.c.2.1.
L.S. Horse (in line)	L.29.b.8.0.
F.G. Horse (in line)	L.23.d.45.70.
R.C. Dragoons (support)	L.29.c.4.9.
Canadian M.G. Squadron	LE VERGUIER.

Brigade in Reserve.-
Sec'bad Dismounted Brigade H.Q.	R.17.a.2.9.
7th Dragoon Guards	L.34.a.3.5.
20th Deccan Horse	R.17.a.2.9.
34th Poona Horse	R.17.a.2.9.
C⁴ FIELD SQDN. RE.	JEANCOURT.

SECRET

LIST OF BILLETS – 5TH CAVALRY DIVISION.
Ref. Map. LENS 11, ABBEVILLE 14, and AMIENS 17.

App 146

Divisional Headquarters	DOMART-en-PONTHIEU
Field Cashier	HALLOY-les-PERNOIS
Signal Squadron	Forward Area
Field Squadron	--do--
C.R.H.A.	--do--
Ammunition Column	--do--
Supply Column	HALLOY-les-PERNOIS
Sanitary Section	DOMART-en-PONTHIEU
A.H.T. Company	ST. LEGER-les-DOMART
Reserve Park	FIENVILLERS - MONTRELET
Railhead Supplies	CANDAS

CANADIAN CAVALRY BRIGADE.

Brigade Headquarters	BERNAVILLE
R. C. Dragoons	FRANSU - LE PLOUY - DOMQUEUR
L. S. Horse	CRAMONT - LE MENAGE - LES MASURES - MESNIL - DOMQUEUR - LONGVILLERS
F. G. Horse	DOMLEGER - AGENVILLE - BEAUMETZ - PROUVILLE
R.C.H.A Brigade	Forward Area
Canadian M.G. Squadron	BERNEUIL - ST. HILAIRE
Canadian C.F.A.	DOMART-en-PONTHIEU
Canadian M.V. Section	GORENFLOS

SEC'BAD CAVALRY BRIGADE.

Brigade Headquarters	BELLOY-SUR-SOMME
7th Dragoon Guards	ARGOEUVES - ST. SAUVEUR - LA CHAUSSEE - TIRAUCOURT
20th Horse	BETHENCOURT - ST. OUEN - BERTEAUCOURT-les-DAMES
34th Horse	HAVERNAS - WARGNIES - NAOURS - VIGNACOURT
"N" Battery, R.H.A.	Forward Area
13th Squadron, M.G.C.	FLESSELLES
Sec'bad I.C.F.A.	VIGNACOURT
Sec'bad M.V. Section	BELLOY-SUR-SOMME

AMBALA CAVALRY BRIGADE.

Brigade Headquarters	LONGUET
8th Hussars	AILLY-le-HAUT CLOCHER - AILLY - BUIGNY-L'ABBE - YAUCOURT
9th Horse	HOUFLERS - VAUCHELLES-les-DOMART - L'ETOILE - BRUCAMPS - VILLER-sous-AILLY
18th Lancers	LONG
14th Squadron, M.G.C.	EPAGNE - EAUCOURT
Mhow I.C.F.A.	Forward Area
Ambala M.V. Section	LONG

No.Q/213/16.

Headquarters, 5th Cavalry Division,
4th February, 1918.

To/
Cavalry Corps "Q".

Forwarded.

E.O'Hara
Captain,
for G.O.C., 5th Cavalry Division.

Copies to:-
Fifth Army "Q".
1st, 2nd, 3rd and 4th Cavalry Divisions "Q".
Usual Billeting List Distribution.

War diary (5)   App. 179

SECRET.   Cav. Corps.   O.B./2160.
               No G.X.319/4.   G.H.Q., 20th Jan. 18.

Fifth Army.

   Under instructions received from the War Cabinet, the 4th and 5th Cavalry Divisions will be broken up, the Indian Units and personnel thereof, together with one Divisional Headquarters, three Brigade Headquarters and certain British units being sent to Egypt.

2.   A list of the units to be despatched to Egypt is given in Appendix I.

3.   The remaining units of the 4th and 5th Cavalry Divisions, excluding the four British Cavalry Regiments, will be disposed of as shown in Appendix II.
   Orders regarding the disposal of the four British Cavalry Regiments will be issued in due course.

4.   Orders for the disposal of all surplus personnel and of all surplus equipment and horses, will be issued by the A.G. and Q.M.G., respectively.

5.   The date on which the movements of personnel from the Cavalry Corps area are to commence is dependent on the tactical situation and will be notified by G.H.Q. in due course.
   The G.O.C., L of C., Area will place the HALLENCOURT Area forthwith at the disposal of the G.O.C., Fifth Army, who will arrange for units proceeding to Egypt to collect in this area as soon as the tactical situation allows.   Units will then be ready to move by rail at short notice.

6.   Any British officers (other than Staff Officers) belonging to Indian Cavalry Regiments in this country, but serving with units mentioned in Appendix II, should rejoin their   Regiments, when their present units are broken up or transferred elsewhere.

7.   Indian R.A. drivers in the 1st Line transport of Silladar Cavalry Regiments, authorised under G.H.Q. letter No A/5538 dated 14th July 1915, will be transferred to Divisional Ammunition Columns of Imperial Divisions under the orders of the Adjutant General.   These drivers will be replaced by Indian Cavalry reinforcements.

           No G.S.790/1.
                                    Headquarters, 5th Cavalry Division.
                                            8th February 1918.
To
   Sec'bad Cavalry Brigade.
   Ambala Cavalry Brigade.
   17th Bde R.H.A.
   5th Field Squadron.
   5th Signal Squadron.
   A.D.M.S.
   O.C., A.S.C.
   D.A.D.O.S.
   Camp Commandant.

       Forwarded for guidance.
                                              Lt. Col.
                                    G.S., 5th Cavalry Division.

APPENDIX I.

TO BE TRANSFERRED TO EGYPT.

Headquarters Fifth Cavalry Division.

Headquarters Fifth Cavalry Division A.S.C.

Headquarters Sialkot Cavalry Brigade.

Headquarters Lucknow Cavalry Brigade.

Headquarters Secunderabad Cavalry Brigade.

Indian Personnel of Headquarters Fourth Cavalry Division.
    "   "   " Headquarters Fourth Cavalry Division A.S.C.
    "   "   " Headquarters Mhow Cavalry Brigade.
    "   "   " Headquarters Ambala Cavalry Brigade.

10 Indian Cavalry Regiments.

Jodhpur Lancers.

10th, 12th and 14th Cavalry Machine Gun Squadrons.

5th Signal Squadron.

Brigade Signal Troops of Sialkot, Lucknow and Secunderabad Cavalry
                                                        (Brigades.

5 Mobile Veterinary Sections (less British personnel of 2 Sections)

5 combined Cavalry Field Ambulances (less British personnel other
    than H.T. and M.T. drivers of Secunderabad and Mhow (5th Division)
    Ambulances).

Cavalry Sanitary Sections (less British personnel other than M.T.
    drivers of No.5 Cavalry Sanitary Section).

Jodhpur Cavalry Field Ambulance.

1st Cavalry Divisional Ammunition Park on War Establishment Part VII.

4th Cavalry Divisional Supply Column on War Establishment Part VII.A.

6 Indian Field Veterinary Sections.

To be held in readiness to proceed to EGYPT.

1 Brigade R.H.A. (17th Brigade R.H.A. and Ammunition Column.
              Two 6-gun Batteries, viz. "The Chestnut Troop" and
              "N" Battery, R.H.A.).

5th Field Squadron, R.E.

APPENDIX II.

SURPLUS UNITS TO BE DISPOSED OF.	HOW DISPOSED OF.
Headquarters Fourth Cavalry Division (less Indian personnel)	To be broken up.
Headquarters Fourth Cavalry Divisional A.S.C. (less Indian Personnel).	To be broken up.
Headquarters Mhow Cavalry Brigade (less Indian personnel).	To be broken up.
Headquarters Ambala Cavalry Brigade (less Indian personnel)	To be broken up.
Canadian Cavalry Brigade	To remain an independent Cavalry Brigade.
4 British Cavalry Regiments	See para.3 of covering letter.
11th and 13th M.G. Squadrons	To be broken up.
British personnel of :- 2 Mobile Veterinary Sections Secunderabad and Mhow (5th Division) Cavalry Field Ambulances. No.5 Cavalry Sanitary Section.	To be disposed of under orders to be issued by A.G.
Headquarters 16th Brigade, R.H.A. 2 Batteries, R.H.A. Brigade Ammunition Column.	To be retained complete at disposal of Cavalry Corps until further orders.
4th Field Squadron, R.E.	To be transferred to Tanks.
4th Signal Squadron. Brigade Signal Troops of Mhow and Ambala Cavalry Brigades.	Dismounted personnel to Tanks. Remainder to Signal Depot.
Transport of 5th Cavalry Divisional Ammunition Park. H.Q. and transport of 5th Cavalry Divisional Supply Column (less Supply Column and Ammunition Park required by the Canadian Brigade.)	To be broken up under orders of the Q.M.G.
4th and 5th Cavalry Divisional Auxiliary Horse Companies. 4th and 5th Cavalry Reserve Parks.	To be broken up under the orders of the Q.M.G. less No.1 Sections of Reserve Parks which will be retained as complete section for General Transport duties.
924th and 925th Divisional Employment Companies	To be broken up.

SECRET   Copy No. 23

Dismounted Divisions Order No. 7.

Dated 12th February, 1918.

1. The 4th Dismounted Division will be relieved on the nights 13th/14th and 14th/15th inst. by the 72nd Infantry Brigade, 24th Division.

   The 5th Dismounted Division will be relieved on the nights 15th/16th and 16th/17th by the 1st Cavalry Division.

   On relief, 4th Dismounted Division will entrain at ROISEL and detrain at SALUX, 5th Dismounted Division will entrain at ROISEL and detrain at LONGPRE.
   Orders for entrainment will be issued by A.A.& Q.M.G., Dismounted Divisions.

2. The following dismounted units, on completion of relief, will move as under :-

   6th Dragoons.   )
   17th Lancers.   )   Huts at MONTIGNY FARM.
   1/1st Yorkshire Dragoons)

   7th Dragoon Guards   )
   8th Hussars.   )   Tents at VERMAND.

   Canadian Brigade (less
   M.G. Squadron)   ... Huts at VERMAND.

   Accommodation will be arranged by Cavalry Corps "Q".

3. Reliefs and moves of M.G. Squadrons will be as follows :-

   10th and 12th M.G. Squadrons, on relief by 24th Division,
                       will move under orders of
                       4th Dismounted Division.

   11th M.G. Squadron will remain in its present position and
                       come under the orders of the 24th Division
                       until further orders.

   On night 13th/14th inst.

   14th M.G. Squadron will be relieved by 1st M.G. Squadron
                       and will then move to VADENCOURT and come
                       under the orders of Ambala Brigade.

   On the 16th inst.-

   2nd M.G. Squadron moves to JEANCOURT and occupies 1st M.G.
                       Squadron's present camp.

   7th., 9th and 13th M.G. Squadrons and Canadian M.G. Squadron,
                       remain in their present positions.

4. The Cavalry T.M. Battery will be relieved on the night of 14th/15th inst., and will be accommodated at BEAUMETZ.
   On relief they will come under orders of Cavalry Corps.
   "Q" Dismounted Divisions will provide lorry transport for personnel and stores.

5. Command of Centre Sector will pass to G.O.C., 24th Division at 10 a.m. on 15th inst.

6. ....

Dismounted Divisions Order No.7 (conTd).

6. Major-General Macandrew and Staff will be relieved by Major-General Mullins and Staff in command of Dismounted Divisions. Command will pass at 10 a.m. on 17th inst.

7. There will be no change in Artillery arrangements.

8. All other details of reliefs in Centre Sector will be arranged direct between 4th Dismounted Division and 72nd Infantry Brigade, and in Right Sector between 5th Dismounted Division and 1st Cavalry Division.

9. Transport (less that of units mentioned in para.2) (and of 11th, 13th and Canadian M.G. Sqdns) will move as follows :-

On 14th inst.	4th Cavalry Division.	To PROYART Area.	via Main VERMAND - VILLERS-BRETTONEUX road.
On 15th inst.	5th Cavalry Division.	- do -	- do -

Any transport required by 4th Dismounted Division on the night of 14th/15th., and by the 5th Dismounted Division on the night 16th/17th., in connection with relief, will be supplied on application to "Q" Dismounted Divisions.

10. All Defence Schemes, Maps, Aeroplane Photos, etc., etc., will be handed over to incoming units and receipts given.

11. A.D.M.S., Dismounted Divisions will make the necessary arrangements for the reliefs of Medical personnel.

12. Completion of reliefs will be reported to H.Q. Dismounted Divisions.

13. ACKNOWLEDGE. (4th and 5th Dismounted Divisions by wire.).

N. T. Hodgson.
Lt-Colonel, G.S.,
Dismounted Divisions.

Issued to :-

Copy No.		Copy No.	
1.	5th Dismounted Division.	13.	Cavalry Corps.
2.	4th Dismounted Division.	14.	24th Division.
3.	Cavalry Divn'l Artillery.	15.	61st Division.
4.	C.R.E., Dism'td Divns.	16.	72nd Infantry Brigade.
5.	M.G.O., do.	17.	1st Cavalry Division.
6.	A.A.& Q.M.G. do.		
7.	A.D.M.S. do.	19.	3rd Cavalry Division.
8.	D.A.D.O.S., do.	20.	4th Cavalry Division (rear)
9.	A.P.M. do.	21.	5th Cavalry Division (rear)
10.	Gas Officer. do.	22.	5th Cavalry Division "Q".
11.	Signals, do.	23 -25.	War Diary.
12.	Camp Comdt. do.	26& 27.	Office.

SECRET.

WAR DIARY
OR
INTELLIGENCE/SUMMARY.
(Erase heading not required.)

5TH CAVALRY DIVISION.

FEBRUARY, 1918.

Army Form C. 2118.

Place	Date	Hour	Summary of Events and Information	Remarks and references to Appendices
BOUVINCOURT	1st.		Moves of Brigades in accordance with O.O.No.51 dated January 25th 1918 continued.	
	2nd.		Moves of Brigades in accordance with O.O.No.51 dated January 25th 1918 completed. Location of units as per attached list of billets.	Appx.178.
	8th.		Orders received that 4th and 5th Cavalry Divisions would be broken up and portions proceed to EGYPT (G.S.790/1 dated 8.2.18)	Appx.179
	11th.		Warning order received from Cavalry Corps to the effect that 1st Cavalry Division will relieve 5th Cavalry Division in the line on the nights 15th/16th and 16th/17th. The 5th Cavalry Division, less 7th Dragoon Guards, 8th Hussars and Canadian Cavalry Brigade,will proceed to their back area. Canadian Brigade and the 2 British Regiments will remain in the forward area.	
	12th.		Orders for relief of 5th Dismounted Division received from Cavalry Corps (5th Dismounted Divn. duly received then from Dismounted Divisions) Dismounted Divisions Order No.7 attached.	Appx.180.
	15th.		Half relief ordered in Dismounted Divisions Order No.7 completed by 6 p.m.	
	16th.		For actions of 5th Dismounted Division see "5th Dismounted Division War Diary" attached.	Appx. 181.
PONT DE METZ. 17th.			Divisional Headquarters established at PONT DE METZ with Brigades as follows :- Canadian Cav. Bde. - Dismounted Brigade under Cavalry Corps in forward area, remainder in billets around BERNAVILLE. Sec'bad Cav. Bdé. = H.Q., BELLOY SUR SOMME, 20th Horse,and 34th Horse and 13th M.G.Squadron billets around BELLOY SUR SOMME. Dismounted 7th Dragoon Guards under Cavalry Corps in forward area. Remainder " " in billets around PICQUIGNY. Ambala Cav. Bde. - H.Q., LONGUET. 9th Horse, 18th Lancers and 14th M.G. Squadron in billets around LONGUET. Dismounted 8th Hussars under Cavalry Corps in forward area. Remainder " " in billets around AILLY-LE-HAUT CLOCHER. 5th Cavalry Division Rear Report Centre closed at DOMART and opened at PONT DE METZ at 1 p.m. 18th	

Army Form C. 2118.

WAR DIARY
or
INTELLIGENCE SUMMARY.   5th CAVALRY DIVISION.

(Erase heading not required.)

Instructions regarding War Diaries and Intelligence Summaries are contained in F. S. Regs., Part II. and the Staff Manual respectively. Title pages will be prepared in manuscript.

Place	Date	Hour	Summary of Events and Information	Remarks and references to Appendices
PONT DE METZ.	18th) 19th) 20th)		Division organising for pending move to EGYPT.	
	18th.		Information received that Canadian Cavalry Brigade would come under Dismounted Divisions from noon to-day and would take over a sector of the line S. of OMIGNON River with H.Q. at VERMAND.	
	19th.		Orders received for Light Section Canadian Cavalry Field Ambulance to move by 3 stages, commencing on 21st., to VERMAND.	
	21st.		Light Section Canadian Cavalry Field Ambulance marched as above. Orders issued for entraining to TARANTO and MARSEILLES to commence on 22nd inst. For details of these moves please see 5th Cavalry Division "Q" Summary.	

Captain, G.S.,
for LT-Colonel, G.S.,
5th Cavalry Division.

SECRET

LIST OF BILLETS - 5TH CAVALRY DIVISION.
Ref. Map. LENS 11, ABBEVILLE 14, and AMIENS 17.

War Diary
Appx 178

Divisional Headquarters	DOMART-en-PONTHIEU
Field Cashier	HALLOY-les-PERNOIS
Signal Squadron	Forward Area
Field Squadron	--do--
C.R.H.A.	--do--
Ammunition Column	--do--
Supply Column	HALLOY-les-PERNOIS
Sanitary Section	DOMART-en-PONTHIEU
A.H.T. Company	ST. LEGER-les-DOMART
Reserve Park	FIENVILLERS - MONTRELET
Railhead Supplies	CANDAS

CANADIAN CAVALRY BRIGADE.

Brigade Headquarters	BERNAVILLE
R. C. Dragoons	FRANSU - LE-PLOUY - DOMQUEUR
L. S. Horse	CRAMONT - LE MENAGE - LES MASURES - MESNIL - DOMQUEUR - LONGVILLERS
F. G. Horse	DOMLEGER - AGENVILLE - BEAUMETZ - PROUVILLE
R.C.H.A Brigade	Forward Area
Canadian M.G. Squadron	BERNEUIL - ST. HILAIRE
Canadian C.F.A.	DOMART-en-PONTHIEU
Canadian M.V. Section	GORENFLOS

SEC'BAD CAVALRY BRIGADE.

Brigade Headquarters	BELLOY-SUR-SOMME
7th Dragoon Guards	ARGOEUVES - ST. SAUVEUR - LA CHAUSSEE - TIRAUCOURT
20th Horse	BETHENCOURT - ST. OUEN - BERTEAUCOURT-les-DAMES
34th Horse	HAVERNAS - WARGNIES - NAOURS - VIGNACOURT
"N" Battery, R.H.A.	Forward Area
13th Squadron, M.G.C.	FLESSELLES
Sec'bad I.C.F.A.	VIGNACOURT
Sec'bad M.V. Section	BELLOY-SUR-SOMME

AMBALA CAVALRY BRIGADE.

Brigade Headquarters	LONGUET
8th Hussars	AILLY-le-HAUT CLOCHER - AILLY - BUIGNY-L'ABBE - YAUCOURT
9th Horse	HOUFLERS - VAUCHELLES-les-DOMART - L'ETOILE - BRUCAMPS - VILLER-sous-AILLY
18th Lancers	LONG
14th Squadron, M.G.C.	EPAGNE - EAUCOURT
Mhow I.C.F.A.	Forward Area.
Ambala M.V. Section	LONG

No.Q/213/16.

Headquarters, 5th Cavalry Division.
4th February, 1918.

To/ Cavalry Corps "Q".

Forwarded.

G. O'Hara
Captain,
for G.O.C., 5th Cavalry Division.

Copies to:-
Fifth Army "Q".
1st, 2nd, 3rd and 4th Cavalry Divisions "Q".
Usual Billeting List Distribution.

SECRET.　　　　Cav.Corps.　　　　　　　　O.B./2150.
　　　　　　　No G.X.319/4.　　　　G.H.Q.,20th Jan.18.

Fifth Army.

　　　Under instructions received from the War Cabinet, the 4th and 5th Cavalry Divisions will be broken up, the Indian Units and personnel thereof, together with one Divisional Headquarters, three Brigade Headquarters and certain British units being sent to Egypt.

2.　A list of the units to be despatched to Egypt is given in Appendix I.

3.　The remaining units of the 4th and 5th Cavalry Divisions, excluding the four British Cavalry Regiments, will be disposed of as shown in Appendix II.
　　　Orders regarding the disposal of the four British Cavalry Regiments will be issued in due course.

4.　Orders for the disposal of all surplus personnel and of all surplus equipment and horses, will be issued by the A.G. and Q.M.G., respectively.

5.　The date on which the movements of personnel from the Cavalry Corps area are to commence is dependent on the tactical situation and will be notified by G.H.Q. in due course.
　　　The G.O.C., L of C., Area will place the HALLENCOURT Area forthwith at the disposal of the G.O.C., Fifth Army, who will arrange for units proceeding to Egypt to collect in this area as soon as the tactical situation allows.　Units will then be ready to move by rail at short notice.

6.　Any British officers (other than Staff Officers) belonging to Indian Cavalry Regiments in this country, but serving with units mentioned in Appendix II, should rejoin their　　　Regiments, when their present units are broken up or transferred elsewhere.

7.　Indian R.A. drivers in the 1st Line transport of Silladar Cavalry Regiments, authorised under G.H.Q. letter No A/5538 dated 14th July 1915, will be transferred to Divisional Ammunition Columns of Imperial Divisions under the orders of the Adjutant General.　These drivers will be replaced by Indian Cavalry reinforcements.

　　　　　No G.S.790/1.

　　　　　　　　　　　　　　　　Headquarters, 5th Cavalry Division.
To　　　　　　　　　　　　　　　　　　　　　8th February 1918.

　Sec'bad Cavalry Brigade.
　Ambala Cavalry Brigade.
　17th Bde R.H.A.
　5th Field Squadron.
　5th Signal Squadron.
　A.D.M.S.
　　O.C.,A.S.C.
　D.A.D.O.S.
　Camp Commandant.

　　　　Forwarded for guidance.

　　　　　　　　　　　　　　　　　　　　　　　　Lt. Col.
　　　　　　　　　　　　　　　　　　　G.S., 5th Cavalry Division.

APPENDIX I.

TO BE TRANSFERRED TO EGYPT.

Headquarters Fifth Cavalry Division.
Headquarters Fifth Cavalry Division A.S.C.
Headquarters Sialkot Cavalry Brigade.
Headquarters Lucknow Cavalry Brigade.
Headquarters Secunderabad Cavalry Brigade.

Indian Personnel of Headquarters Fourth Cavalry Division.
    "   "   " Headquarters Fourth Cavalry Division A.S.C.
    "   "   " Headquarters Mhow Cavalry Brigade.
    "   "   " Headquarters Ambala Cavalry Brigade.

10 Indian Cavalry Regiments.

Jodhpur Lancers.

10th, 12th and 14th Cavalry Machine Gun Squadrons.

5th Signal Squadron.

Brigade Signal Troops of Sialkot, Lucknow and Secunderabad Cavalry
                                                                           (Brigades.

5 Mobile Veterinary Sections (less British personnel of 2 Sections)

5 combined Cavalry Field Ambulances (less British personnel other
    than H.T. and M.T. drivers of Secunderabad and Mhow (5th Division)
    Ambulances).

2 Cavalry Sanitary Sections (less British personnel other than M.T.
    drivers of No.5 Cavalry Sanitary Section).

Jodhpur Cavalry Field Ambulance.

1st Cavalry Divisional Ammunition Park on War Establishment Part VII.

4th Cavalry Divisional Supply Column on War Establishment Part VII.A.

6 Indian Field Veterinary Sections.

To be held in readiness to proceed to EGYPT.

1 Brigade R.H.A. (17th Brigade R.H.A. and Ammunition Column.
                Two 6-gun Batteries, viz. "The Chestnut Troop" and
                "N" Battery, R.H.A.).

5th Field Squadron, R.E.

&&&&&&&&&&&&&&&&&&&&&&&&

APPENDIX II.

SURPLUS UNITS TO BE DISPOSED OF.	HOW DISPOSED OF.
Headquarters Fourth Cavalry Division (less Indian personnel)	To be broken up.
Headquarters Fourth Cavalry Divisional A.S.C. (less Indian Personnel).	To be broken up.
Headquarters Mhow Cavalry Brigade (less Indian personnel).	To be broken up.
Headquarters Ambala Cavalry Brigade (less Indian personnel)	To be broken up.
Canadian Cavalry Brigade	To remain an independent Cavalry Brigade.
4 British Cavalry Regiments	See para.3 of covering letter.
11th and 14th M.G. Squadrons	To be broken up.
British personnel of :-	
2 Mobile Veterinary Sections Secunderabad and Mhow (5th Division) Cavalry Field Ambulances.	To be disposed of under orders to be issued by A.G.
No.5 Cavalry Sanitary Section.	
Headquarters 16th Brigade, R.H.A.	To be retained complete at disposal of Cavalry Corps until further orders.
2 Batteries, R.H.A.	
Brigade Ammunition Column.	
4th Field Squadron, R.E.	To be transferred to Tanks.
4th Signal Squadron.	Dismounted personnel to Tanks. Remainder to Signal Depot.
Brigade Signal Troops of Mhow and Ambala Cavalry Brigades.	
Transport of 5th Cavalry Divisional Ammunition Park.	To be broken up under orders of the Q.M.G.
H.Q. and transport of 5th Cavalry Divisional Supply Column. (less Supply Column and Ammunition Park required by the Canadian Brigade.)	
4th and 5th Cavalry Divisional Auxiliary Horse Companies.	To be broken up under the orders of the Q.M.G. less No.1 Sections of Reserve Parks which will be retained as complete section for General Transport duties.
4th and 5th Cavalry Reserve Parks.	
924th and 925th Divisional Employment Companies	To be broken up.

SECRET   Copy No. 24

Dismounted Divisions Order No. 7.

Dated 12th February, 1918.

1. The 4th Dismounted Division will be relieved on the nights 13th/14th and 14th/15th inst. by the 72nd Infantry Brigade, 24th Division.

   The 5th Dismounted Division will be relieved on the nights 15th/16th and 16th/17th by the 1st Cavalry Division.

   On relief, 4th Dismounted Division will entrain at ROISEL and detrain at SALUX, 5th Dismounted Division will entrain at ROISEL and detrain at LONGPRE.
   Orders for entrainment will be issued by A.A.& Q.M.G., Dismounted Divisions.

2. The following dismounted units, on completion of relief, will move as under :-

   6th Dragoons.   )
   17th Lancers.   )   Huts at MONTIGNY FARM.
   1/1st Yorkshire Dragoons)

   7th Dragoon Guards   )
   8th Hussars.   )   Tents at VERMAND.

   Canadian Brigade (less
   M.G. Squadron)   ... Huts at VERMAND.

   Accommodation will be arranged by Cavalry Corps "Q".

3. Reliefs and moves of M.G. Squadrons will be as follows :-

   10th and 12th M.G. Squadrons, on relief by 24th Division, will move under orders of 4th Dismounted Division.

   11th M.G. Squadron will remain in its present position and come under the orders of the 24th Division until further orders.

   On night 13th/14th inst.

   14th M.G. Squadron will be relieved by 1st M.G. Squadron and will then move to VADENCOURT and come under the orders of Ambala Brigade.

   On the 16th inst.-

   2nd M.G. Squadron moves to JEANCOURT and occupies 1st M.G. Squadron's present camp.

   7th., 9th and 13th M.G. Squadrons and Canadian M.G. Squadron, remain in their present positions.

4. The Cavalry T.M. Battery will be relieved on the night of 14th/15th inst., and will be accommodated at BEAUMETZ.
   On relief they will come under orders of Cavalry Corps.
   "Q" Dismounted Divisions will provide lorry transport for personnel and stores.

5. Command of Centre Sector will pass to G.O.C., 24th Division at 10 a.m. on 15th inst.

6. ....

Dismounted Divisions Order No.7 (conTd).

6. Major-General Macandrew and Staff will be relieved by Major-General Mullins and Staff in command of Dismounted Divisions. Command will pass at 10 a.m. on 17th inst.

7. There will be no change in Artillery arrangements.

8. All other details of reliefs in Centre Sector will be arranged direct between 4th Dismounted Division and 72nd Infantry Brigade, and in Right Sector between 5th Dismounted Division and 1st Cavalry Division.

9. Transport (less that of units mentioned in para.2) (and of 11th, 13th and Canadian M.G. Sqdns) will move as follows :-

On 14th inst. 4th Cavalry Division. To PROYART Area. via Main VERMAND-VILLERS-BRETTONEUX road.

On 15th inst. 5th Cavalry Division. - do - - do -

Any transport required by 4th Dismounted Division on the night of 14th/15th., and by the 5th Dismounted Division on the night 16th/17th., in connection with relief, will be supplied on application to "Q" Dismounted Divisions.

10. All Defence Schemes, Maps, Aeroplane Photos, etc., etc., will be handed over to incoming units and receipts given.

11. A.D.M.S., Dismounted Divisions will make the necessary arrangements for the reliefs of Medical personnel.

12. Completion of reliefs will be reported to H.Q. Dismounted Divisions.

13. ACKNOWLEDGE. (4th and 5th Dismounted Divisions by wire.).

H. T. Hodgson.
Lt-Colonel, G.S.,
Dismounted Divisions.

Issued to :-

Copy No.		Copy No.	
1.	5th Dismounted Division.	13.	Cavalry Corps.
2.	4th Dismounted Division.	14.	24th Division.
3.	Cavalry Divn'l Artillery.	15.	61st Division.
4.	C.R.E., Dism'td Divns.	16.	72nd Infantry Brigade.
5.	M.G.O., do.	17.	1st Cavalry Division.
6.	A.A.& Q.M.G. do.		
7.	A.D.M.S. do.	19.	3rd Cavalry Division.
8.	D.A.D.O.S., do.	20.	4th Cavalry Division (rear)
9.	A.P.M. do.	21.	5th Cavalry Division (rear)
10.	Gas Officer. do.	22.	5th Cavalry Division "Q".
11.	Signals, do.	23-25.	War Diary.
12.	Camp Comdt. do.	26& 27.	Office.

No.G.A.141.

Headquarters, Dismounted Divisions,
13th February, 1918.

To/
All recipients of Dis.Divns Order No.7.

Reference Dismounted Divisions Order No.7.

Cavalry Corps wires 13th begins :-

" 11th and 13th Machine Gun Squadrons
will now move with Divisions concerned
and will not be at disposal of Dismounted Divisions."
                                    ends.

Divisions concerned will make all necessary
arrangements.

Captain, G.S.,
Dismounted Divisions.